CARDINAL HUME
and the changing face of English Catholicism

CARDINAL
HUME

and the changing face
of English Catholicism

PETER STANFORD

GEOFFREY
CHAPMAN

Geoffrey Chapman
An imprint of Cassell Publishers Limited
Villiers House, 41/47 Strand, London WC2N 5JE
387 Park Avenue South, New York, NY 10016–8810

First published 1993

British Library Cataloguing-in-Publication Data
A catalogue record for this book is available from the British Library.

Library of Congress Cataloging-in-Publication Data
Available from the Library of Congress.

ISBN 0–225–66658–8

Typeset by Colset Private Limited, Singapore
Printed and bound in Great Britain by
Mackays of Chatham PLC

Contents

To Pete Walker
1963–1992

1

Not a bad story

Cardinal Basil Hume doubted my wisdom in trying to define English Catholicism when I visited him to talk about this book. Yet he could see – admittedly with less than total detachment as Archbishop of Westminster and leader since 1976 of the English and Welsh Church – the fascination of the subject, the thrill, even the romanticism of the chase. 'Ours is not a bad story. No Church has been so persecuted for so long. And everyone knows about John Fisher and Thomas More. They're household names. There's a great respect for that tradition.'

The Cardinal has been helpful in the preparation of this book. Yet I should make it clear from the outset that it does not carry, nor have I sought, his imprimatur.

The Cardinal's doubts about my setting down in black and white the characteristics of the Church he leads concerned his fears that any survey might be anecdotal. Well, this book is most certainly a personal view, the fruits of nearly a decade working for Catholic newspapers, the past four years as editor of the *Catholic Herald*. But this isn't just a jigsaw of old clippings, diary entries and fleeting impressions I have picked up while pursuing some hot story.

The blow-by-blow historical survey will come in future years when academics evaluate the integration of what was once an excluded, persecuted and largely immigrant minority into the mainstream of British national life. The fusion is so complete that the joins are already beginning to be invisible to the naked eye. In the interim this is the viewpoint of a journalist – with all the strengths and flaws of that profession.

I feel in many ways a product of the changing face of English Catholicism. Cardinal Heenan, Basil Hume's predecessor, and the sort of enclosed, introspective Catholic world that is now described as the 'fortress church' were as much a part of my childhood as Valerie Singleton, cream soda from the Corona man and *Animal*

1

Magic. And in a more extended perspective my family history leads back to the days of persecution and inevitably enough, like that of well over a quarter of English Catholics, to Ireland. Yet my adult life – and my working life too for that matter – has been spent as part of an outward-looking, confident Catholic Church, fundamentally at ease with its environment. I haven't been made to feel different because I'm a Catholic in a society where Anglicanism remains the Established Church and agnosticism is increasingly the norm. My creed may lead me to make different choices but it has never been a disadvantage. As far as I am aware it has never closed any doors to me, save marriage to a member of the Royal Family, and I can say, without a hint of modesty, that I haven't been overwhelmed with offers from that direction. Professionally it has been a boon, a subject of endless interest to explore in print. Indeed from university days onwards I have been aware of a certain fashionable halo surrounding a creed that is, by repute at least, so uncompromising.

My mother was one of eight Catholic children growing up in inner-city Liverpool in the pre-Second World War years when Orange marches were taken for granted each July and school children would throw stones at each other along denominational lines. The Liverpool I now return to is – leaving aside its economic abandonment by successive national and local governments – the showpiece of ecumenism not just for this country, but for the world. Archbishop Derek Worlock was able to hold his head high and tell the Synod on Europe in Rome in the autumn of 1991 about how he and his Anglican counterpart Bishop David Sheppard have conquered the prejudices of old. In their place they have turned the Church into a positive agency and lobby for their city and its future well-being, uniting in the process factions that once were as far apart as the warring communities of the north of Ireland.

Such contrasts within two generations have inspired – if that isn't too portentous a word – this book. The result probably won't please everyone. One of the fruits of the new-style Catholicism is that dissent, disagreement, everyone having his or her own viewpoint, has become the norm. The one, holy, Catholic and apostolic Church that we profess to believe in when we say the *Credo* is today in effect several different factions, as argumentative and competitive as any group of political parties.

This book is also written in the aftermath of a previous and debated offering, *Catholics and Sex*, which I co-authored with Kate Saunders in 1991. There we looked at many of the absurdities and difficulties of being a Catholic in a Church where the official line, on sexual morality at least, is sometimes semi-detached from the reality of people's lives. We were accused of washing dirty linen in public. Here, on the other hand, are some of the more choice items, some shining examples of the benefits of being a Catholic, the things that make all the rest if not bearable then not something easily rejected like an imperfect piece of china whose flaws are exposed one bright summer's day. After having climbed on my soap box about the Pope and the pill in a radio interview, I was asked why I didn't opt for a creed that is a little more tolerant of human nature and celebratory of the joys of the flesh, a faith that doesn't wrap every duvet in a bouquet of barbed wire. It's not something I can even begin to contemplate: once a Catholic and all that.

If English Catholicism comes out of this scrutiny looking a little too comfortable, a little too Establishment, able to gloss over the divisions of the past in pursuit of peace and prosperity, then bear in mind that past and recognize the achievement. And, however cosy it may now be, mixed up in there are, I feel, elements of the radicalism that fired the first apostles.

A final word of thanks to all those who have helped in this project. To the Franciscan Friars of the Atonement for the wonderful and quite unexpected treasures to be found in the basement of the Catholic Central Library (if you are near Westminster Cathedral, pay them a visit); to Joanna Moorhead, Shannie Ross, Kate Saunders, Martin Stanford, Imogen Parker, Cristina Odone, Helen Lederer, Caroline Willson and all those who gave advice when asked; to Clare Dixon, Nicholas Coote, Bruce Kent, Fr Anthony Churchill, Viviane Hewitt, Michael Walsh, Jean Judge and Professor Simon Lee for their top tips on the manuscript: and to my editor Ruth McCurry for her enduring patience.

Before I am assailed with howls of anguish from the valleys of Wales, I have for ease of expression talked about the English Church when I mean the English and Welsh Churches. They are as one in the Vatican's eyes, and though there is a distinct tradition of Celtic Christianity running down through the ages, that is not the subject of this book. Cardinal Hume is president of the Bishops' Conference of England and Wales. As for Scotland, Basil Hume's word is not law there. Scotland is an entirely different set-up, with its own hierarchy, its own structures and its own relations with Rome. The Scottish National Party would approve of such independence within a worldwide church.

2

The reluctant Archbishop

Just by being there, friendly and unfrightening, Basil Hume has
exorcised some of the nightmares in the English subconscious
about the Catholic Church.

(Clifford Longley, *The Times*)

Dom Basil Hume, the 52-year-old Benedictine Abbot of Ampleforth Abbey in Yorkshire, was settling down to a peaceful dinner
with his fellow monks on the evening of 5 February 1976 when the
telephone rang. The call was to transform his life and herald in a
new era for both English Catholicism and the nation as a whole.

The voice on the other end of the line told Dom Basil, an unas-
suming intellectual whose long Plantagenet face and diffident smile
was little known outside the corridors of monasteries, bishops'
palaces and Curial offices, that he had been named the next Archbishop of Westminster and leader of the Roman Catholic Church in
England and Wales. 'When I got the news I was rather shattered,
rather distressed. I must confess I didn't enjoy the rest of the meal',
he recalled. Although his name had been mentioned as a possible
successor to the long-serving and recently deceased Cardinal
Heenan, the fact that the two were in so many ways chalk and cheese
had made his candidacy in 1976 seem as unlikely as the thought of a
Pope who was not Italian.

John Carmel Heenan was a forceful, outspoken and occasionally
abrasive shepherd, sure in his views and equally at ease in radio and
TV broadcasts or among his flock. He was every inch a prince of the
Church, comfortable as the lynchpin of elaborate ceremonies and a
man conscious of the dignity of his office. His robust if often
introspective brand of Catholicism built on the tradition maintained by successive Archbishops of Westminster since the restoration of the English and Welsh hierarchy by the Vatican in 1850. The

Catholic Church with Cardinal Heenan at the helm was usually to be found standing apart from the mainstream of national life, semi-detached from the great political debates of the day.

Basil Hume, by contrast, shunned the limelight and talked often of searching for God amid doubt and uncertainty. This silver-haired, tall monk, once likened to a gentle ecclesiastic carved in the portals of Chartres Cathedral, had pioneered practical ecumenism as a member of the local Ryedale Council of Churches and welcomed and encouraged the setting up of an Orthodox house a stone's throw from the Benedictine Abbey. He was a close friend of the Anglican Primate Donald Coggan when the latter was Archbishop of York.

Heenan came from working-class Ilford. Although he was an East Ender by adoption, his family's roots were in Ireland where his parents had met and married. He served his apprenticeship in thriving, if poor, parishes. His climb up the ladder of ecclesiastical preferment had been as conventional as it was swift: studies in Rome, parish postings, a spell running a church organization, Bishop of Leeds, Archbishop of Liverpool, and then the top job at Westminster and the cardinal's hat that customarily goes with it.

Basil Hume was that rare creature for his generation, a middle-class Catholic. The son of a Protestant, Scottish-born heart consultant, Sir William Hume, and a French Catholic mother, he was at home among the British ruling classes. He had grown up in comfortable surroundings in Newcastle and had mixed since he first went to Ampleforth as a schoolboy at the age of ten with the privileged elite of English Catholicism, Evelyn Waugh's *Brideshead* generation and their offspring. He had never been a bishop and his role in the hierarchical structure of Catholicism was that of backroom counsellor rather than leader. As he later admitted, with characteristic understatement: 'I hadn't cut any figure in public life and I wasn't known. And I really didn't think I had done anything particularly significant.'

If Basil Hume was shattered and distressed by the news of his elevation, British Catholics were more than a little puzzled by what the *Daily Telegraph* described as 'an ecclesiastical bombshell'. They were not quite sure what to make of their new leader with his sombre demeanour and thoughtful manner, the first monk to be Archbishop of Westminster since 1850. His obvious reluctance to take on the job could not have reassured them. Dom Basil said at the time that he had accepted it 'under obedience' as a monk. 'A monk doesn't choose what he does. He does what he is told by the authorities who are above him. And what I felt about it, what I thought about it, was as far as I was concerned as a monk irrelevant.' The new Archbishop gritted his teeth and only broke into a smile after a private audience with Pope Paul VI, where his doubts were laid to rest.

Why, it was asked at the time, had the Vatican, not a multi-national known for taking bold or radical steps in the personnel department, as Cardinal Heenan's sainted progress demonstrated, decided to pass over the entire bench of English and Welsh bishops in favour of a little-known abbot? It was not as if there were not outstanding candidates, well acquainted with the ropes, among the hierarchy. Bishop Derek Worlock of Portsmouth, previously secretary to three Archbishops of Westminster, was a man who had attended the reforming Second Vatican Council of the 1960s and imbibed deeply of its spirit. He was given the Archdiocese of Liverpool, Catholicism's equivalent of York instead of Canterbury, and condemned to be the Denis Healey of English Catholicism, the best leader it never had. And there was the bookmakers' favourite, Bishop Alan Clark, then an auxiliary in Northampton and later Bishop of East Anglia. His calling card at Lambeth Palace and Canterbury, if Rome was looking for a man to ease relations with the Church of England, was without blemish. But Rome chose Abbot Hume. It seemed to many Catholics like a sign from the ecclesiastical big-wigs that change was on the agenda. They weren't quite sure what to expect, but the days of Cardinal Heenan were history.

More than 17 years on, as Cardinal Hume celebrates his seventieth birthday, such questions have been, at least in part, answered. A final and full evaluation will not come until Dom Basil has retired. His promise, soon after taking office, to do the job for only ten years has fallen by the wayside. But not on account of any clinging to the trappings of office by the Cardinal. His palatial new home at Archbishop's House in Victoria, huge, very dark and about as welcoming as a North Country station hotel during a period of national mourning, can scarcely be keeping him away from Ampleforth and the North Yorkshire Moors.

Basil Hume is without personal ambition – though he has admitted to a touch of vanity occasionally. (He has let it be known that

7

cartoons featuring his prominent nose do not raise a laugh in Archbishop's House, and he once remarked: 'I never know what hurts
most – flattery or criticism'.) If it was a monk's obedience that led
him to accept the challenge of leadership of the English Church, it
is the same devotion that keeps him in an office that is notorious for
breaking its occupants. Cardinal Griffin, the youngest of Basil
Hume's predecessors, was plagued by ill-health, while even the
robust John Carmel Heenan suffered in his later years.

Yet the reluctant archbishop, Rome's dark horse, has succeeded
in winning the respect and affection not only of his Catholic constituency but of the whole country, to an extent not achieved by any
of his predecessors at Westminster. And his lack of personal ambition has been a key factor in that. He has been described as the
spiritual leader of the nation – though some of the Tory MPs issuing
the plaudit more often than not uttered it as a rebuke to Robert
Runcie, for eleven eventful years Archbishop of Canterbury and
traditional holder of the country's moral conscience. When Basil
Hume takes to the national stage – backs humbly into the limelight, as one commentator once put it – he commands attention
and respect.

Product or cause?

It would be wrong to credit Cardinal Hume with single-handedly
changing the face of English Catholicism, a beast that defies
attempts at precise definition. In many ways his appointment was
more a product than a cause of social and theological changes
already afoot. With the Second Vatican Council of the mid-1960s,
the global Catholic community was encouraged to look outwards, to
open a window on the world, in the words of Pope John XXIII, who
instigated the reforms.

The message was not lost on Catholics in England. The advent of
Abbot Hume in 1976 came less than 200 years on from the Gordon
Riots, when Protestant fanatics crying 'No popery' had taken to the
streets to protest at the Catholic Relief Act of 1778. But over that
period the Church of Rome and its British adherents had slowly and
sometimes falteringly ceased to be outcasts in their own land –
though they were still regarded with some residual puzzlement,
occasionally bordering on suspicion, by their fellow countrymen
and women.

With the Catholic Emancipation Act of 1829 had come the restoration of civil and legal rights taken away at the time of the Reformation and its bloody aftermath. Although its main effect was in Ireland, where the Catholic majority were able to have some say in their government, the new legislation also lifted remaining sanctions on the estimated 80,000 'Romans' living in England.

Exactly when English Catholics became known as Roman Catholics is unclear. The Puritan poet John Milton scoffed at the title, calling it 'one of the Pope's bulls'. But the term was certainly never devised by the Vatican, and English Catholics have never been fond of it for precisely John Milton's reasons. It carries with it an air of foreignness, of a narrow sect like the Seventh Day Adventists.

In 1850, with the re-establishment of the hierarchy with the Archbishop of Westminster at its head, the Catholic clergy brushed off the last cobwebs from the priestly hiding holes in recusant houses where the candle of faith had been kept burning, often in secret, despite the persecutions of the post-Reformation period. By the middle of the nineteenth century, Catholics made up about 5 per cent of the population, their numbers boosted by a vast tide of Irish immigration into the north-west of England after the famine in Ireland.

That eminent Victorian John Henry Newman's very public abandonment of the Church of England for Rome in 1845 gave Catholicism an intellectual and moral authority it had been lacking. Following Newman's conversion Catholicism also acquired a certain fashionable attraction for the intelligentsia and the upper reaches of society, although the former Oxford University vicar was not followed in his 'going over to Rome' by nearly as many Anglicans as he had imagined. The 'second spring' he talked of never blossomed in his lifetime, though the trickle did become a flood in the twentieth century, with almost three-quarters of a million converts swelling the ranks between 1900 and 1960.

At the other end of the scale from Newman, Cardinal Henry Manning's crucial intervention in the London dock strike of 1889 on the side of the workers made him a popular hero whose image figured alongside that of Karl Marx on trade union banners. His social radicalism certainly cut a dash in Victorian England, though his staunch defence of papal infallibility made him mistrusted among the Establishment.

Irish independence in the 1920s removed a major grievance

against the British authorities among English Catholics with close ties with Ireland, although the issue of Northern Ireland continues to be of concern to the hierarchy in Britain.

In the 1930s and 1940s writers like Evelyn Waugh, Graham Greene, Hilaire Belloc and G. K. Chesterton began to disentangle the mythology surrounding Catholicism, which had made it in many people's minds a popish fifth column with strange rituals and 'foreign' allegiances. These fashionable journalists and novelists through their published works brought Catholicism's beliefs and attendant strains to a wide audience. Novelist Anthony Burgess, himself a cradle Catholic, recently wrote: 'The British Protestant middle class of the present age became casually interested in Catholicism when it began to read the novels of Graham Greene and Evelyn Waugh. Catholicism became not merely respectable but glamorous. In *Brighton Rock*, Greene seemed to affirm that only Catholics were capable of good and evil, whose secular equivalents – right and wrong – were the mere rags of a morality that had rejected God.'

By the late 1940s there were Catholics like Frank Pakenham (now Lord Longford) in the inner circles of government, Catholic MPs and Catholics in senior positions in the civil service. The Church had been given a major role – and ultimately a favourable financial deal – in the state schools system by R. A. Butler's Education Act of 1944. Day-to-day running costs were met in full out of the public purse, while the Church had to find 50 per cent – reduced in 1959 to 15 per cent – of capital costs. In return the bishops and clergy retained effective control and, in the process, became used to dealing on a regular basis with Whitehall, Westminster and local town halls. And working-class Catholics, still the bulk of the community, were given the educational opportunities to propel them up the social ladder.

The fortress model

If Catholics were beginning to come out of their shells by the early 1950s, there was still a part of their make-up that made them feel different, apart from rather than above the rest of society around them. At the 1980 Synod on the family, Cardinal Hume described this period of English Catholicism as according to 'the fortress model'. The history of persecution of English Catholicism remained too fresh in many memories and in the folklore of the Church. A residual defensiveness, a closing of ranks, looking within for support, was the order of the day.

The Church itself reinforced this siege mentality by being authoritarian and hierarchical in structure. The gaze of the bishops was fixed on Rome. This Ultramontane tendency contributed to the general suspicion that Catholics were in some way less than wholehearted in their patriotism, in their loyalty to Crown and constitution, in their connection to the rest of society, taking their cue from a foreign power. The slurs used against the Catholic John F. Kennedy in the 1950s when he was running for the White House – the image of him sitting in the Oval Office ringing the papal apartments for his instructions – were also thrown at the English Church in the same period.

Outsiders were excluded from the fortress and there were strict and unbending rules for those within. They were bound together by their liturgical devotions – vast processions behind statues of the Virgin Mary – and common practices that made them distinct from the rest of the population, most notably their hunger for fish as part of Friday abstinence.

If Catholics tended to stick together, they were encouraged to do so by their leaders and by the very nature of their belief. Because Catholicism centres so much on the Mass as a communal act of worship, parish communities thrive. For many the parish was the main focus of social activity. For a viewpoint on a wider world, Mass-goers could purchase in the church porch Catholic newspapers like the *Universe* and *Catholic Herald*, which reached their peak of circulation in the 1950s – 300,000 plus and 100,000 plus respectively – preaching a message that no Catholic home was complete without their weekly diet of news, comment and analysis from within the institution about the institution. The chief foreign correspondent was of course based in Rome.

The ties forged across the pews found echoes outside the church precincts in a variation on the practices of the Freemasons. Firms built their reputations on being run by Catholics serving a Catholic market, when their professional skills in practical terms involved no distinction on the basis of religion. There were 'Catholic' solicitors like the London firm of Witham Weld, 'Catholic' doctors, architects, bank managers and so on.

Increasingly from the 1930s onwards the professions had opened

11

their doors to a new generation of young men and women, the products of the fledgling Catholic middle class and schools like Ampleforth, where headteacher Dom Paul Nevill's criterion in this period was that the education on offer should be as good as – if not better than – that offered by any comparable non-Catholic school. Cardinal Hume, himself a pupil at this time, recalls that his Protestant father was convinced of the benefit of a Benedictine education for his son, rather than a place at his own *alma mater* Repton, by the scholarly standards maintained at the Yorkshire abbey.

Marrying out continued to be frowned on – in practice if not in the rule-book. In the eyes of all but a small band of liberal priests – the Jesuits in Farm Street in central London had a reputation for being especially sympathetic – nice Catholic girls were expected to marry nice Catholic boys and vice versa. Many of those who defied this injunction, like my own parents, learnt the cost in hurried, weekday marriage ceremonies in side-chapels, with no music, no flowers and an unspoken disapproval.

It was only in 1957 that Cardinal Heenan, when he arrived as Archbishop of Liverpool, tackled head-on such second-class treatment. But even then there were many priests who thought he was being far too lenient in letting down the drawbridge around the fortress. In a letter to his clergy, the future Cardinal acknowledged that 'some priests whose opinions I value greatly may deplore any relaxation of the present regulations', but went on to order that mixed marriages be accorded not 'a small altar obscurely sited' but centre stage. Any discrimination could lead to bitterness in the Catholic partner and hostility in the non-Catholic, he noted.

If there were the first signs of a relaxation in the 1950s before the altar, in the often adjoining Catholic schools segregation remained absolute. Anthony Burgess recalls of his Manchester Catholic childhood (before the 1950s, but still relevant): 'Pupils of Anglican schools jeered "Cat-lick" at us and we learned to respond with "Proddy dog" '. The atmosphere contributed to a sense of Catholic apartness while in practical terms the 'Penny Catechism' remained the standard teaching tool, preparing its readers for verbal onslaughts on the faith from Protestants and non-believers. The two were considered almost akin in an age when 'the conversion of England' remained a prayer on every Catholic's lips.

This situation has been slow to change. On a recent television discussion programme on the thorny question of priestly celibacy, an otherwise articulate, open-minded Catholic participant reacted to the result of a telephone poll of viewers overwhelmingly endorsing the right of clerics to choose to marry with the retort that 'it must be Protestants ringing in'. Yet her sense of persecution is thankfully rare today. When a visiting preacher asking for funds for the Converts' Aid Society went to a local parish in 1990, he based his appeal on the idea that Catholics still suffer discrimination. The response in the collecting tins was small – a sign that such ideas no longer have the power to excite. Catholics in the 1990s no longer feel a persecuted minority. Indeed the sense of oppression that lived on for so long was often more in the minds of the would-be victims than in the hearts of their persecutors.

The Catholic teachers who until the 1960s put such notions in tender minds were themselves products of the fortress mentality. They had been through the segregated system and gained their professional qualifications at Catholic teacher-training colleges. The pinnacles of the higher education system, Oxford and Cambridge, continued to be viewed not as dreaming spires but as Protestant recruiting grounds. The same suspicion that had foiled Newman's plans in the 1860s to establish an Oratory in Oxford lived on years after his death. As recently as 1980, my Christian Brother tutor told me to apply for a certain Oxford college because 'they're not too bad on discriminating against us'. I, of course, took his advice, but throughout my three years I couldn't detect a trace of bigotry or even a flicker of prejudice against my denominational background.

A new broom

With Vatican II much of this paranoia was swept away at the highest level, and the foundation of the fortress was fatally undermined. No longer was praying for the salvation of souls deemed to be adequate contact for Catholics with a wider world. The old missionary ideas were replaced with a new pastoral–cultural strategy that demanded the building of bridges. Ecumenism buried the ghost of the Reformation and the Tyburn martyrs. Liturgy in the vernacular began to chip away at Catholic specialness, its outward signs of an inner apartness. Dialogue with politicians and leaders of society, and an outspoken contribution to the world in which the Church existed were the order of the day. Although the trickle-down effect has been slow to penetrate some bastions of traditional Catholicism – a dwindling bunch of ultra-conservatives continue to gather in clearly identified churches like London's Brompton Oratory to yearn together for the Latin, lace and incense of the old rite and its attendant certainties – the walls of the Catholic ghetto began to come tumbling down.

In England and Wales, for the most part, the bold new directives coming from Rome as a result of Vatican II received an enthusiastic response: sometimes too enthusiastic, as some clerics and even Cardinal Heenan thought. With the benefits of education, a new generation of Catholics had been encouraged to think for themselves, no longer to accept slavishly the dictates of their priests. The fruits of the Council inspired them.

Parallel to the process of the Church opening up to the world – *aggiornamento* as John XXIII dubbed it – the world opened up to Catholics. English Catholics have become increasingly socially mobile. At the turn of the century there was only a tiny Catholic professional middle class. The vast bulk of Catholics came from Irish roots, many of them exiles from the famine of the 1840s. They were characteristically working-class, and large numbers were grouped in the north-west of England around the entry ports of Liverpool and Preston. This immigrant group had little in common with the small number of long-suffering landowning Catholics who had maintained the faith down the ages in spite of persecution – families like the Vaughans, the Welds, the Mostyns, and most notably the Dukes of Norfolk. There wasn't an Irish vowel in the lot of them. They looked not to Ireland but to continental Europe for their spiritual cousins in the faith. They formed alliances with European Catholic families whose names featured in the *Almanach de Gotha*.

Two literary images – both admittedly exaggerated – sum up the two threads of English Catholicism that have finally been woven together in the age of Basil Hume. Flora Thompson in *Lark Rise to Candleford*, her memoir of childhood in Oxfordshire at the end of the nineteenth century, wrote of the 'old Irishers', dishevelled men of strange appearance who worked on the expanding railway network or as labourers in the fields. They were a remote group with their own rituals, which she describes as revolving around the pub and the church. On Sunday these navvies and farm hands would process, stiff-gaited in a line, past Lark Rise to hear Mass at the Catholic church at Hethe. At the other end of the scale is Evelyn

Waugh's *Brideshead Revisited*. The author, a convert to Catholicism, tells the tale of Charles Ryder's friendship with the charming, irrepressible Sebastian Flyte and his eccentric Catholic family – believed to be modelled on the Howards, part of the Norfolk clan. Days of champagne and privilege at Oxford and stately homes with chapels in their grounds give way, as Sebastian's health deteriorates, to questions of religion and morality, love and the Catholic faith. Charles woos Sebastian's sister, Julia, but she prefers God.

Down the generations from those days at Lark Rise the Catholic working class spread its wings throughout the land and underwent embourgeoisement. With the benefit of an education at the hands of academically gifted monks and nuns, Catholics climbed up from the foot of the economic ladder to join the middle classes. The 1944 Education Act, providing a sound financial base for Catholic schools and a place for every Catholic child up to age 15, no matter what his or her parents' means, substantially speeded up this process.

From being just 5 per cent of the population in the 1850s, Catholics had increased by the time of Cardinal Hume's appointment to constitute 11 per cent of the nation. Immigrants from Ireland continued to provide a boost to numbers, but they were augmented by converts and a new wave of refugees from eastern Europe, in particular in the post-war years. The Catholic Church's total ban on artificial birth control – the Church of England dropped its objections in 1930 – was an added factor in this demographic growth, although, as we shall see later, acceptance of the papal ban on the pill has not been the norm.

When Cardinal Hume took command of the English Church, it was already in social, economic and political terms well on the road to assimilation. His surprise promotion, given his background, was recognition of that process. But he has also acted as an accelerator.

A middle-class church

The small number of Catholic pundits who had called for Basil Hume's appointment in 1976 as Cardinal Heenan's successor were notable for having gained positions of authority within the English Establishment. Their religion was no longer a bar to their advancement. Men like Norman St John-Stevas, later to become a Cabinet minister in Margaret Thatcher's first government, and William

Rees-Mogg, then editor of *The Times*, were enthusiastic backers of the Abbot of Ampleforth. (The identification of the Duke of Norfolk, whose seat is at Arundel Castle, with this informal lobbying group – though he had seemed during the interregnum to be throwing his not inconsiderable influence behind Fr Michael Hollings, the press-termed 'simple priest from Southall' – led one supporter of Bishop Worlock to complain that their candidate had been 'dished by the Arundel and Brighton blue-blood set'.) With such links – not forgetting that the former Cabinet Secretary, Lord Hunt, is his brother-in-law – Cardinal Hume has moved the Catholic Church closer to the Establishment. He has made it another comfortable bit of the furniture in the national drawing-room. As *The Times*'s long-serving religious affairs editor, Clifford Longley, once wrote: 'Just by being there, friendly and unfrightening, he has exorcised some of the nightmares in the English subconscious about the Catholic Church'.

For those who claimed no denomination, there was something in the new Archbishop of Westminster in 1976 that appealed to the English psyche. He was after all a sportsman, pictured jogging on Wimbledon Common, a regular squash player and a fan of Newcastle United who revealed in a TV interview that he wanted the *Match of the Day* theme played at his funeral. And in his honesty, simplicity and directness he buried at once the stereotypes of Catholic prelates as akin to the Borgias – bloated, power-crazy princes of the Church.

In specific terms, Basil Hume replaced the age-old injunction, dating back to the restoration of the hierarchy, to pray for the conversion of 'Mary's Dowry', the somewhat provocative phrase used to describe the godless nation of lost souls that in the Reformation had turned its back on devotion to Christ's mother and destroyed her shrines at places like Walsingham in Norfolk. The Abbot of Ampleforth dispensed with such talk and brought to hisnew job an unflinching commitment to ecumenism. Although Cardinal Heenan had taken significant steps along the road to the inter-church understanding demanded by Vatican II, Basil Hume by a single dramatic gesture at the very start of his leadership took an enormous stride in the direction of unity. And in the process he made it clear that no longer was Catholicism seeking to undermine the national Church, or to deny its right to call itself a Church.

Two hours after his installation as Archbishop of Westminster on

16

17 February 1976 he took the ecumenically revolutionary step of leading a party of monks from his new cathedral on the short walk to Westminster Abbey, once a Benedictine centre. During Evensong, the first time in 400 years that the Abbey had heard the Latin plainchant of vespers sung by Catholic and Anglican monks, he spoke of the two churches as 'two sisters, estranged, not on speaking terms, quarrelsome, misunderstanding each other'. Referring to the graves of the sister Queens Elizabeth and Mary in the Abbey, he spoke of the inscription on their tomb – 'in the hope of one resurrection' – and looked forward to Christian unity.

For the diehards in Catholic ranks, the Cardinal might have been seen as replacing one idea of conversion with another. Conversion to Benedictines means the interior spiritual change in themselves to which all Christians must attend as a daily duty. Monks take a vow to work to their own conversion, unceasingly. It is an emphasis rather more acceptable to the other English churches than that of dragging them over to Rome.

Yet an equally important part of the Cardinal's success and his moral authority has been in upholding his detachment from the rough-and-tumble of daily political battle. While he followed in Cardinal Heenan's footsteps in using private diplomacy with ministers to raise matters of concern – though arguably on a wider range of issues and more frequently than his predecessor – Cardinal Hume has been at pains to stress that the Church is above party. At times his Anglican and Methodist colleagues, while paying lip service to the same principle, have not been so clear-sighted in their practice, with the result that their Churches have been compromised in the public's eye, stereotyped as opponents of the government, Her Majesty's Loyal Opposition in the cloisters. Cardinal Hume, by contrast, has managed to avoid such charges and in common with only a tiny handful of others – the Queen Mother, Gary Lineker, Delia Smith – has never suffered a bad press during his long spell in the national spotlight.

His face is known and respected in the corridors of power in Whitehall. A combination of immaculate preparation, caution in picking his issues and the implicit threat of going public and throwing his national moral weight against the government has taught ministers to sit up and take notice when the Cardinal approaches them. They also know that he is a man with whom they can do business without it ending in a blaze of publicity. He is 'one of us'. And

Basil Hume has pulled off some notable coups, not the least of which was to persuade the Home Secretary to re-open the files on the Guildford Four and Birmingham Six, a victory that led to their release in the late 1980s. Such an intervention on an issue that in no way falls within the brief of 'religious' would have been unthinkable for Basil Hume's predecessors, with the possible exception of Henry Manning.

The former abbot has achieved for the Catholic Church an elevated status above party politics through unambiguous gestures, such as turning down a seat in the House of Lords when it was mooted (officially because Catholic clerics are not allowed, by the 1983 Code of Canon Law, to hold any sort of political office). But more telling has been the Cardinal's demeanour. His leadership is often exercised more by what he is than by what he says. When he appears in public he is every inch the man of God. It is almost as if God is there in his shadow, and no amount of self-effacement can disguise the fact. Another of his enthusiastic backers in 1976, Bishop Gordon Wheeler of Leeds, once remarked of his protégé: 'Although even in the great national events on television one sees him tucked away behind pillars, the impact of his image cannot be said to diminish'.

While other clerics may choose to steal the politicians' clothes and try to talk their language, Cardinal Hume's public statements manage to be both specific and at the same time rooted in a set of generally accepted Christian principles of justice and morality that give them tremendous authority. He is not afraid to speak of spirituality in the way that most bishops prefer to talk about schools or diocesan finance – as something real, tangible and accessible to all.

In Basil Hume, the broader meeting between English Catholicism and English culture has found eloquent expression. The Cardinal is a very English man of God. No longer does the English Catholic Church have at its head a variation on the theme of the Jesuit warrior of the Counter-Reformation, champing at the bit to win back Mary's Dowry for the Holy Father. This peaceful Benedictine is the antithesis of the zeal of a Newman, a Manning or even a Heenan. With the Church coming out of its fortress and Catholics taking their place at every level of society, he has been a mirror for the changes. He has been a conciliator, with Lambeth and Whitehall. He has brought in an era of peace and prosperity for the English Catholic Church after the ravages of its past and the divisions of the immediate post-Vatican II years.

But peace brings its own price. When a minority feels persecuted it bunches together. Differences are forgotten. When Cardinal Hume signalled the end of a long history of standing on the outside, Mass attendance, the acid test of the fortress church, began to decline. A 1991 survey showed that Catholic churchgoing in England and Wales is decreasing faster than that of any denomination except the tiny United Reformed Church. Between 1979 and 1989 it dropped by 14 per cent. In 1979 there were 1.5 million adult Catholic Mass-attenders, representing 40 per cent of the Catholic population; in 1989 the figure was 1.3 million, just 31 per cent. The survey forecasts that the figure will have dropped to 1.1 million by the year 2000 in spite of the current 'decade of evangelization'. (A small comfort is that Catholics still make up the largest group of regular churchgoers in the country.)

The blame does not lie entirely at Cardinal Hume's door – or indeed at those of his fellow bishops and priests. Social and theological changes have combined to fashion a very different Church from that of the 1850s or even 1950s. The education that brought Catholics out of the ghetto mixed with the reforming notions of the Second Vatican Council to produce a more articulate, questioning laity.

The Cardinal is, as ever, pragmatic in facing up to declining Mass attendance. He finds hope in the fact that the survey quoted above also revealed that 65 per cent of people in England profess some allegiance to what they called 'notional Christianity'. 'I wonder about that word "notional" ', the Cardinal said at the time of the survey's publication. 'I believe profoundly that every person is not only a social animal but a religious animal, and there are many, many ways in which people are actually in pursuit of God, in their own way, very often unconsciously. I come across people who say their prayers and are very much involved in social action, but who have a very different view of going to church than we have.' For the modern Cardinal, Mass attendance is not the *sine qua non*. Although not happy about empty pews where once Catholics had to stand in the aisles, he can see beyond the yawning gaps and is not one to resort to generalized appeals for a return to Sunday observance.

A questioning laity

The high point of lay involvement – and perhaps the final nail in the coffin of the fortress Church – came four years into Cardinal

Hume's period in office with the 1980 National Pastoral Congress in Liverpool. Some 2,000 delegates, representing parishes, deaneries and dioceses from up and down the land, gathered to debate what the Church should be doing and saying, to stake their claim to be authentic leaders of their Church, as much 'the people of God' as clergy.

Top of their list of complaints was the papal teaching on birth control. Cardinal Hume and Archbishop Worlock were delegated to tell the forthcoming Roman Synod on the family about the level of disagreement on this issue. The predictable message came back from Rome: No change. But because of its opening up, its embourgeoisement, the Catholic community was no longer going to take Rome's rebuff as the final word. The middle classes have a tendency towards liberalism and with liberalism comes a lessening of the fear of authority. The Pope may want to assume the ostrich position when it comes to matters of sexual morality, but Catholics are determined to shape the ideals of the Vatican's teaching to the reality of their own consciences and their lives and needs. At a more general level, Cardinal Hume's own readiness to admit that he hasn't got all the answers – he has made it a policy not to plug the official line on sex in his sermons, for instance – has encouraged an educated and articulate laity to think for themselves.

In place of the Ultramontane attitudes of the fortress Church, Hume's people have favoured a form of its polar opposite, Gallicanism – sorting out a response appropriate to the national circumstances. Survey after survey now shows that the vast majority of Catholics make up their own minds on subjects like birth control, remarriage after divorce, and pre-marital sex, but stay within the institution. Whereas in the days before the Second Vatican Council the attitude was 'if you want to be a member of the club keep the rules or leave', today's English Catholics are refusing the tag 'lapsed' when they make a moral decision in good conscience that conflicts with the rule book.

With an end to its persecution and its self-imposed isolation, the Catholic Church has undoubtedly lost some of its fire. Those who continue to press Rome to canonize Cardinal John Henry Newman cannot fail to be struck by the contrast between today's calm and the fervour that inspired him to write of the Church of his age: 'She holds that it were better for sun and moon to drop from heaven, for the earth to fail, and for all the many millions who are upon it to die of starvation in extremest agony, as far as temporal affliction goes than that one soul, I will not say should be lost, but should commit one single venial sin, should tell one wilful untruth or steal one poor farthing without excuse'.

Getting to grips with the modern age has its price. A kind of customary Catholicism is developing where the Church's regulations, especially with regard to sexual morality, are filtered through personal experience and need, and adapted or quietly ignored as a consequence. A new generation is deciding that they can still be good Catholics, leading moral lives, without keeping to the letter of the law. Some would say they can still be Catholic without going to Mass every Sunday, a factor that is clear from the statistics quoted above. However, for such a process to be truly deemed Gallicanism, the people would have to carry their bishops and priests with them. And the liberal tendencies of English Catholics in certain areas of life – notably those traditionally associated with the bedroom – have not won any sort of public endorsement from the hierarchy. (In the privacy of the confessional, where pastoral considerations rather than outward shows of unity are the main concerns, it is a different story.)

While fundamentalism and authoritarianism are antipathetic to the Catholicism of both the majority of the laity and Cardinal Hume, they are not shunned in the Vatican. The Cardinal and his bishops have therefore had to walk a tightrope between their people and their superiors in Rome. The Church has begun to operate on three levels: Rome, the people and, torn between the two, the pastorally sensitive bishops and priests.

The result of such tensions in English Catholicism – and they are by no means unique to this country – has been a liberal pastoral practice together with a public acceptance of the party line by the bishops. This has angered both radical and traditional laity at the poles of the church, but suited the majority of the faithful. More importantly for Cardinal Hume, it has demanded a wholly new type of leadership.

In response he has had to preside in a distinctly English manner, no longer the general with his troops marching in neat columns behind, but the guide, the counsellor, for the most part standing shoulder to shoulder with his people, occasionally gently nudging them in the right direction. Compared with other Catholic Churches in the developed world there has been an air of unruffled reasonableness and serenity in English Catholicism. After the trials and tribulations of the past, the English bishops tend to keep a low profile. This fits in with the Vatican view that what goes on in these islands is now a bit of a side-show on the Catholic world map. The theological debates that have torn the German, American and Dutch Churches asunder haven't happened here. English theology remains – rather like the English – unambitious and resolutely practical.

It is the brew distilled from these practical manifestations and changing tones, called English Catholicism, the faith of Cardinal Hume's people, that is the subject of this book. Education, ecumenism, Europe, relations with Rome, Whitehall and West-minster are all areas where a distinctive contribution has been made, a contribution that shows marked contrasts with the past practice of the Catholic Church from its restoration in 1850 to the 1960s. But before we look at specific areas, a glance at the back-ground of the Archbishopric of Westminster and the holders of that office will help to illuminate the transformation from what was initially dubbed 'the Italian mission to the Irish' and greeted with thinly veiled intolerance to a post that in the hands of Cardinal Hume has come to rival the Archbishopric of Canterbury in national religious leadership.

3

A break with tradition

At present the requirement demanded by the Vatican in the case of high appointments in Great Britain is that the candidate should be an efficient administrator of a religious minority and nothing more. This dates back to the time when indeed nothing more than this was expected of the Archbishop of Westminster.

(Foreign Office document, 1943)

In the marmoreal interior of Westminster Cathedral, you can read of the Archbishops and Cardinals of England, starting with Augustine of Canterbury in 601, under the portentous banner 'Chief Pastors of the Catholic Church in England showing their communion with the Apostolic See of Rome'. The list breaks off abruptly with Thomas Cranmer, who was deprived of the seals of office by the Pope for heresy in 1533. 'The only good thing I ever heard about Cranmer', wrote Hurrell Froude, friend of Newman, 'was that he burnt well' (a tribute to Cranmer's final, possibly unexpected, courage).

The brutality that accompanied Henry VIII's abandonment of his papal allegiance, and the subsequent intolerance of his children and their courts, left scars that have been nearly 400 years in the healing. It has only been in the era of the last name on the list in Westminster Cathedral, George Basil Hume, that Catholicism and its leader can be said to have found a wide-ranging national role to accompany its specific denominational responsibilities.

After Cranmer the Roman Catholic Church went underground – with a brief if bloody respite under Mary Tudor and her henchman Cardinal Pole, who together showed a lamentable faith in the persuasive powers of burning Protestants. That aside – and the ferocity of Henry VIII's elder daughter in trying to turn back the

23

clock on the Reformation probably contributed in no small measure
to what was later visited on her fellow Romans – Catholics, with
their priest holes, became a persecuted minority, teetering on the
brink of extinction.

After Pole there were no more Cardinals, only archpriests who for
practical reasons hid their lights under a bushel. It was not until
1753 that the first tentative steps towards a Catholic leadership were
made when the Pope divided the country into four districts, to be
overseen by Vicars Apostolic, answerable directly to Rome. The next
100 years saw Catholic priests increasingly free to go about their
business, tending to a flock of recusant families, swollen in the
middle years of the nineteenth century by the first wave of Irish
immigration. Bishop Richard Challoner, one of the eighteenth-
century Vicars Apostolic, crops up in contemporary chronicles
of London life. But they did without any Roman pomp and circumstance. Cranmer and Pole would not have recognized them as men
of God. They wore dark suits but never a Roman collar. They
eschewed titles like Father or Reverend for fear of exciting anti-
Catholic hysteria, which remained close to the surface. Their Masses
were simple events in discreet, out-of-the-way places. Only in
cosmopolitan London could one hear a Mass with music, and then
only in the chapel of the old Sardinian Embassy.

The fanfare blaring out from the Vatican to announce the full
restoration of the hierarchy in 1850 therefore jarred somewhat the
ears of English Catholics. Because of its policy of circumspection,
the rump of the Catholic Church had kept its horizons narrow.
Rome, its attentions and its strategies, had all seemed a long way
away. Pope Pius IX's decision to name an Archbishop of Westminster took most of his future flock by surprise. Others were simply
angry. 'The cause of religion, I am convinced, is thrown back at least
a century by this proceeding', wrote one cleric at the time. If there
was bemusement in Catholic circles, the appointment provoked a
national backlash, with the Prime Minister, Lord John Russell,
joining Anglican bishops and marauding street mobs to denounce
the 'insolent and insidious' action of Pope Pius IX in naming the
Vicar Apostolic of the London district, Nicholas Wiseman, as Archbishop of Westminster.

After 300 years of persecution, Wiseman's reply to the papal
summons – a shrill and less than subtle claim that the Roman
Catholic branch was the one true Church – stuck in the English

palate like an indigestible continental delicacy. His regal manner increased the malaise, while his staunch adherence to the letter as well as the spirit of every statement coming out of God's business address on earth won the fledgling Catholic hierarchy only mistrust and dislike. To whom was their first loyalty, it was asked in Parliament, the Crown and the constitution or a foreign power?

Wiseman left little room for doubt about the answer and was to set the Catholic Church on a course of triumphalism. It reached its peak under Cardinal Vaughan, with the 1895 bull *Apostolicae Curae* declaring Anglican orders null and void. The Church of England, the spiritual backbone of Victorian England, was, according to this weighty document (still on the statute book), not a proper Church at all. The Archbishop of Canterbury was little more than a dubiously baptized heretic. The damage done by this confrontation with the Church of England took many years to be repaired. It was only on Cardinal Hinsley's death in 1943, for example, that the Archbishop of Canterbury attended a Catholic leader's funeral, and even in 1963 the *Catholic Herald* wrote in Cardinal Godfrey's obituary that he had 'become Archbishop of Westminster, successor to the Catholic Archbishops of Canterbury'. Those who take today's ecumenism for granted do not have to cast their minds back very far to see a wholly different set of attitudes.

The restored English Catholic hierarchy was not dubbed 'the Italian mission to the Irish' out of affection. Rather than an asset to be cherished, part of the landscape like those dark satanic mills, it was for its first hundred years regarded as an irritation to be tolerated. Hinsley's patriotism during the Second World War began to turn the tide but it was not until the eras of Heenan and Hume that perceptions began to change.

Cardinal Nicholas Wiseman (1850–1865):
The triumphalist

Nicholas Wiseman radiated such a strong sense of the dignity and mission of his office as the first Archbishop of Westminster, following the restoration of the hierarchy in 1850, that he prompted Queen Victoria, on reading his remarks, to ask 'Am I Queen of England or am I not?'

Born in Seville in Spain, the scion of a clan of Irish Catholic merchants who plied their trade between the Iberian peninsula,

France and Ireland, Nicholas Wiseman was educated at Ushaw College in Durham, still a Catholic seminary today, and the Venerable English College in Rome, likewise still the destination of bright young sparks among each year's crop of recruits for the priesthood. In 1840 he became Vicar Apostolic of the London area and ten years later was named by Pope Pius IX as the first leader of the newly restored hierarchy. His scholarship was much admired in the Vatican.

As was his way – and, to be fair, that of many princes of the Church at the time – the new Cardinal Archbishop of Westminster embarked on a stately progress from Rome to what he naively imagined would be the welcoming embrace of his new flock. In regal fashion, he sent ahead a message of greeting to England in late October 1850, entitled grandly *From Out the Flaminian Gate*. Its tone was about as discreet as that of a Cardinal in full regalia walking into a Quaker gathering. It was a trumpet call for the successors of Gordon rioters of seventy years before to dust down their placards and stoke up their ire. The period of persecution since the Reformation had been but the blinking of an eye, the new Archbishop seemed to imply. 'Catholic England has been restored to its orbit in the ecclesiastical firmament, from which its light had long vanished, and begins now anew its course of regularly adjusted action round the centre of unity, the source of jurisdiction, of light and of vigour.' And he did not mean the Archbishop of Canterbury.

The response in Britain from the other side was immediate and no less intemperate. *The Times* weighed in with an editorial accusing Wiseman of being 'in the service of a foreign power'. It went on: 'If this appointment be not intended as a clumsy joke, we confess that we can only regard it as one of the grossest acts of folly and impertinence which the court of Rome has ventured to commit since the crown and people of England threw off its yoke'. Publication of *From Out the Flaminian Gate* coincided with 5 November, the anniversary of Guy Fawkes's 1605 attempt to blow up the Houses of Parliament and restore a Catholic to the throne of England. The then traditional effigies of the Pope that were burnt on bonfires were joined by crude representations of Wiseman. Back in the hallowed columns of *The Times* – where 125 years later Basil Hume would become a star contributor of opinion pieces – Lord John Russell, the Prime Minister, added to the howls of protest at papal presumption from the Anglican bishops, although he had been aware for two years that Rome planned to restore the English hierarchy and had given this move the green light. (His opposition now had something to do with his desire to swim with the tide and not a little to do with his disillusion as a liberal statesman with Pius IX, who, though seemingly open-minded and modern, had in 1848, the year of revolutions in Europe, sided with those reactionary forces who wished to preserve the status quo.)

On 11 November, Wiseman arrived in England and at once set to work on repairing some of the damage his ill-considered message of greeting had caused. He published a pamphlet that was as carefully worded as *From Out the Flaminian Gate* had been ill-considered. It categorically denied that the new Catholic hierarchy had any plans to encroach upon the privileges and role of the Church of England and rebutted charges that by setting up a diocese at Westminster the Catholic authorities had their eyes on reclaiming the former Benedictine establishment at Westminster Abbey.

Wiseman was reasonably successful at damping down the fire his own initial thoughtlessness had caused. But some of the embers would stay aglow for years to come. One result of the furore was a bill introduced into Parliament in February 1851 making it an offence for any body but the Church of England to assume an existing ecclesiastical title. Hence Catholicism boasts a Bishop of Salford, not of Manchester, since there was already an Anglican with that title, and a Bishop of Shrewsbury, not Chester, for the same reason. The legacy of this legislation still haunts the Catholic bishops and is currently the subject of planned legislation by the Major government.

Despite his chastened tone, the new Archbishop saw little need to allay some of the more deep-seated suspicions of Catholic ambitions that had taken root in England since the Reformation. His Vicar-General, Robert Whitty, wrote after Wiseman's death about how he loved a show, travelling round London in an 'old fashioned carriage with its gorgeous trappings . . . to him the natural and right accompaniment to his dignity; and any modification of it in concession to English tastes was to yield to ''No Popery'' prejudices'. It was all a far cry from the discreet saloon car Cardinal Hume favours today. The worldly lifestyle of the Catholic leader attracted some attention. Robert Browning satirized Wiseman's 'lobster salad side' while even his biographer, Richard Schiefen, admits that the Cardinal was a mass of 'human failings and undeniable eccentricities'.

Wiseman's relations with his fellow bishops began badly and got

27

worse. Many of them grew to resent his grand manner, which they saw as undoing all their good work in keeping their heads down in the preceding years. His slavish devotion to Rome was damaging, they thought, to the character of the national Church, which during its persecution had developed a thoroughly independent turn of mind. Wiseman's task was further complicated by the fact that although he was to be the only Archbishop in the hierarchy (a state of affairs which lasted until 1911), and hence the natural leader, Rome did not name him Primate with the attendant authority such a title bestows. He – like his successors to this day – was essentially *primus inter pares*. While a show of unity was maintained at the first two national synods organized by Wiseman after the restoration, which aimed at building a Catholic infrastructure in schools and churches, by the time of the third in 1859 he had become a lonely figure, waiting in his room for the other bishops to come and – metaphorically – sit at his feet. He need not have held his breath. They did not oblige.

His staunch allegiance to Rome cost Wiseman dear throughout his time as Archbishop. With the moves towards Italian unification, and in particular the assistance offered to that fledgling nation by Emperor Napoleon III of France in the 1859 war, the Papal States were all but swallowed up. Pius IX was reduced as a temporal potentate to the city of Rome. Wiseman made plain his bitter opposition to this, adding to the gulf dividing the Catholic Church from the nation, which welcomed Italian unity.

When he tried in the following year to set up an Accademia of the Catholic Religion, his fellow bishops, including his successor Manning, who dubbed it 'an engine for infusing the Roman spirit into the cultivated laity', saw it as a means of arguing on the national stage for support for the Pope in defending his lands. Such a strategy, they predicted, would go down badly with the English, and the Accademia was still-born. Wiseman, incidentally, saw the Accademia much more as a think-tank where a Catholic response to challenges like Darwin's *Origin of Species*, published in 1859, could be articulated. He had clearly not taken on board the residual non-intellectualism, some would say anti-intellectualism, of the English Church.

By his support for the Pope and the Papal States, Wiseman compromised his own position. He had invoked the principles of *laissez-faire* liberalism to argue that English Catholics should be allowed their own hierarchy, but was then seen to be standing against the Europe-wide tide of that same liberalism by holding that the pontiff had to cling to his temporal powers to the detriment of a united Italy.

Wiseman increased his personal isolation by clashing with the darling of English liberalism, John Henry Newman, one of the leading lights in the Anglican Oxford Movement, who had converted to Catholicism in 1845. When Newman drew up plans for an Oratory at Oxford, his erstwhile home, Wiseman intervened decisively to block them. He believed that the presence of Newman at the Oratory would be like a magnet to young Catholics, encouraging them to go to Oxford University, which, to Wiseman, was a bastion of Established Anglicanism and anti-Catholic prejudice. An Oxford education would 'weaken the faith' of tender minds, he declared in 1864. The Oratory idea was to sit on the shelf until 1989 when it was revived by Birmingham Archdiocese – another testament to Newman's vision.

Another source of disharmony came in 1857 when the Association for Promoting the Unity of Christendom was set up, with Catholics, Anglicans and Orthodox Christians as members. It received a cool response from Wiseman. He recorded his antipathy in a memo to Rome. His principal objection was that the association treated 'the three great denominations . . . of Christianity, i.e. Catholics, Greeks and Anglicans, as though they were all equal and could treat of religious union upon a footing of equality'. In 1864, he asked the Holy See to condemn the ecumenically minded association, to the dismay of his fellow bishops.

The benefits of hindsight, however, should not obscure the scale of the task Wiseman faced. When he arrived in 1850 the new Archbishop found English Catholics as a body accustomed to being on the defensive. He was at least bold in staking a claim for a more equal situation, though it was not until the advent of Basil Hume that English society wholeheartedly took the Catholic Church to its bosom. In practical terms he inherited a Church with few priests, even fewer buildings and a perception of its national role that did not stretch much beyond keeping its head below the parapet and above the pulpit. Cardinal Wiseman oversaw a substantial growth in the number of Catholic churches and schools in the country, and vocations increased thanks to his careful nurturing. The concession by Parliament of the need for Catholic prison, army and navy chaplains was a substantial achievement.

By the time of his death his eccentricities no longer caused anger so much as interest, bordering on bemusement, among the general public who lined the route of his cortège when he was buried in 1865. *The Times* on 23 February claimed that not since the funeral of the Duke of Wellington, victor at Waterloo over Napoleon and a former Prime Minister, had the people shown so much interest in watching a coffin. And, in marked contrast to its editorial greeting his appointment by the Pope, the *'Thunderer'* described Wiseman as 'an eminent Englishman and one of the most learned men of his time'.

Cardinal Henry Manning (1865–1892):
The workers' friend

Cardinal Henry Manning is unique among the Archbishops of Westminster of modern times – not to mention distinctly unusual among Catholic bishops worldwide – in having been married. His wife Caroline died in 1837, four years after their wedding and 14 years before her husband, then an Anglican clergyman, decided to 'go over to Rome'.

Lytton Strachey created a thoroughly disagreeable picture of Manning that reflects many of the prejudices the English Establishment felt about the restoration of the Catholic hierarchy in the nineteenth century. Manning, the second Archbishop of Westminster, was a ruthless megalomaniac, with more than a hint of hypocrisy, according to the author of *Eminent Victorians*. It is a portrait revealing the antipathy the average Englishman of the period felt towards the Church of Rome. Manning was, like his predecessor Wiseman, a champion of papal authority and hence a target of the author's 'papal fifth column' paranoia; he was, according to Strachey, a scarlet-robed, sinister, intriguing dogmatist whose intensity was distasteful to the English way of doing religion.

The truth was rather different. For a start Manning was very English. The son of an MP, he converted to Catholicism in 1851 just as his career in the Church of England was taking off. A friend of Gladstone's from Oxford – his *alma mater* was Harrow – the young Archdeacon of Chichester seemed destined for high office in the Anglican world, some even talking of him as a future Archbishop of Canterbury. Gladstone never quite got over the shock of his friend's conversion and though the two remained in contact – and indeed shared much in their political and social outlooks – they were never as close again. Manning, by becoming a Catholic, put himself outside the Establishment. By naming such an outsider as Archbishop, Rome effectively emphasized the outsider status of English Catholicism.

Despite his Anglican background, Manning did little better than Wiseman at easing relations with the Church of England. When he spoke in disparaging terms of those who stayed within the Anglican fold, emphasizing 'their want of truth', his old friends saw a reflection of the kind of triumphalism that Wiseman had come to symbolize. The papal bull *Apostolicae Curae*, condemning Anglican orders as null and void, was published in 1895 after Manning's death, but he was certainly influential in shaping the thinking behind it – thinking that appeared to the Anglicans of Victorian England to confirm all their worst suspicions about the restored Catholic hierarchy.

If Manning and Wiseman shared an insensitivity to the Church of England, they were opposites in many other ways. Manning had radically different enthusiasms from his predecessor. He was above all a practical man rather than a thinker or a writer, and was certainly not one to stand on his dignity. Where Wiseman saw his task as to establish the Catholic Church and bring England back to the one true faith, Manning's mission was to alleviate the sufferings of the poor, particularly the recently arrived Irish who were transforming the face of English Catholicism. Neither crusade eased the task of the restored hierarchy in a hostile environment.

Manning's was a mission that had the added drawback that it won him few friends among the Catholic aristocracy. To them the Irish were an embarrassment, a hindrance as the one-time recusants strived for the acceptance and political advancement that emancipation had promised. They found that other great convert to Catholicism, John Henry Newman, much more to their taste.

Relations between the two Cardinals were no easier than those between Wiseman and Newman. Manning was in public always polite to Newman and paid tribute to him for his intellectual contribution in re-establishing English Catholicism. 'No-one who does not intend to be laughed at will henceforward say that the Catholic religion is fit only for weak intellects and unmanly brains', he wrote of his colleague. While Newman was liberal and progressive in his thinking – his ideas are often held to have inspired the reforming Second Vatican Council of the mid-1960s – Manning was a theological conservative, decidedly Ultramontane in his attitude to Rome and papal power. He was therefore as intolerant as Wiseman of the more relaxed attitude abroad in the English Church, encouraged by Newman in his famous letter to the Duke of Norfolk: 'If I am obliged to bring religion into after-dinner toasts I shall drink – to the Pope if you please – still, to Conscience first, and to the Pope afterwards'.

If Manning courted the role of the outcast, he certainly found a home among his fellow outcasts. To the working classes Manning was a hero and it was his commitment as a social radical that contributed most to his unpopularity among the powerful.

English Catholicism in the latter years of the nineteenth century was overwhelmingly working-class in composition because of the waves of Irish immigration, and Manning geared his policies – often with an iron will and intransigence that exasperated those around him – to that fact. And since to the Establishment the political devotion of the Irish to the Crown and constitution could not be relied upon, their champion was similarly suspect. He challenged the social pretensions and political conservatism of Victorian England.

Social radicals do not usually thrive in the English Church and Manning stands alone in this respect among the Archbishops of Westminster. The habitual trend of the Church has been towards the conservative in matters of state and society, and the liberal in theology. Manning turned this formula on its head.

While Victorian England took pride in being the workshop of the world, Manning denounced capitalism as a 'tyranny' and the Industrial Revolution as 'one hundred years of selfish political economy'. He argued, with just a hint of the Marxist analysis that the current Pope finds so distasteful in Latin American-style liberation theology, that labour and skills were just as much capital as financial investment was. 'I claim for labour and the skill which is acquired by labour, the rights of capital. It is capital in its truest sense.' Profits, he said, had to take second place to the rights of workers. This radical line of Manning's was not as out of step with Vatican thinking as today's liberation theologians are with Pope John Paul II. For 1891 saw the publication by Pope Leo XIII of the encyclical *Rerum Novarum*, every bit as critical of the exploitation of workers as Manning had been in his utterances on the subject. Indeed Leo XIII is said to have been impressed and influenced by Manning's work.

The encyclical's appearance contributed to the image of Catholicism as an intoxicating and dangerous drug for those on the bottom rung of society.

Manning did not confine himself to fine words, or even to making sure that other people did what he said was right. He set an example. So when he decided that drink was bad for the health, especially of working men, he became a fervent teetotaller himself. Such exacting standards often made relationships with his fellow bishops difficult for, contrary to Lytton Strachey's charge, Manning was anything but a hypocrite.

When the rich and powerful suggested that the new Archdiocese of Westminster needed a cathedral to rival the nearby Abbey, he played for time. The money would be much better spent on building schools to educate the children of the poor in London. When in 1884 he sat on the Royal Commission on the Housing of the Working Classes, along with the Prince of Wales, he was dubbed 'our only revolutionary' by the chairman. He earned the epithet by suggesting prisons, factories and ironworks be moved to the suburbs to make more space available for housing in the inner cities. Because of his outspokenness, Manning earned the label of socialist from his detractors. Yet for all that it summed up much of his social outlook, this term did not convey the contradictions that made him so authoritarian and conservative in upholding the infallibility of the Pope when the doctrine was promulgated in 1870.

Perhaps Manning's most famous gesture of solidarity with the poor against the wealthy – an outsider siding with the outsiders – came in 1889 during the London dock strike. His intervention with the employers was decisive in reaching a compromise over pay and conditions that was greeted by the workers as a victory. In the May Day procession of 1890, his portrait was carried alongside that of Karl Marx.

The Cardinal's involvement with the workers, and especially with the Irish urban poor, led him, logically enough, to become interested in the fate of their homeland. He has been, so far, the only Archbishop of Westminster to take such a close and sustained interest in Irish matters. Despite their earlier differences, Manning and Gladstone shared an enthusiasm for Home Rule for Ireland, although Manning railed more against the injustices of the colonial rule from Dublin Castle than did Gladstone. As both found to their cost, to stand up for the Irish in Britain was to court unpopularity.

For Manning it also meant incurring the displeasure of Rome. For many years the British government had put pressure on the Vatican to act as a restraint on Irish radicalism through the power of the pulpit in Irish society. In 1888 Pope Leo XIII yielded and sent a commission of inquiry to Ireland, which came down against illegal practices in the campaign to win rights to land ownership for local people. Manning responded to Leo's endorsement of the report by stating that the principle of keeping within the law was the right one, but that the Pope was mistaken in the case of Ireland. The pontiff was not infallible in matters of fact, his erstwhile champion said, and Leo XIII simply didn't know the facts about Ireland.

Manning's stewardship of Catholic England was an uncomfortable time for the powerful, both within the Establishment and among the Catholic elite. When he died in 1892, they determined that his radicalism should die with him. His robust willingness to take on the politicians on issues not directly 'religious', to get involved at a practical level, would not be seen again until Abbot Hume arrived at Westminster.

Cardinal Herbert Vaughan (1892–1903):
A safe pair of hands

Herbert Vaughan couldn't have been more different from Henry Manning. The new Cardinal was Catholic to the core, a member of a recusant family who had kept the faith alive at their Courtfield home in Herefordshire since the days of Elizabeth I. The Vaughans were certainly a devout clan. The eldest of thirteen, Herbert had five sisters who were nuns and five brothers who were priests (the other two tried out their vocations in seminaries). He was a pious, energetic, straightforward man who shared with Wiseman and Manning a loyalty to the dictates of Rome. As his biographer wrote: 'Herbert Vaughan's simple rule of conduct, his easy test for Catholic loyalty, was always, and under all circumstances, to stand on the side of Rome'.

His distaste for the brand of English Catholicism that saw fit to debate papal decrees in the light of conscience became apparent when he used his personal wealth to become editor and proprietor of the Catholic weekly review, *The Tablet*. He would allow no discussion in its columns of the papal claims to infallibility that emerged in the later part of the nineteenth century, much to the chagrin of liberals.

In some ways he was more open than his predecessors. Soon after taking office in 1893 he rescinded Wiseman's ban on Catholics going to Oxford and Cambridge. Yet his theology was undoubtedly conservative and traditional, as his spiritual writings make abundantly clear, and he shared little of Manning's zeal for improving the lot of the working Irish. He saw his task primarily as an administrator, fitting the description by the Foreign Office official quoted at the beginning of this chapter.

Vaughan's great work, indeed his monument, was Westminster Cathedral. Where Manning had stalled plans to build a great church, preferring to spend his money on schools, Vaughan took up the plans with gusto. Catholic life in England and Wales must have its centre, he argued, its house of prayer. Until Westminster had a cathedral the successful restoration of the hierarchy would not be complete. His priority was bricks and mortar and it proved to be a popular policy. To this day English Catholicism cannot but envy the Church of England its great cathedrals. With a few notable exceptions – like the medieval St Etheldreda's in central London, bought back by the Church in more recent times – there is little of inspiration in the architecture of Catholic churches in England, all of which were built since the restoration of the hierarchy. Westminster Cathedral did not make good that absence, but at least tried to provide one showpiece.

Vaughan, perhaps with a premonition that his reign would not be a long one, determined that the cathedral should be built quickly – within five years was his target. He therefore selected John Bentley's Byzantine design. It would be cheaper and faster to erect than a Gothic or Baroque alternative. It also had the advantage of being radically different from Westminster Abbey, quashing forever those rumours that had haunted Cardinal Wiseman of a Catholic desire to reclaim the former Benedictine centre.

With his easy *entrée* into the wealthy upper echelons of English Catholicism Vaughan was able to raise the money needed to get started. Indeed the image of a builder, a man who left monuments for future generations, is an appropriate one for Herbert Vaughan. As Vice-Rector of St Edmund's College at Ware, he had guided an overhaul of the methods used for the training of priests. Later he established St Joseph's Missionary Society at Mill Hill in north

London, still active to this day. Vaughan harboured an abiding resentment that his stated desire to go and work in the mission fields was frustrated first by his superiors and then by having high office, as he saw it, thrust upon him.

For a man who was born in 1832, the year in which the Great Reform Act took the first step towards universal suffrage, Vaughan was singularly lacking in the spirit of his age. He was no liberal reformer or radical. His eleven years at Westminster saw the Church slip from the forward, if exposed, position it had taken under Wiseman and Manning into a backwater where it slept peacefully and securely in its liturgical devotions and separateness until the Second World War provided a rude awakening.

Cardinal Francis Bourne (1903–1935):
The quiet Cardinal

Francis Bourne's biographer, the former *Tablet* editor Ernest Oldmeadow, claimed that because his subject preferred the softly-softly approach he was judged to have done nothing during his long reign – some would say interregnum – at the head of English Catholicism. Quietness should not be equated with mediocrity, Oldmeadow emphasized, not altogether convincingly.

A former rector of Wonersh Seminary near Guildford and Bishop of Southwark, Francis Bourne witnessed as Archbishop some of the most traumatic years of the century in world and national history. Yet his contribution to easing the pain of those events, providing a Christian witness, was a limited one. He repeatedly appealed during the First World War for a just peace but did little to press home his message. To his mind that was not the Catholic Church's role. During the General Strike of the mid-1920s, he showed not a glint of the Manning of old when he declined to intervene, and then castigated those refusing to go back to work. English Catholicism under Bourne became conservative in all things, issuing censorious condemnations when it was occasionally pricked into action.

A great deal of Bourne's energy was taken up in feuding with his fellow bishops. In 1911, in response to not infrequent bickering within the English hierarchy, the papal instruction *Si qua est* made Bourne (and his successors) as Archbishop the president of the bishops' conference but not the Primate. The notion in the Vatican's mind of collective action, of liberals nudging conservatives forward

36

and the traditionally minded restraining the more radical, was not borne out by the facts. It was a recipe for inaction and introspection.

The most notorious disagreement came over Bourne's attempts to swallow up his former see of Southwark – which covers the London region south of the Thames – into Westminster. Bishop Peter Amigo of Southwark, appointed by Bourne in the belief that he would be placid and easy to manipulate, resented the Cardinal's plans and his high-handed interference in local matters. The public row between the two reached such a pitch that the Holy See made its displeasure known. In 1929, when Bourne travelled to Rome to be briefed on the Vatican's view of the Concordat it had just concluded with Mussolini, in order then to relay the details to the Foreign Office, he received a very frosty welcome. He was upset by the experience and turned to one of the Vatican officials with special knowledge of England, Cardinal Gasquet, for support. Gasquet's biographer notes that 'when coldly received at Rome, Bourne asked Gasquet what he had done, he was frankly told that his relations with Southwark were a scandal'.

Amigo was later to take the lead in pressing Rome for the appointment of an Apostolic Delegate to England, conveying to the Holy See the opinion of many of the bishops that a papal representative would act as a counterbalance to the ambitions and power of the Archbishop. This campaign achieved its goal in 1938, just three years after Bourne's death.

The 1930s in particular were a somnolent period for English Catholicism. Ill-health and personal inclination pushed Bourne more and more into his shell. The growing threat in Europe, industrial stagnation and mass unemployment loomed large in many lives, but were rarely addressed by the Cardinal, who to many appeared trapped in the pre-war days of his youth. The first flowering of an educated middle-class laity caused him only alarm and he blocked all attempts to allow Mass-goers a greater say in affairs in their parishes.

The Cardinal was, however, vocal in his dislike of the emerging Labour Party. On the eve of the 1931 election, which was to see significant gains for Labour and the formation of the National Government, Bourne travelled to London's East End and the bizarrely named Premierland Hall. There, while stressing that Catholics could join the Labour Party if they had to, he told those who did 'to set your faces against anything in the nature of a denial of the right to private property and anything in the nature of class warfare'. He touched briefly on the problems of unemployment, which was soaring in the area at the time. His chosen solution was that more land should be put under plough to provide jobs. That somewhat eccentric notion was followed, after a fleeting reference to the on-going battle with the government over the position of Catholic schools (of which much more in later chapters), by Bourne launching a far-sighted appeal for the building of a Channel tunnel.

The following year, on one of his trips to Rome, Bourne was taken ill. He never really recovered his health and he lingered on, a lame duck leader, for two more years before dying on the first day of 1935, largely unmourned beyond the dictates of politeness. A year before his death, the government had decided that the King would not be represented at Bourne's funeral. Archbishop Cosmo Lang of Canterbury told the King's private secretary at the time that it could not be said that Bourne 'with all his merits has occupied a place of very distinguished leadership in national life compared with Cardinal Manning. He is more in the position of Cardinal Vaughan though not even as prominent as he was in general social life.'

Cardinal Arthur Hinsley (1935–1943):
Churchill's tip for Canterbury

Arthur Hinsley was living in semi-retirement in Rome when he received the summons from the Pope to return to his native England, after an absence of 18 years. The 69-year-old Archbishop of Westminster had spent much of his life as Apostolic Visitor to British Africa and while his lack of knowledge of the domestic scene and his age were severe handicaps in carrying out his new task, his experience of dealing with British officialdom – and its with him – were to prove invaluable during the early stages of the Second World War when the Vatican struggled to distance itself from Mussolini's Italy that surrounded it, and from Il Duce's allies in Berlin.

Hinsley came from Irish stock. His father had been a carpenter in his native Yorkshire. The future Cardinal showed great promise as a teacher after ordination – he founded St Bede's Grammar School in Bradford despite the opposition of the local bishop – and was quickly marked out for preferment when he moved to the Venerable English College in Rome as Rector in 1917. After a decade there, during which he saw the rise of Mussolini and was not much impressed, he moved on to his wandering brief in British Africa.

A Foreign Office official who followed affairs in the Holy See, Stephen Gaselee, commented at the time of Hinsley's surprise appointment that 'his selection shows that the Vatican still pays attention to the influence and sentiments of the old *English* Roman Catholics, by passing over the more distinguished Archbishop of Liverpool, Dr Downey, who represents the Irish Roman Catholic immigrants now forming so important an element of Roman Catholic life in the rest of the British Isles'.

While it is true to say that Downey, Irish-born and with a proven record in tackling the religious sectarianism that had plagued Liverpool, would have gone down very badly with certain influential elements in English Catholicism, to consign Hinsley to the camp of the landowning families is to overlook his humble origins. The demarcation line, in any case, had by this stage become harder to draw. While the two camps of English Catholicism were straying on to each other's territory, no true integration had yet taken place.

Where Gaselee's comments ring true (as has been very readably and very comprehensively shown by Dr Thomas Moloney in his book *Westminster, Whitehall and the Vatican*) is in pinpointing Hinsley's role in the immediate pre-war years. Catholics within the Foreign Office, and those increasingly concerned by the growing threat from Germany and Italy, had grown impatient with Cardinal Bourne's stubborn refusal to face up to the events shaping Europe. In Hinsley, men like the Duke of Norfolk saw someone with a knowledge of how both Foreign Office and Vatican diplomacy worked, and therefore with the credentials and skill to align British and Holy See interests against Mussolini, who had been claiming that the Rome–Berlin Axis had God on its side.

Working with a small group of influential Catholic peers and senior civil servants, Hinsley was able to perform that task, though often his advances were met with obstacles from both sides. Mussolini's invasion of Abyssinia in 1936 and the Vatican's somewhat equivocal attitude to it hampered Hinsley early on, while the naming of a papal representative to London in 1938, the first step towards the full diplomatic relations which finally came in 1981 when the Apostolic Delegate became a Pro-Nuncio, was effected largely over the Cardinal's head.

When war finally came, Hinsley was a diligent pastor who stayed at his post, alongside his people. His radio broadcasts were a source of inspiration and won him if not quite the love and admiration then certainly the respect of the nation.

His impact on other aspects of the domestic scene was limited by his preoccupation with what was going on around the world. His relations with his fellow bishops were always difficult. They resented the fact that he had been, as they saw it, foisted on them. His presence was a constant reminder that the Vatican had not considered any of them up to the task and had chosen instead a 69-year-old in semi-retirement. When he turned to them for support and advice on national and local affairs, like the growing debate on the education issue, they displayed their irritation that he was so out of touch. Archbishop Downey and Archbishop Mostyn of Cardiff were particularly difficult in this regard. When he tried to act without their advice they felt he was trampling on their authority.

Hinsley wasn't entirely successful or even single-minded in his attempts to move Catholic England on from the secure world of the *Catholic Fireside*, popular in the parishes at the time as a pious, introspective journal that carried on as if there were no war clouds gathering on the horizon. But at least he recognized the need. On a personal level he refused to follow the example of his two predecessors and remain censorious and disapproving in the safe backwater of his home and community. When the going got tough, he got going on a national stage.

Symptomatic of Hinsley's willingness to look outwards at a time of trial was his sponsorship of the 'Sword of the Spirit' movement. In his letter to his fellow bishops of August 1941, Arthur Hinsley made clear his reasons for the setting up of this body: the fall of France; the shock to Catholic sentiment of Italy's entry into the war; the insidious allurements of a Latin Catholic bloc; and above all the exhilarating but frightening realization of Britain's isolation. The aim was to 'secure more united and intense prayer, study and work among Catholics in the cause of the Church and of our country'. The patriotism of Hinsley's appeal struck a chord in an England that had always doubted the allegiance of a mainly Irish Catholic community to the English Crown. As the Cardinal himself put it in his letter: 'I had reason to fear propaganda against British Catholics if steps were not taken to forestall it'. In the parishes there was enthusiasm. The suggestion that thought should be given to the shape of post-war Europe proved particularly alluring.

The birth of Sword of the Spirit came after a radio broadcast by Hinsley of the same title at the end of 1940. A group of influential Catholic lay people – including the historian Christopher Dawson and the writer Barbara Ward, who went on to be an adviser to two Presidents of the United States – visited the Cardinal and suggested starting a movement, open to all regardless of denomination. Hinsley agreed and at first Sword of the Spirit thrived, its high point being the summer 1941 gathering at the Stoll Theatre on the Strand. But when it was decided to draft a constitution for the movement, Hinsley's fellow bishops insisted that it be specifically Catholic. They didn't like the idea of too much lay involvement, as they had told Cardinal Hinsley on many occasions. Cardinal Bourne could be relied on to keep the laity in its place. Anglicans enthusiastic about Sword of the Spirit tried to work around the Catholic bishops' prejudices. A parallel organization was set up – Religion and Life – and it held its meetings jointly with Sword of the Spirit.

Despite the grassroots popularity of the movement, in particular with those serving in the forces, Hinsley's enthusiasm was not enough to carry the day, especially when in June 1941 his fellow bishops nudged the new Apostolic Delegate, William Godfrey, to preach a sermon in Birmingham reaffirming the boundaries for co-operation between Catholics and other faiths.

Arthur Hinsley was a man ahead of his time who recognized the changes afoot in the world but who, in the final analysis, did not have the physical strength or the strength of character to carry the Catholic community and his fellow bishops with him. He saw that the English Catholic community would have to come out of its ghetto of parish socials, simple truths and liturgical fervour. He realized that an increasingly educated laity was beginning to demand a role and tried in the Sword of the Spirit to give it one. He recognized that windows had to be opened, the musty smell of incense let out and the heady odours of the new world order that was to come after the war let in.

He won many admirers during his brief time as Archbishop. Evelyn Waugh, never a gentle judge, wrote: 'The succession of Archbishop Hinsley in April 1935, though he was an old and ailing man, was a grateful refreshment to English Catholics inside and outside the archdiocese'. Winston Churchill admired Hinsley's wartime record and patriotism so much that when the request came to 10 Downing Street to appoint a new Archbishop of Canterbury he commented 'A pity we can't have the old man at Westminster'. And, as if out of gratitude, the new Anglican Primate in 1943 broke with precedent and attended Hinsley's funeral.

The omens were good for the future. The first signs of a shift out of the ghetto had appeared.

Cardinal Bernard Griffin (1943–1956):
Full of early promise

When he received a letter bearing the papal coat of arms in 1943, Bernard Griffin, the young auxiliary Bishop of Birmingham, suspected it would contain news of a promotion. But his ambitions stretched only as far as heading the neighbouring vacant diocese of Northampton. The 44-year-old had not even entertained dreams of translation to Westminster to lead English Catholicism.

Hinsley's death had come at a crucial juncture in the war. The tide was starting to turn the Allies' way. The Luftwaffe had been defeated. The Italian campaign was proving successful. Thoughts were beginning to turn towards the aftermath of the war and the new world order that would result. It was with an eye to planning for the future that Rome in effect skipped a generation and chose Bernard Griffin, an obscure but talented provincial auxiliary bishop, to be Archbishop of Westminster. 'Of the future no-one could say very much except that it was going to pose great problems, international, national and social', wrote Michael de la Bedoyère, editor of the *Catholic Herald*. 'The Pope selected to face them, whatever they might be, a young bishop in the flower of health and energy.'

Griffin's diocesan work had covered all aspects of the social problems post-war Britain was to face. And his own background, Birmingham-born of lower middle-class stock with roots in Ireland and the countryside but forced into the city to find work, was considered ideal to give him a clear understanding of the challenges ahead.

One of the first tasks for the new Archbishop was to follow the progress of R. A. Butler's Education Bill through Parliament. There had already been many heated discussions about the role of the Catholic schools in the state system that Butler was proposing. Griffin shared Hinsley's misgivings about the deal the Catholic Church was being offered and argued, to no avail, that such a major reform should not be introduced in wartime when the electorate had no way of making its feelings known. Eventually he reluctantly agreed to the compromise whereby Catholic schools joined the state system and had all their day-to-day running costs met by White-hall, but had to find 50 per cent of capital costs in return for the bishops retaining overall control of what went on in the classroom. Griffin was later to refer to Butler's legislation as 'a hotch potch sort of an Act' and in 1950 spoke darkly of the changes being a 'death sentence' for Catholic schools. What he was complaining about was the strain placed on the Catholic community in raising its 50 per cent contribution to the building of new schools. Although the strain was undoubtedly real, such florid language – which with hindsight can be seen to have been unjustified – did little to endear the Catholic hierarchy to the Whitehall mandarins over-seeing the new system.

With Aneurin Bevan's introduction of the National Health Ser-vice, Cardinal Griffin had a more difficult task. He did not want the 70 or so Catholic hospitals that had grown up to serve the Catholic community – another feature of the ghetto mentality – lumped in with the new system. In his heart he clearly still saw the Catholic community as a group apart, parallel to the rest of the nation, contributing and exchanging ideas, but not integrated.

Bevan, who was a great admirer of the Catholic institutions and who had been a patient at St John and St Elizabeth's Hospital in north London, was keen that it and similar institutions should join in. A largely amicable debate between the two men, who were brought together by Richard Stokes, a Catholic in the Labour government, resulted and was only resolved when Griffin threat-ened to use his office to warn off the Irish (Catholic) nurses who were to be the backbone and the powerhouse of the NHS from crossing the Irish Sea to work. The Catholic system, with its special ethos, was saved – though it should be noted, in judging Griffin's wisdom, that of the 70 hospitals only a handful now remain.

Griffin based his post-war policy on the primacy of the family. In his first major sermon as Archbishop he said that the disruption and dislocation to family life in the wartime years had to be tackled. The permissiveness – shocking by the standards of the 1940s if not by those of today – that had occurred in the heat of battle and on snatched leaves from the front line had to stop, Griffin emphasized. It was a theme he would return to repeatedly. 'A nation depends for its well-being on sound family life; therefore we should endeavour to remove all those obstacles that exist to the restoration of Christian family life.'

Griffin did not lose sight of the need Hinsley had identified for the Catholic Church to move more into the mainstream of society, though his chosen form of action was the block vote. Lay people were encouraged to get involved in local and national politics but Griffin's channels for this were special Catholic groups within trade unions. Under the banner of the Association of Catholic Trade Unionists, the faithful would act as a lobby within their own unions. The walls of the ghetto were slow to tumble and the first tentative steps outside were to be taken roped together for safety. It should be noted that Griffin in particular, and the English Church in general, resisted the trend of continental Catholicism towards specifically Catholic trade unions, a tradition which many historians today hold responsible for the alienation of the working classes from the Church in Europe. Within the parish Griffin encouraged the separatist old-style devotions of figures like Fr Peyton, and his Rosary Crusade, or pilgrimages to the restored shrine of Our Lady of Walsingham in Norfolk.

In 1949 Griffin had to withdraw at the last minute from a Catholic protest rally in the Albert Hall about the plight of Cardinal Mindszenty, the Hungarian Primate who was being persecuted by the Communist authorities. Officials at Westminster said Griffin was suffering from nervous exhaustion. It was in effect the end of his active leadership of English Catholicism. Although he recovered a little and took the stage again, the energy and dynamism of old had gone and the Cardinal came increasingly to rely on his close circle of advisers. The demands of the job had broken his health.

Of this later period, Ronald Knox remarked in his tribute on the Cardinal's death in 1956 that he had been 'encased in too much velvet'. The ailing Cardinal had become distant from his people, a remote figure venturing out of Archbishop's House to his favourite spot in London, the Queen Mary Rose Garden in Regent's Park, and then driving back home listening to *Mrs Dale's Diary* on the radio. The Cardinal bore his suffering with great courage and humility but his earlier reputation as a man of action was inevitably overshadowed. The momentum he had built up was lost.

Cardinal William Godfrey (1957–1963):
A man of another age

William Godfrey, who had been the first papal delegate to Britain in 1938, and from 1953 onwards Archbishop of Liverpool, was the natural choice as Griffin's successor. It was his reward for covering for the ailing Cardinal in his last years. But Godfrey came to the job in his late sixties, an age when most working men had retired, and in his six years as leader he was able to do little to shake off the image of lethargy and drift that had afflicted English Catholicism in the latter part of Griffin's cardinalate.

The social and educational changes transforming the Catholic community were gathering pace. There was a rising middle class and a growing call for more lay involvement, for reform, for true integration with the outside world. But William Godfrey, though a diligent pastor, was unable fully to comprehend or harness these changes, which, on an international scale, came to a head when Pope John XXIII summoned the Second Vatican Council for 1962. Indeed Godfrey once remarked to his colleague Bishop Cashman that it was only during the preparations for the Vatican Council that he had realized how out of touch he was with the modern Church. Cardinal Godfrey, like Griffin and Hinsley, stood on the brink of the modern world, but each, for his own reasons, instinctively held back.

When he was appointed as Apostolic Delegate to Great Britain in 1938, Godfrey was the first papal emissary to reside in the country since Cardinal Pole in the time of Mary Tudor 400 years earlier. The Vatican newspaper, *L'Osservatore Romano*, trumpeted 'a new and glorious stage of the church in that noble nation' and even such faintly triumphalistic language could rouse little more than the odd question in Parliament from some of the more dogmatic Protestant members, and a Protestant Truth Society protest at 'the dangerously strong Roman Catholic influences in the Foreign Office'. But the age of the Gordon rioters was over. The extremist voices no longer struck a chord in their listeners.

Godfrey was another of those efficient administrators who worked diligently as a pastor in both Liverpool and Westminster. In later years he devoted much of his energy to the Central Preparatory Council for the Vatican Council, a labour that sapped his health and contributed to the heart attack that took his life in January 1963.

Cardinal John Carmel Heenan (1963–1975):
Caught in a storm

John Carmel Heenan was the first modern Archbishop of Westminster. His predecessors had lived in a cocoon, and had kept English Catholicism frozen in time. Here was a man unafraid of the challenge of the new. Yet Heenan was a victim of circumstance and those long-suppressed cries for reform. Much of his energy at Westminster was spent not in bringing the new spirit that he recognized as necessary but in coping with the fall-out of disputes within the Church universal as it attempted to get to grips with the modern world at the Vatican Council and afterwards. It was a period of turbulence not seen in English Catholicism since the days of the Reformation.

The Council was already meeting in Rome when Heenan was appointed. The winds of change were blowing through the universal Church. In England and Wales this would mean that Catholicism's leading light, rather than taking the constructive, liberating, modernizing role that was anticipated for him, had to battle to keep his Church in one piece as the wholesale reforms of the Council left Catholics veering between confusion, expectancy and division.

Heenan had to hold the line and keep his flock together. Where reasoned argument failed he was seen on occasion to resort to old-style coercion, albeit with a modern face and a smile for the cameras. As the outside world was invited into the *cordon sanitaire* surrounding the English Catholic parish, its culture of sodalities, Children of Mary and grand processions began to crumble. In the face of this change, John Carmel Heenan's role became essentially reactive, coping with each new challenge as it arose, dishing out reassurance and rules in equal measure. It was an exhausting and dispiriting task and by the end of his life, his health broken, he admitted to his close colleagues that for the first time he had suffered doubt and bouts of despair at the direction the Church and English Catholicism was taking.

Born in Ilford, to the east of London, of Irish parentage – his mother and father met in Ireland and were married there – Heenan had grown up in a very different Church from the one which he bequeathed Basil Hume in 1975. He reflected on those changes in his 1971 autobiography, *Not the Whole Truth*. 'The great hero of my youth was Fr Palmer, the parish priest. A minister of religion in Ilford today would probably be little known. He would not be regarded as an important figure unless he had rare gifts. It was not so in the Ilford of my childhood. Fr Palmer was the best-known man in the little town. . . . He had so many prospective converts that it was impossible for him to take them.'

Heenan's origins and his affections were with the working-class first- and second-generation Irish who peopled his childhood and youth. He recalled that when he was growing up in Ilford, 'the welfare state was not yet even on the horizon. Most Catholic parents were poor and found difficulty in supplying all the extras.' Even when he became Cardinal, the fusion between this mass of immigrant Catholics and their descendants and the older English gentry was not yet complete. The two factions were being diffused as a growing number of middle-class Catholics and converts took their places in the pews. But it was in the simple, pious faith of the Irish, which at times bordered on Jansenism in its righteousness, that Heenan had his roots.

His climb upwards into the higher echelons of the Church was rapid. While still a parish priest in the East End, he was called in by Cardinal Hinsley and marked out for preferment. In 1936 Hinsley supported Heenan, over the head of his local bishop, in his trip to the Soviet Union, giving the young priest permission to leave his Roman collar and breviary at home and travel incognito, disguised as a psychologist. This was a bizarre episode, characteristic of a restless curiosity in the future Cardinal and a desire to see things at a practical, first-hand level – in this case why Communism was gaining converts from the Church. He was shocked at what he witnessed – Stalin's reign of terror was at its height – and one lasting result of the trip was to awaken Heenan's interest in Catholic–Jewish relations.

During the Second World War, Heenan began to make his mark as a broadcaster with his talks entitled 'Britain speaks' on the World

Service. He appeared occasionally alongside Barbara Ward on the *Brains Trust* and was also a keen journalist, building a church hall with the fees he received for his articles in the *Daily Sketch*. That gift for communicating was used after the war when Fr Heenan was appointed in 1947 to run the Catholic Missionary Society, set up by Cardinal Vaughan in 1901 to win converts 'by means of sermons in churches and lectures in halls' and by the mid-1940s moribund. Heenan took up the task with gusto, criss-crossing the country with a mobile display housed in a caravan. As an early sign of the sort of modernization he thought the Catholic Church needed in the post-war era, he changed the focus of the society's work from seeking new converts to strengthening the faith by preaching to the converted. No longer were there dreams of reclaiming Mary's Dowry.

Heenan's dynamism and talent for administration did not go unnoticed and in 1951 he took the first step up the ecclesiastical ladder when he was named Bishop of Leeds. His first months there were unhappy ones. He felt the diocese had grown too sleepy and set in its ways and he embarked on a wide-ranging programme of transferring priests to new parishes and bringing in new blood. The changes weren't popular with the clergy – they remarked bitterly that he had kept the local removal firms in business for many years – but did Heenan's reputation no harm. In 1957 he was promoted to the Archdiocese of Liverpool.

There he showed similar energy, tackling the sectarian divides that had plagued the city since it became the focus of Irish immigration in the mid-nineteenth century. He also resolved the problem of the city's cathedral with a typically daring gesture. In the pre-war days Edwin Lutyens, the architect of New Delhi, had been commissioned to design a cathedral and had come up with a towering, marble-clad edifice to rival St Peter's in Rome. War-time shortages and a lack of funds meant that by the time of Heenan's arrival construction had got no further than the crypt. He decided to abandon the plan. After all, it was asked at the time, was such a triumphalistic outpouring still appropriate to the place of an English Catholic Church keen to integrate? In its place Heenan launched a competition and awarded the task to Frederick Gibberd, whose revolutionary glass and concrete circular cathedral, known affectionately as 'Paddy's wigwam' or 'the Mersey funnel', took its place on the Liverpool skyline in 1967.

By that time John Carmel Heenan was in Westminster, where his power-house-of-activity approach was in marked contrast to the cautious reign of Cardinal Godfrey. When Heenan discovered, for example, that there was a backlog of marriage annulment cases before the diocesan tribunal, he moved at once to speed up the process to get them cleared.

While his early years at Westminster were spent in the heady and optimistic environment of the sessions of the Second Vatican Council, his time thereafter was dominated by the struggle to deal with its practical effects and the momentum and expectations it created. Although Heenan was single-minded in implementing the Council's decisions, introducing English in the liturgy, re-ordering churches, encouraging priests to go out among the people and not remain isolated in their presbyteries, he grew to despair of those theologians who took their cue, as he saw it, from the Swinging Sixties, and demanded an end to all authority in the Church.

In his autobiography, he wrote in unhappy and blunt terms, characteristic of the manner employed in his many television and radio appearances: 'There has been a radical alteration of outlook on theology in the years following Vatican II. I am thinking not of the content of theology but of the attitude of theologians. Today much theology can be called exciting in the same way that daring new designs are said by architects to be exciting. It is the result not so much of the Council as of the conscious turning away from authority in the years following the Council – a phenomenon not exclusively religious. This attitude of mind was common to illiterates and academics alike after the middle sixties. It involved a rejection of authority but was not primarily anarchic. It was, however, self-assertive and tended to be violent. Beatles, hippies, death-of-God theologians, student demonstrators, skin-heads and the sex-obsessed were all children of their time. Whatever had once been cherished must be wrong since change can be only for the better. Only a cretin can prefer Mozart to pop. The popular theologian need take little notice of what popes have said. Insights are the modern guide and, as everyone knows, scripture can be quarried to find texts for any opinion. Charismatic theologians are fun but they are not safe guides to the faith. Speculation which used to be largely restricted to philosophy now acknowledges no theological limits.' There were clearly many aspects of the modern world that Heenan would have preferred to see kept at arm's length by the Church.

If he was dismayed by the practical effects Vatican II triggered off within his Church, he found himself in very hot water when Paul VI's encyclical *Humanae Vitae* was published in the summer of 1968. This long-awaited document dealt with the issue of birth control. Many Catholics – as David Lodge amusingly catalogues in his novels *The British Museum Is Falling Down* and *How Far Can You Go?* – believed that Rome, as part of the reform process begun by Vatican II, was about to allow artificial birth control to be used. For them *Humanae Vitae* was a bitter pill to swallow. The papal message, with a de Gaulle-like finality, was no change.

In response to the cries of anguish from his flock and from some of his bishops, and in the face of hostile media, Cardinal Heenan tried to walk a fine line. He had, in fact, been a member of the commission which had advised the Pope in advance of the publication of *Humanae Vitae* to relax traditional Catholic teaching. Now the Cardinal had to give the papal encyclical his full assent, though he strove in public to modify its rigours by an evident pastoral concern and charity. He emphasized the phrase in *Humanae Vitae* which said that the rights of conscience were to remain sacred. However, the depth of the divisions that the publication of the encyclical revealed, and the subsequent decision of many English Catholics either to turn their backs on the Church or to stay within the fold but to pay little attention to the dictates of Rome, came as a cruel blow to Cardinal Heenan. In particular he was dismayed at the number of priests renouncing their vows. 'It has become the fashion in certain circles to make little of the priesthood. Today some priests cast it aside as a layman throws up his job.'

In these times of trouble, dissent and division, Cardinal Heenan came to rely more and more on the old truths of his younger years. He had little time for those who claimed that there was room for doubt, for following one's own path within Catholicism. 'I had known before becoming a priest that some Catholics miss Mass. I now think that most of these lapsed Catholics had lost the faith, or, more probably, had never had it. The Mass-missers were almost feckless in everything they did, or rather failed to do. Those whose homes were dirty, whose children were neglected, were rarely practising Catholics. The lapsed were usually also in arrears with rent and hire purchase agreements', he wrote in his autobiography of his days in the East End, but with a clear slant on the times in which the book was published (1971).

If his later years were clouded by disappointment and increasingly by poor health, Cardinal Heenan did break new ground in many of his practices, taking initiatives that Cardinal Hume was then able, in more peaceful times, to exploit and develop. It was Heenan, for example, who can be said to have begun the practice of regular behind-the-scenes diplomacy with Whitehall, taken up by Hume. Heenan was not a man for great public fights with ministers. His relationship with Harold Wilson, in particular, was a good one. They were in many senses birds of a feather, from similar backgrounds, men who had risen by their own merits and wits. Wilson, canny as ever, saw the vote potential among what was still a largely working-class Catholic Church.

Heenan had several briefing sessions with the Labour leader in advance of the 1967 Abortion Act, which legalized provision for women to end their pregnancies. Although Wilson listened with interest and concern to the points the Cardinal raised, it should be noted that the campaign against the legislation, in which the Catholic Church played a prominent role, was unsuccessful.

While Cardinal Heenan maintained many of the still rather triumphalistic trappings of office when he arrived in Westminster, he did away with enough to let the people see that he was more than a scarlet-robed prince of the Church. Rather as Wiseman had done in an earlier age, Heenan used to travel around London in his early days in office in a limousine with the papal flag flying and often with the light on inside so that people could see him. He ran Archbishop's House along the lines of the papal household and there were too many uniforms around for many people's liking. But Heenan would defend such grand gestures by saying that his people expected them. As Ronald Knox used to claim, the Church has a duty to put on a good show for the poor living in the slums.

There was another side to Heenan. The sacred purple sat lightly on his shoulders and did not constrain his humanity and his spirit. While he would brook no false modesty – he knew he was talented and would not apologize for it – he was patently a man of prayer. His secretaries used to say that if you couldn't find him at his desk, he would be on his knees in the church or listening to someone's problem and trying to find a solution.

Heenan's death in the autumn of 1975 was not unexpected. In 1973 and 1974 he had suffered heart attacks. While his passing left the Catholic Church in England more integrated into the mainstream of national life than ever before, it still had not quite arrived. The death of John Carmel Heenan was also the end of an era. Many of his closest colleagues among the bishops – the towering figures of the troubled post-Vatican II years – were also on the way out. Archbishop George Beck had resigned from the country's second see, Liverpool. Archbishop John Murphy of Cardiff was in poor health.

In Rome, Pope Paul VI, in an unusual gesture as a mark of his personal esteem for Heenan, sent a special message to the Venerable English College. Yet whatever his liking for the dead Cardinal, just four months later the Pope named as the new Archbishop of Westminster a man who was radically different from Heenan – Abbot Basil Hume.

The present Cardinal Archbishop lacks many of the qualifications that apparently advanced his predecessors. He was never a seminary rector and was not resident for any significant period of time in Rome. His training and his ministry have been in England and have given him an independence from Rome that his predecessors lacked (this is discussed further in a later chapter). He has not in any sense climbed up the ladder of preferment in the time-honoured fashion. Among those who have gone before him, even the youthful Bernard Griffin had got as far as auxiliary bishop before being singled out for greater things. While the office of abbot can be seen as on a par with that of bishop, Basil Hume was not part of the hierarchy and had no designs or ambitions in that direction. That fact has given him a certain freedom in how he has interpreted his office. And he hails from neither of the poles of English Catholicism, the Irish immigrants and their descendants or the aristocratic recusant families of old, and has therefore been able to close forever those old wounds and divisions. His was a decidedly middle-class upbringing – upper middle-class admittedly – but he is a product of the new style of English Catholicism, one of those who by education and profession had found a position within society.

Where previous Archbishops had struggled with the English Establishment, Basil Hume understood it and had, in a sense, grown up with it. His father was an influential, respected man, knighted for his services to medicine. The young George Hume attended a private school and later studied at Oxford, an experience denied to young Catholics in Newman's day.

While it would perhaps be stretching a point to say that Cardinal Hume is part of the Establishment – surely to enter a Benedictine monastery means to turn your back on the world of such conventions – his knowledge of how it works has enabled him to move the Catholic Church into the mainstream of national life to an extent his predecessors couldn't have dreamed of in those dark days when Wiseman returned home to mobs on the streets. How that has been achieved in terms of policy is a subject to which we must now turn.

4

What the Pope doesn't see

He's the Pope, he decides. If I can't go along with it in my
personal thoughts, I toe the line.

(Cardinal Hume, Thames TV interview)

The fortress Church of the 1950s was often seen by its members as a
club. When they objected to any of its rules, dissidents were told
that if they didn't like them, they could leave. Catholicism was an
all or nothing thing. Relatively little differentiation was made
between the core beliefs (encapsulated in the *Credo*, matters of
faith and morals), papal infallibility, the ban on contraception, and
disciplinary rules such as Mass attendance and fish on Fridays. It was
a package deal, to be taken or left.

The Second Vatican Council and the subsequent debates over
contraception in the late 1960s undermined that uniformity. When
many believers decided to make up their own minds on the pill it
was the hole in the dyke that brought down the whole defensive
structure. In Cardinal Hume's Church pluralism has blossomed,
what one priest describes as *à la carte* Catholicism, in which you
pick and choose the items you can live with but stay within the fold.

The more pluralist – or more liberal as it is often called – Church
has reacted against the old authoritarian structures. And top of the
pile in the hierarchy of the Church is Rome and the Pope. The three
decades since the closing of the Second Vatican Council have seen
English Catholics – in common with their co-believers in many
other nations – adopting a more critical attitude to what comes
from the Vatican. Where once the Pope's word was law, today
Catholics listen attentively to his concerns, but filter them through
their own experiences and needs.

During the 1982 papal visit, the sociologist Michael Hornsby-
Smith interviewed people attending the various functions. He

reported: 'Although the bulk of our interviewees were regularly practising Catholics, and although they were virtually unanimous in their positive evaluation of Pope John Paul II as a person, their responses to his teaching spanned the whole spectrum from unqualified acceptance to complete rejection. For some the Pope had to be obeyed, otherwise "we might as well give up our religion". Such beliefs were sometimes recognised as being the result of their Catholic upbringing. Others were prepared to accept the Pope's teaching when he was speaking *ex cathedra* (from the chair of office) on doctrinal issues but not on social or moral issues. Most Catholics in practice made up their own minds on most matters, recognising the Pope's teaching as offering authoritative guidelines to action.'

Such research would suggest that there is a difference between *English* Roman Catholicism and *Roman* Roman Catholicism. It has been Cardinal Hume's task to juggle the two. In his public pronouncements he defends the official line, what the Vatican says. Yet at the 1980 Synod on the Family in Rome, he referred to the 'special authority in matters concerning marriage' of married couples. In helping individual Catholics whose circumstances fall short of the ideals set out by Rome, the Cardinal has shown a degree of tolerance unthinkable in the 1950s.

The majority of English priests take their cue from their leader and follow a very relaxed pastoral line while in public being seen to endorse Rome's rulings. The private thoughts Cardinal Hume refers to in the passage that opens this chapter inform their performances in the confessional. They may not stand up in the pulpit and challenge Vatican documents and directives, as do their colleagues in the United States or Germany. The English Church is by tradition and by inclination not congenial to great movements of theological dissent like the 1989 Cologne Declaration, signed by 160 central European clerics and academics, protesting among other things at the papal line on contraception. But neither does the English Church apply the letter of the law with the rigidity of more staunchly Catholic countries like, perhaps, Ireland. As Cardinal Hume once remarked: 'The Church has always got to be very, very strict on principles and endlessly compassionate with individuals'.

Obviously, for every generalization there are plenty of exceptions. There are some priests who feel the English bishops should be a little tougher in imposing the papal line. On the eve of John Paul II's visit to these shores in 1982, for example, the traditionally minded Pro Ecclesia et Pontifice – the Latin name, meaning 'For Church and Pope', giving a clue as to its orientation – launched a well-publicized attack on the bishops for being 'too wishy-washy' in their teaching. Their appeal to John Paul to give the English hierarchy a public dressing down went unanswered.

Today, among the clouds gathering on the horizon for Cardinal Hume and his fellow bishops is the presence of a younger generation of clergy, fresh out of seminary, many of whom are more traditionalist and Ultramontane in their tastes than their chiefs. It is a disturbing symptom of the malaise in the Catholic Church that such pressure from below is not for change and reform but for retrenchment and reaction. No longer does the old rule of thumb apply – when in trouble seek out the young curate who will be more liberal and understanding than his parish priest – in some cases quite the reverse.

There has, however, historically been an underlying tendency in English Catholicism towards flexibility in interpreting the will of Rome. Before Henry VIII's spectacular break with the Pope, the Vatican had seemed a long way away from the English Church. The Pope's orders could only be relayed across half a continent as swiftly as the fastest horse. Because of the geographical position of Britain on the outer edge of Europe, most decisions had to be taken at a local level. In the darkest hour of the persecutions that followed the Reformation, the embattled recusants had little opportunity to listen to the voice of the Pope and his Cardinals. The result was that, with the restoration of the hierarchy in 1850, the natives grew restless at the attempts of Wiseman, Manning and their successors to make them toe the official line. Wiseman, because he had spent so much of his early career in Rome, was seen very much as the Pope's man by his clergy. For much of his time as Archbishop he was treated with suspicion by local priests and bishops who were used to considerable autonomy. The Pope may have been on the verge of declaring himself infallible in 1870, but many English Catholics thought they knew better.

Their situation was rather like that of the Church in Eastern Europe today. From the Second World War onwards it was persecuted by the Communist authorities. In countries like Hungary and Czechoslovakia it in effect went underground, surviving in the local equivalents of priest holes. Communication with Rome was impossible and decisions were taken at a local level to meet local needs.

When in 1989 the Iron Curtain came crashing down – a scenario in which the persecuted Churches played a significant role – the Catholics who stepped out of the shadows had developed their own credo. Caught in a liturgical time warp, still using the Latin that had been abandoned by the rest of the Church after the Second Vatican Council, they had been forced to take steps that Rome did not like at all. In Czechoslovakia, for example, where the ranks of the clergy were reduced by successive waves of arrests and detentions, married men and at least one woman risked their lives and liberty by being ordained as priests.

With the coming of freedom, they have found themselves, in one sense at least, less free. While it congratulates the Catholics of Eastern Europe on keeping the flame of faith flickering in the face of the Communist storm, Rome also wants to re-impose its will. So far the Czechoslovakian priests and people have shown a marked reluctance to comply – notably over the question of allowing their married priests to be defrocked or transferred into the Eastern-rite Churches (in communion with Rome but preserving their distinctive traditions, including married secular clergy).

While the issues facing Rome in its dealings with the English Church in the 1850s were different, the grassroots resistance to submitting to a distant authority was similar. The triumphalism of Wiseman and Manning, followed by the Ultramontane approach of their successors, never entirely extinguished that independence, that niggling resentment of Rome telling the local Church what to do and think. The fortress Church buried thoughts of independent thinking, but the 1960s saw a renaissance.

London and Rome

Cardinal Hume assumed the leadership of the English Church at a time when taking the teaching of Rome and interpreting it according to individual and local needs – customary Catholicism as it was once dubbed – was again taking a firm grip after a gap of 125 years. No longer was repeating what the Pope decreed enough to ensure that it happened. A more complex situation had developed, with, in many important areas, the Vatican working on one level and the people on another.

For today's bishops and priests in general, and for Cardinal Hume in particular, the task has been to reconcile the two factions at every level of leadership, or, more to the point in recent years, to act as an intermediary, linking the ideals coming out of the Vatican to the reality of English Catholics' lives. The Cardinal clearly has to be aware of how Rome might interpret his actions, and any latitude he applies in putting into practice its rulings. Yet he has been anxious to dispel the notion of the Pope's having eyes everywhere. He has repeatedly placed great emphasis on the role of local bishops. 'As a bishop I don't feel the weight of a monolithic authoritarian person on top leaning on me and directing me all the time. I feel that I have enormous responsibility and very considerable power', he said in an interview in 1989.

In other parts of the Catholic universe such attempts to apply the principles of what we would all now call subsidiarity (the post-Maastricht era having popularised a word once confined to Catholic social teaching) have been strongly resisted by the Vatican. Liberal bishops – like Archbishop Raymond Hunthausen in the United States, who took a pastorally sensitive line on sexual morality in his Seattle diocese – have been disciplined. When those prelates who have doubted the Vatican's wisdom have reached retirement age they have been replaced by others who may be more conventional. Whole bishops' conferences in countries like Brazil, the Netherlands and Austria have been re-created to fit in with the mood of centralization in the universal Church.

England and Wales have somehow escaped such rough justice. There have been no imposed candidates and little in the way of disciplinary sanctions. Rome did indicate its displeasure in 1984 over a book by the Jesuit moral theologian, Fr Jack Mahoney, *Bioethics and Belief*, which carried the Westminster diocesan imprimatur. Although the old Index of books that Catholics were not to read has long since disappeared, clerics writing on faith and morals have a duty in canon law to seek their local bishop's approval or imprimatur for their work. Fr Mahoney's book, on the dialogue between medicine and religion, got the required go-ahead from the Westminster diocese, but some of his thoughts on the moral status of the embryo, soon after conception, were not in line with Rome's teaching. The disparity was brought to the attention of the Vatican

authorities, who then pressed Westminster to withdraw its imprimatur. It agreed, but the announcement bent over backwards to
stress that Fr Mahoney was a faithful son of the Church and that his
'professional integrity' as a moral theologian was not being called
into question.

The English Church thereby kept the Vatican happy while not
looking heavy-handed or authoritarian. Perhaps it is their capacity
for knowing just how far to push things that has protected the
English bishops. In Brazil, the Netherlands and Austria, outspoken
clerics have simply stood up and told John Paul II that he has got it
wrong. Then again, perhaps it is because, with just four million
Catholics, England and Wales have been considered less important
by the Vatican. There are no troublesome Catholic universities
here, fomenting theological dissent akin to that generated by
church faculties in Germany and Switzerland. Or perhaps it is
because the Vatican sees a need to show sensitivity in the heartland
of the Anglican Communion that England is treated as a special
case. No longer is Mary's Dowry seen as a desirable prize. Pope John
Paul II is reported, by an English monsignor in the Curia, to have
been in a state of high anxiety as he prepared for his 1982 visit to
Britain. Not only was the political delicacy of the visit, with war
under way in the Falklands, worrying him, but also the danger of
re-opening historical wounds. 'It would be so easy to say the wrong
thing', John Paul is said to have remarked on the flight over.

Whatever its reasons, Rome has given Basil Hume a fairly free
hand in running the English Church. And there must be an
element in that policy of official esteem for him. Over the vexed
question of bishops' appointments, for example, he has been
remarkably successful in getting the men he wants named by the
Holy See. The decision, in theory at least, is largely shaped by the
Pope's representative in London, the Papal Nuncio, who, after local
consultations, sends the Vatican a *terna*, or list of three names, from
which the Congregation for Bishops makes its choice. Yet if one
looks down the bench of bishops chosen during Basil Hume's time
at Westminister, his hand can be seen at work in shaping a hierarchy where extremes of opinion are avoided and consensus is by
and large the order of the day.

Among the rising stars of the bishops' conference are two of his
protégés: John Crowley, once his secretary, and Vincent Nichols, a
former general secretary to the hierarchy and a close confidant of

the Cardinal. Basil Hume's successor as Abbot of Ampleforth, Dom Ambrose Griffiths, was in 1992 named as Bishop of Hexham and Newcastle. Men like Crispian Hollis in Portsmouth, Christopher Budd in Plymouth and the long-serving and underrated Cormac Murphy-O'Connor in Arundel and Brighton are very much in the Hume mould: friendly, unfrightening, patently men of God, above politics but with a vocal concern for injustices in the society around them.

It would be stretching the point to say that the bishops' conference is always a haven of harmony. Some appointments – notably that of the conservative and taciturn former Cambridge University chaplain Maurice Couve de Murville as Archbishop of Birmingham – have advanced characters outwardly more in tune with the dominant mood in Rome. And Cardinal Hume is known occasionally to get exasperated with those of his colleagues who stand on their dignity, waving their pectoral crosses and issuing great gusts of hot air. But his irritation is characteristically understated and his displeasure well veiled. The story is told that at a gathering of the bishops' conference one auxiliary bishop pontificated at length on the timing of holy days of obligation – feasts on which Catholics should go to Mass. At the end of his oration, the Cardinal looked round the table and asked: 'Well, has anybody got anything sensible to say about this problem?'

There are naturally and rightly differences of opinion on some issues among the bishops. Bishop Patrick Kelly of Salford, for example, has adopted a radical policy on the age at which children should be confirmed, while some of his fellows strongly hold different views. At the height of the national debate about nuclear deterrence, with the Catholic bishops' attitude much scrutinized because of the role of Cardinal Heenan's former secretary, Mgr Bruce Kent, at the head of the Campaign for Nuclear Disarmament, the hierarchy could not agree on a single position. It was left to the Cardinal to make his own view clear in an article in *The Times* (of which more later).

Then there was the unhappy episode in the diocese of Northampton that followed the early death in 1989 of one of the very few theologians to make it into the hierarchy, Bishop Francis Thomas. It was 18 months before a new bishop was named, almost double the usual delay. Rumours and speculation abounded. The eventual appointment of Bishop Leo McCartie, a kindly but elderly man who

had been quietly beavering away as an auxiliary in the neighbouring Birmingham diocese, did little to quieten those who claimed
that the Vatican had sought to impose a candidate more conservative than the English bishops could stomach. Bishop McCartie was
taken to be the compromise and his links with Archbishop Couve
de Murville, his former boss, were much remarked upon.

There was even talk that Rome had sought – as it has in many
other countries around the world – to name a member of the
secretive church organization Opus Dei as the Bishop of Northampton. This would undoubtedly have gone down very badly with
Cardinal Hume. Quite who the Opus Dei candidate could have
been is difficult to pinpoint. Philip Sherrington, their regional
vicar in Britain, and Stephen Reynolds are two of the leading lights
of the organization, but as one priest remarked, Opus Dei headquarters in London are a bit like the Chinese Embassy, so wrapped
in secrecy and double bluff that the gardener is in fact the
ambassador.

Pope John Paul has heaped praise upon the ultra-traditional
Opus Dei and its 80,000 members worldwide who include both
priests and laity. In May 1992 he bestowed the title 'Blessed' – one
step short of sainthood – on its widely criticized founder, Mgr
Josemaria Escrivá, despite an international outcry from, among
others, the former president of the Spanish bishops' conference,
Cardinal Tarancón.

Escrivá had died only in 1975, making this the fastest ever
beatification in recent times, overtaking even such blameless figures
as St Teresa of Lisieux. Evidence was produced to show that Escrivá
had spent a great deal of time preparing to be honoured after his
death – writing diaries to make himself look a picture of Christian
charity, falling into an ecstatic trance. His former secretary reported
that the only time she could recall seeing him 'transported' was
when he flew into a rage. But most concern revolved around the
recruitment methods Opus Dei uses to attract young people into its
houses, techniques that have been likened by parents who have
'lost' their children to the alleged brain-washing of the Moonies.

Many of the mothers and fathers of English recruits to Opus Dei
have told their tales of woe to Cardinal Hume. Aware of their plight
and by nature not one to admire the fanaticism that inspires Opus
Dei, he has taken a tough line on the organization, in effect
disagreeing with Rome. In 1981 he issued guidelines for Opus Dei

recruitment, recommending that no one under 18 make a full-time commitment to the movement, and suggesting that anyone considering membership should seek the advice and consent of his or her parents.

In 1992, on the eve of Escrivá's beatification, one of the Cardinal's advisers, Fr Vladimir Feltzmann, for 20 years a member of Opus Dei until he left the movement, attracted international headlines when he turned the spotlight on Blessed Josemaria's darker side. In particular he mentioned Escrivá's ambivalence towards the Holocaust. 'He said "Hitler never killed six million. It was not more than four million" ', Fr Feltzmann recalled. He stressed that he was speaking in a personal capacity and not as the Cardinal's adviser. However, callers to the Cardinal's office at the time were told that he – and not Fr Feltzmann, who had been in the headlines – 'was very busy with Opus Dei'.

Rome is clearly aware of Cardinal Hume's distaste for the conservative organization. If the Curia was trying to impose its will by selecting an Opus Dei priest as Bishop of Northampton, it failed. If Bishop McCartie is a compromise, then the Cardinal saved the day and the people of the diocese have a diligent, if not an inspirational, pastor.

The most significant difference of opinion between Cardinal Hume and the Vatican in the matter of the appointment of bishops has been over Basil Hume's own tenure of Archbishop's House, Westminster. He made it clear when he somewhat reluctantly took the job that he only wanted to do it for ten years, when he would be within two years of the secular retirement age. He is without ambition and hankers for home, Ampleforth Abbey. And, as we have seen, the leadership of English Catholicism is a burdensome task that has sapped the strength and health of his predecessors. Yet after a decade in the job, the Cardinal did not keep his pledge. The reason, however, was not a lack of willingness on his part but, apparently, Rome's opposition. They didn't want to lose him and turned down his soundings about retirement, he told his Westminster priests. And with the monk's obedience that brought him south in 1976, he has shelved plans to return north. With Rome so fond of the English Cardinal, he may have to wait until 1998 to settle down again at Ampleforth. Bishops in the Catholic Church retire from their dioceses at 75 – unless the Pope decides otherwise. Extensions are not unprecedented.

Poles apart?

Pope John Paul II, of course, was not the one who chose Abbot Hume to lead English Catholicism. It was the old guard, in the final years of Paul VI, that was responsible for his arrival at Westminster. Indeed Cardinal Hume had scarcely got his feet under the table at Archbishop's House when the Catholic Church was rocked by the 'year of three popes', 1978.

The death of Paul VI in the summer of that year took Basil Hume to the traditional conclave of Cardinals in Rome. They elect the new Pope and all holders of the red Cardinal's hat under the age of 80 have the right to vote. Their choice, announced in traditional fashion by clouds of white smoke appearing above Michelangelo's Sistine Chapel, was the Patriarch of Venice, Cardinal Albino Luciani. He paid tribute to the achievements of his two predecessors, John XXIII who summoned the Second Vatican Council and Paul VI who put its teaching into action, by taking the name Pope John Paul I.

At first he was dubbed 'the smiling Pope' because of his sunny disposition in public. But soon he was to become 'the 33-day Pope' when he died after just over a month in office. The suddenness of his demise led to later speculation that he was murdered by corrupt Curial officials, caught with their fingers in the tills of the Vatican Bank and fearing exposure. But a comprehensive investigation, with the help of senior Vatican figures, by *Observer* journalist John Cornwell showed conclusively that a combination of ill-health and the strains of a job that is to all practical purposes beyond the capacity of one man, and an OAP at that, saw off John Paul I. The cardinals returned to Rome in the autumn and, to the surprise of the world, chose Karol Wojtyła, the 58-year-old Archbishop of Cracow.

Both conclaves drew the attention of the world's media and in England at least led to feverish speculation that Basil Hume was about to be elected Pope. It marked the peak of his personal popularity in this country and was a mark of his success, in the two years since becoming Archbishop, in capturing the public's imagination and laying to rest the ghosts of old anti-Catholic prejudices. But to the self-effacing Cardinal the whole chapter was an embarrassment. Despite favourable bookies' odds as the date of the second conclave that chose John Paul II approached, Basil Hume described talk of himself installed in the papal apartments, high above St Peter's Square, as 'quite lunatic'. Without a trace of the false modesty that some pushy churchmen show to further their cause, Basil Hume remarked at the time: 'I have always been profoundly convinced in life that I have been over-estimated, over-assessed. I was over-estimated to be put into this job. It is quite lunatic to think of the other. I fool a lot of people a lot of the time, but not all of the time.'

There is in that remark just a note of panic that the press speculation was about to be proved true. After all, Basil Hume had no doubt been saying much the same from his office at Ample-forth to those who thought to ask him in the days and weeks before he was called to Westminster. And Cardinal Luciani was an unlikely candidate – a simple man whose few claims to distinction included composing an imaginary correspondence between God and Pinocchio.

Those who argued that an Englishman couldn't be made Pope because there had not been a pontiff from these isles since Nicholas Breakspear in the twelfth century might have reflected after the choice of Karol Wojtyła that Poland had been waiting even longer to get one of its own installed in the Vatican. However, Basil Hume wasn't elected. There was palpable relief in his comments years later when he joked about the bookmakers before the 1978 conclaves: 'I was most hurt when the odds started to widen'.

His task as the leader of English Catholicism has been to work with John Paul II as Pope. Soon after his election, John Paul showed his respect for Basil Hume. He was appointed to several significant Vatican committees. And the years do not appear to have dimmed John Paul's admiration for the former abbot. In August 1992, while he was recovering from surgery to remove a potentially cancerous tumour, the Pope paid the English Cardinal the great compliment of sending him as his personal representative to an international gathering of Catholic youth in Poland. In his message to those at the rally, John Paul described Cardinal Hume as 'a great friend of young people'.

A capacity to get on well with the young, to speak to them in language they will understand, is a shared trait of the Pope and the Cardinal. The two have other things in common. They are both keen sportsmen – Basil Hume played squash and went running on Wimbledon Common until a hip replacement operation put paid to his exertions. John Paul II was a footballer in his youth (a central defender!) and a skier and Alpine walker into his sixties.

Both have stood out in an introspective Europe by showing a passionate and practical concern for the Third World. They share a vision of a reunited Europe, held together by a common religious and cultural heritage. On occasion they have worked well together at a practical level – co-ordinating their efforts to effect the release of the kidnapped English tourist Annabel Schild in Sardinia in the late 1970s. On a personal level they are believed to get on well, though the plain-speaking Pope often finds Cardinal Hume's coded messages – such as his Martin Luther King-like 'I have a dream' address to the 1980 Synod on the Family – a little confusing.

There are profound differences between the Archbishop of Westminster, a Benedictine pragmatist, and the Pope, a Polish dogmatist. The latter has made his mission the uniting of the 900 million Catholics worldwide behind a single set of beliefs. On his travels – and he has broken all the conventions by regularly visiting his far-flung flock around the globe – John Paul has pinned his colours to the mast on issues like contraception, precisely the area where English Catholics, in line with many in the developed world, have gone their own way. Though he is a clever and academically gifted man who trained in philosophy in Paris, John Paul II belongs to the muscular branch of Christianity, which sees black and white, good and bad. He pitches his appeal at the lowest common denominator, and, sure in his faith, will not countenance any dissent on the basic principles around which he has chosen to unite his universal Church. His experiences in a Poland ruled by the Communists have left him with a profound distrust of all variations on the theme of socialism. This legacy of his formative years has caused no end of trouble with liberation theologians in Latin America. There bishops and priests argue that using Marxist analysis can help define the Church's 'option for the poor'. John Paul's reaction has been to silence those who insist on such a course and to marginalize those he suspects of privately supporting them.

His has been a determinedly centralizing period in the Catholic Church's history, with Rome drawing in the strings of its authority. Yet this trend from Rome has come at the same time that English Catholics have been asserting their independence. Indeed many would argue that it is the pluralist tendencies in the European and

North American Church that have prompted John Paul's centralizing drive. Whatever the origin, it has been Basil Hume's task to reconcile the Roman trend with the changing face of English Catholicism in the post-Vatican II years.

His Benedictine background has been crucial in that process. The order of St Benedict has been at the heart of Catholicism – geographically and spiritually – since their founder started his first monastery at Monte Cassino, between Rome and Naples, in the sixth century. Yet the Benedictines have also blended in with the English landscape since they arrived in Britain in Anglo-Saxon times. Pope Gregory the Great sent 40 Benedictine monks from Rome to the Isle of Thanet in 598. Basil Hume's abbey, Ampleforth, can trace its history back to the pre-Reformation Westminster Abbey. The Ampleforth community arrived in north Yorkshire from Dieulouard in Lorraine at the time of the French Revolution, having earlier left England to avoid the persecutions that accompanied Henry VIII's change of faith.

Basil Hume's own formative studies made him wary of Roman centralization and sympathetic to new liberal, outward-looking trends that were shaping Catholicism in the 1940s and 1950s. His English superiors decided to send him not to the monastery of Sant'Anselmo in Rome, with its prevailing regime of conservative German monks, but instead to Fribourg in the Swiss mountains where the lectures – in Latin – anticipated many of the changes that came with the reforming Second Vatican Council.

His natural inclination, shaped by his Benedictine training, is not to be an authoritarian figure in the mould of John Paul II, laying down the law and ensuring that others obey. The abbot in a Benedictine community is not the boss but the servant of all. St Benedict's Rule says: 'his [the abbot's] goal must be profit for the monks and not pre-eminence for himself . . . let him strive to be loved rather than feared'. The abbot should be 'discerning and moderate . . . arranging everything so that the strong have something to yearn for and the weak nothing to run from'.

Basil Hume took this guidance to heart at Westminster, but he had earlier tested it as Abbot at Ampleforth. He piloted the community of 153 monks through the turbulent times of the Second Vatican Council, easing the tensions between liberals and conservatives, losing some along the way, but ensuring that Ampleforth came through a testing period united behind its commitment to the modern Church, with its retreats, lay involvement in parishes, sex education in its classrooms and growing ecumenical links. It was a trying period for the future Cardinal – Derek Clark's portrait of him at that time, now hanging in the monastery's refectory, has an air of strain and even El Greco-like gloom about it. But it was equally a time that prepared Basil Hume for the challenge ahead of reconciling the will of Rome with that of four million English and Welsh Catholics.

The Benedictine tradition shrinks from the fanatical, from displays of power and authority. Its way is more peaceful, more moderate, harnessing humanity and not riding rough-shod over it. The product of that tradition, as the leader of English Catholicism, has been at pains to make it clear that there is room for all in the Church, whatever their personal circumstances. He talks of searching for God. He doesn't give prescriptions as to how to find Him.

His public comments are orthodox in their theology. In a letter to *The Times* of 30 October 1985, he rebutted claims that John Paul had made the Church too papal-orientated, too centralized. But it is his tone, inviting and understanding, not hectoring or giving orders, that characterizes his leadership. That has not always been the impression given by Rome, and to get round that dichotomy his habitual stance has been to avoid being emphatic on matters of great debate. When he came to Westminster in 1976 he decided at once, he recalls, to keep quiet about sex. 'Soon after I arrived in London', he told me, 'I made a decision never to talk about sexual ethics. I'm not an expert on the subject. I'm very conscious that I am a celibate and my comments will be interpreted because of that.'

When he has travelled to Rome, to take part in synods, Basil Hume has consulted his flock, showing that he is prepared to listen. For the 1987 Synod on the Laity, for example, there was a national consultation, through the pages of the various English Catholic newspapers, on the various themes of the forthcoming gathering. A response from the English Church was prepared and the Cardinal's contributions to the debate in Rome reflected what the laity had said.

In 1980 the Cardinal and Archbishop Derek Worlock of Liverpool, fresh from the National Pastoral Congress, arrived at the Synod on the Family in Rome. At this landmark Congress, free and uncensored discussion took place on a variety of subjects. The customary Catholicism of England showed its true colours. The Roman line was criticized by a laity showing its radical edge, in effect burying the supine self-preoccupation of the past. Cardinal Hume sat and listened as the hierarchy was challenged to make its own 'option for the poor' by standing up for the oppressed and marginalized in society. His subsequent record on issues of social justice (to be discussed later) gives the lie to accusations that once the Congress was over he buried its conclusions.

Most importantly, he and Archbishop Worlock were challenged by the delegates to register at the forthcoming Roman synod the unhappiness of English Catholics with the ban on contraception and the treatment of the divorced by a Church that refuses to acknowledge that marriages break down. (Its annulment process is lengthy and can be distressing. The focus of the clerical tribunals who examine marriages and decide whether the Church can grant an annulment often seems to be on maintaining the claim that Catholic marriages last forever. By granting an annulment the Church is in effect saying that marriages that do break down were not real marriages in the first place.)

At the autumn synod, Archbishop Worlock pleaded for the readmission to communion of those whose marriages had ended and who had married again, without recourse to annulment. The Synod, he said, 'must listen to the voice of priests, rich in experience, and laity' about what was actually happening in the parishes. The Cardinal tackled the more delicate question of contraception. Those who could not accept the ban, he said, were often good, conscientious and faithful sons and daughters of the Church. 'I hope and I pray that as a result of this Synod, I shall be better able to give guidance to those married people who are looking to the Church for help.' The Cardinal then went on, in a famous address, to place the question of contraception in the wider context of what form the modern Church should take. With Pope John Paul taking notes, Basil Hume contrasted two models of the Church, one that could be taken for a rough sketch of how English Catholicism was until the Second Vatican Council, and one of how he wanted it to develop.

During some of the synodal debate, the Cardinal boldly admitted, he had fallen asleep and had dreamt. 'I saw in my dream . . . a vision of the Church. I saw a fortress, strong and upstanding. Every stranger approaching seemed to those who defended it to be an enemy to be repelled. From that fortress the voices of those outside could not be heard. The soldiers within showed unquestioning obedience – and that was much to be admired: "Theirs not to reason why, theirs but to do and die." It seemed thus in my dream, and then I remembered, upon awakening, that dreams distort reality. They exaggerate.'

'Then I had another vision. It was of a pilgrim, a pilgrim through history and through life. That pilgrim was the Church. The pilgrim was hastening towards the vision, towards all truth. But he had not yet reached it. He limped along the road. But meanwhile there were signposts to show the way, or rather they told you that this or that road was not the right one. The pilgrim is always in search.'

Then he described another vision. 'I saw with great clarity that the insight of Paul VI in the encyclical *Humanae Vitae*, confirming the traditional teaching of the Church, was surely right. But alas we did not know how to speak to the people. The road-signs point the way, but signposts become weatherbeaten, and new paint is needed. It takes time to get the work done. My dream became a nightmare, for I saw the wrong paint being put on the signpost, and the last state was worse than the first.'

Just what John Paul wrote down at the end of the speech will never be known. But the Cardinal had masterfully been all things to all men. To the traditionalists, he said that *Humanae Vitae* was right. To the liberals, he said that the message wasn't being put across. Quite what message he would like to see stressed he didn't make clear.

The appeal was a balanced one that demonstrated the tightrope he has had to walk between his local Church and his loyalty to Rome on so many issues. He suggested that there was space for change and development – as Catholics at the Congress in Liverpool had requested – without undermining the authority of Rome, a concern for any Cardinal in John Paul II's Church. It was sadly – though inevitably in the current climate in Rome – an appeal that fell on deaf ears. The Cardinal knew better than to labour the point, though many who had taken part in the exuberant Liverpool gathering felt let down.

Stand up and be counted

There have been moments when Basil Hume has felt obliged to stand up and be counted, to clash with Rome. These struggles have not been splashed all over the front pages of newspapers. As in his dealings with Whitehall, the Cardinal prefers collective pressure and quiet diplomacy to vulgar brawls in public.

His capacity to argue his corner has been boosted considerably by his European and international standing. None of his predecessors as Archbishop of Westminster cut much of a figure in the world of the universal Catholic Church. Their concern was with the British Isles. For them international affairs meant the missions. Basil Hume, however, has been a man ahead of his time in his commitment to breaking down European barriers. His spell as leader of the English Church has coincided with a period of unprecedented European togetherness. While some voices in Britain have urged the country to remain semi-detached from the moves towards greater co-operation, the Cardinal has seen developments in the political and economic spheres of the European Community as an opportunity to encourage his domestic Church, and the international Catholic community, to realize the potential for a broader meeting of minds and spirits across the continent.

He started this task with a marked advantage over those who had sat in Archbishop's House before him. Where their roots lay in Ireland, even more remote from continental Europe than England, and Vaughan and Hinsley had left their hearts in the missions, Basil Hume's mother was French and had brought up her children to be bilingual. He moved at the age of ten from one family with a European tradition to another, the Benedictines. As a young man they sent him not to Rome but to Switzerland, where he became acquainted with new trends in European theology.

As Abbot of Ampleforth he headed the International Monastic Ecumenical Committee and later the Commission for Monastic Renewal, forging global links. In 1979, confirming perhaps that speculation in the previous year about Cardinal Hume being chosen as Pope may not have been so wide of the mark, he was appointed President of the Council of European Bishops' Conferences, a body whose brief stretched from Ireland to the Urals. He was re-elected in 1983 for a second term and relinquished the post only in 1986. For the first time in the modern period, English Catholicism had at its head an international statesman of the Church, able to command attention in the corridors of power in Rome.

Cardinal Hume used his European role to promote some causes close to John Paul II's heart. The need for effective evangelization – getting the message over – has been a constant theme of both men. Hume stressed, prophetically, the need to bring together the two halves of a divided continent. And he seized the opportunity provided for the Church by the development of the European Community to lobby the Brussels bureaucrats for greater attention to the plight of the developing world. This was most marked after his 1984 visit to famine-struck Ethiopia, when he won the backing of bishops all over the EC for an appeal for food aid from the notorious mountains of surplus, subsidized produce to be sent to those in desperate need.

In November 1981 he spoke to the Christian Forum in Ghent about the role of the Catholic Church in working for change in Europe. 'The Catholic community, east and west, must explore ways of putting into practice their collegial responsibility for evangelising the continent. We must not perpetuate the religious divisions of the past.' Ten years later the political map of Europe had been redrawn. Speaking to the Catholic Theological Association of Great Britain in Leeds in September 1991, Cardinal Hume reflected on the change and stressed one of the abiding themes of his leadership, that Christianity offers a viable alternative to the prevailing capitalist and communist ideologies of the day: 'The East after decades of lies, poverty and oppression looks to the West for political models and economic expertise. It will look alas in vain for values and vision. Both halves of our European family have for different reasons largely lost their souls and suffer an inner emptiness and loss of spiritual vitality. This presents us with an inescapable challenge and opportunity. The Church's response needs to go to the very heart of the divine mystery we profess.'

Interestingly, at a time when the Polish Pope was busy praising the abiding faith and spiritual values of the East, condemning Western secularism and materialism, and telling the pampered Catholics in the West to learn the value of fidelity from their brethren's struggles in the countries behind the Iron Curtain, Cardinal Hume was presenting a more rounded vision. Both halves of Europe were sick – the West for reasons already identified by John Paul. But the East had its problems too, notably in its reborn virulent nationalism, as was soon to become apparent in the disintegrating Soviet empire, in Czechoslovakia and especially in Yugoslavia.

In his Leeds speech the Cardinal went on: 'Europe is a continent in search of identity, meaning and purpose. State communism is being consigned shamefacedly to the scrap-heap. Liberal capitalism successfully meets many material needs but is extravagant in its use of irreplaceable resources and has little to say to the spirit of man. The peoples of Europe may well seek in religion and nationalism the answer to their deeper needs. But only a more spiritual, contemplative, truly renewed faith will save Europe's soul.'

Later that same year, at the specially summoned Synod of European Bishops in Rome, Cardinal Hume developed the point for 126 of his colleagues. The way ahead for the continent must be through ecumenical endeavour, he stressed. 'We are all burdened in our relationships with other churches by theological controversy and past events. If we are serious about ecumenism we shall address both of these with some urgency.' True man of the Second Vatican Council that he is, the Cardinal pointed to a way ahead for the Churches to work together for the good of Europe. He quoted a remark made by Pope John XXIII at the opening of the Council: 'The substance of the ancient deposit of the faith is one thing, and the way in which it is presented is another'. In seeking a common faith to inspire the continent, the Catholic Church must be flexible, he said, while remaining true to its traditions. The implications of his point for Catholicism's stalled relationship with the Anglicans cannot have gone unnoticed and will be explored in the next chapter. But his comments could also be seen as linked to the unhappy state of Catholic–Orthodox understanding in the post-Cold War age.

Never a man to confine himself to words, Cardinal Hume expanded his ecumenical vision by donning the mantle of diplomat. When the collapse of the Soviet empire had left Eastern-Rite Catholics, persecuted since the days of Stalin, and the Orthodox who had compromised with the system at loggerheads, Cardinal Hume travelled to Russia at Easter 1992 to meet the recently appointed Catholic Archbishop in Moscow and the Orthodox Patriarch Alexei. He tried, in a private capacity, to reconcile the two warring sides. No doubt his credentials as the abbot who encouraged the setting up of the Orthodox house of St Symeon's at Oswaldkirk near Ampleforth stood him in good stead in his mission.

Defender of the Council

Basil Hume's most important role as leader of the European bishops was to forge an alliance of senior churchmen who were not prepared to see any deviation from the course of the progressive development of the Church after the Second Vatican Council. Although Karol Wojtyła had been one of the most enthusiastic voices for reform at the Council, in the mid-1980s he was beginning to suspect that the changes had come too thick and fast, without sufficient thought and co-ordination. It was to give voice to these fears that he called an Extraordinary Synod for November 1985 to celebrate the twentieth anniversary of the closing of Vatican II and review its progress. Cardinal Hume was among those alarmed that the meeting might be used by conservative forces to 'put the clock back'. He emerged in Europe as a figure around whom the 'progressive' side could rally.

With a delicacy of touch that left him, with characteristic modesty, to claim that he had not done anything much, Basil Hume took the high ground and defended it in his dealings with Rome. Rather than shout from the rooftops along with dissident European theologians like Professor Hans Küng, who preceded the Synod with an outspoken attack on 'the seven lean years' of John Paul's pontificate, the Cardinal quietly but effectively applied diplomatic pressure.

In public he showed himself as Rome's obedient servant. He rebutted Professor Küng's claims of revisionism. The synod would, he told reporters in Rome when he arrived in advance of the gathering, 'recapture some of the enthusiasm, idealism and unity' of Vatican II and would 'see how far and with what success we have managed to put the teaching of the Council into practice, and point out for the people of God the surest way ahead'. Yet in private he shared some of Küng's fears and was working with his senior colleagues to make sure they didn't come true. Particularly significant was a conference in Rome in mid-October, attended by key European figures, just before the Extraordinary Synod began. The European meeting, presided over and 'animated' by Basil Hume, as it was put at the time, set the tone for the one to follow. The movement for reaction never really got going.

On the always vexatious issue of liturgy, Basil Hume played a significant role in preventing a retreat from the Council. A small but vocal minority of Catholics in the developed world regretted the outlawing of the ancient Tridentine rite, which followed the Council's enthusiastic endorsement of Mass in the vernacular. Although modern translations of the Mass could be said in Latin, the Tridentine format, with its clouds of incense and the priest with his back to the congregation muttering in a language few could understand, became a rallying point for many who found it hard to accept the changes of Vatican II.

Principal opponent of the reforms was the former head of the Holy Ghost Fathers, the French Archbishop Marcel Lefebvre, who attracted substantial numbers of traditionalist Catholics to his Society of St Pius X because he offered the banned Tridentine rite. In fact he was also backing a cocktail of policies that rejected wholesale the teachings of Vatican II on issues like ecumenism. The rebel Archbishop labelled Pope John Paul II 'the anti-Pope'. It was in an effort to win back those who wanted the Tridentine rite of their childhood, but who didn't want to follow Lefebvre down the road to schism – as he eventually went in 1987 when he ordained four bishops without the Pope's permission – that the Vatican began suggesting in 1986 that it would once again allow the use of the ancient Mass.

Cardinal Hume, with a sizeable domestic Lefebvrist community centred on Wimbledon and a much larger conservative minority who yearned for the old way of celebrating the Mass, at once saw the danger. Any concession by Rome would encourage, not diminish, such groups. It would boost their attempts to recruit younger members to their largely aged ranks and would give the impression that the Vatican was intent on 'putting the clock back' as some had suggested on the eve of the 1985 Extraordinary Synod.

As ever, his strategy was not confrontation but diplomacy. He travelled to Rome and persuaded the Pope and Curial officials that any relaxation in restrictions on the Tridentine rite had to be carefully controlled or it would get out of hand. Vatican II must not be seen to be compromised. The Lefebvrists must not be allowed to gain the initiative.

The compromise solution was that at certain churches on certain occasions the Tridentine rite would be used. Otherwise it could only be used with the express permission of the local bishop. In the Cardinal's own Westminster diocese six churches were earmarked. For the first month or so the pews were packed with the curious. But congregations soon dwindled. The number of churches was reduced and the whole episode passed off without the forward momentum of the Church being challenged.

It would be a mistake to see the clashes between Rome and Westminster, between the Cardinal and the Pope, as being between liberal and conservative. Both men are rather more complex than simple tags suggest. John Paul II has a radical side while Basil Hume's moderation, his reasonableness, can occasionally make him unquestioning.

This was never better demonstrated than in the tense period between August 1990 and the outbreak of the Gulf War in February of the following year. Cardinal Hume, assuming what had become his habitual position at times of national emergency alongside the Archbishop of Canterbury, visited Prime Minister Major at Downing Street to discuss the escalating hostilities. While deploring the devastation that war could bring, and urging all sides towards a peaceful solution, the two Church leaders essentially told Mr Major to do what he had to do with their blessing.

The Cardinal soon found himself out of step with some of his fellow British Catholics. A series of Church petitions, signed by religious leaders and several of his fellow bishops, demanded that United Nations sanctions against the Iraqi occupiers of Kuwait be allowed time to take effect. Disagreement among the English Catholic hierarchy on war and peace was nothing new. The bishops had never been able to agree a common stance on deterrence and disarmament, for example. The Cardinal was well practised in side-stepping such divisions and presenting a consensus position. Things got more difficult when opposition to hostilities surfaced in Scotland and Ireland, with their Catholic leaders – Archbishop Thomas Winning of Glasgow and Cardinal Cahal Daly of Armagh – taking a strong anti-war stance.

The bombshell came at Christmas 1990, when Pope John Paul belatedly entered the international debate. In the past, Basil Hume and John Paul II had taken similar positions on war and peace, adopting, for instance, the same pragmatic line of giving nuclear deterrence their conditional and unenthusiastic backing. John Paul had been, it would be fair to note, willing to exert a little more pressure than the Cardinal to achieve consensus with his fellow churchmen on the matter. In 1985, the internationally respected Pontifical Academy of Sciences delivered a report to John Paul, its patron, criticizing the American 'Star Wars' defence system. The Pope suppressed the document and refused to allow it to be published.

In his careful line on the Gulf conflict, Basil Hume could have expected to be following the same policy as John Paul. But just as the Western world was preparing for what the Cardinal seemed prepared to concede was a just war, the Pope found an unexpected radicalism and spoke the words that afterwards covered the walls of Italian cities on posters and in aerosol paint, and were echoed in international capitals: 'War: a journey without return'. The Pope's pacifism grew stronger with every one of his 55 public pleas for peace: 'End this pointless slaughter'; 'Have the courage to end this war!' he challenged the world's leaders. 'Abandon this bellicose road. Negotiate! Collaborate!' Those who manufactured arms – and it was Western weapons that made possible Saddam Hussein's territorial ambitions – were sinners, said John Paul II.

It was a very difficult time for Cardinal Hume and one we must return to when considering his position on defence questions. But part of his discomfort at the time had to do with his relationship with Rome. With the press providing continuous news coverage of a war in which there was for much of the time very little action, the differing views of the Cardinal and the Pope, domestic and international leaders of Catholicism, were much discussed.

Basil Hume tried to put a good – if anguished – face on it. When the Pope in mid-February reiterated his plea for peace with justice, but began to back down on his earlier comments and disowned attempts to paint him as a pacifist, the Cardinal sent for a copy of his speech. And he manoeuvred carefully, if not wholly convincingly, to get himself off the hook.

In an interview with *The Times*'s religion editor, Clifford Longley, Basil Hume contended that he and John Paul II were effectively saying the same thing. Both were taking their teaching from *Gaudium et Spes*, the Vatican II document which legitimizes war in defined circumstances, but declares 'Divine Providence urgently commands us to rid ourselves of the ancient slavery of war'. That was, according to the Cardinal, what the Pope was in effect saying.

And the papal speech, disowning pacifism, proved the point. 'It would have been wrong of him to take sides.' But until that address, 'people could have put him on one side and me on the other side'.

It has been a running theme of his time as Archbishop never to be seen to be going against the Pope. Indeed the struggle to reconcile Rome's wishes with the needs of English Catholics has been a central, if discreetly waged, battle for Basil Hume.

The papal visit

The outward appearance has always been one of unity of purpose. And the crowning moment of such an image was the papal visit in 1982, described by one Vatican observer of long standing as 'the one totally successful journey of this pontificate'. It was also a personal triumph for Basil Hume.

The invitation for John Paul II to visit Britain was issued in 1980. It would be an unprecedented journey, symbolically healing the wounds of 400 years and marking the final acceptance and integration of the Catholic community into the bosom of English society. A handful of ultra-Protestant bigots raised a protest at what Ian Paisley, with one eye as ever on the Battle of the Boyne, called 'a direct violation of the Williamite revolution settlement'. But such cries were whispers in the face of wall-to-wall television coverage and an atmosphere akin to national rejoicing in those last days of May 1982.

The scene was set in January, with the upgrading of diplomatic links between Britain and the Vatican to ambassadorial level – in effect removing a historical anomaly dating back to days when the Holy See was still viewed in Whitehall with a degree of suspicion. Money was collected among the Catholic community to pay for the events on John Paul's programme – though plans for an open-air Mass in Richmond Park had to be dropped when an estimate of £1.5 million landed on Cardinal Hume's desk. An itinerary was drawn up including both Scotland and Wales. In February, Cardinal Hume was describing the visit in the context of a renewal of the English Church, following on from Vatican II and the National Pastoral Congress. Some of those who had taken part in the Congress came to believe that the papal visit was a way of deflecting attention from the implementation of their decisions.

The aims of the visit outlined by the Cardinal – spiritual development, affirming unity among Churches and showing that there was more than material gain to life (themes, it will be noted, in his own work) – had by April changed dramatically with the outbreak of hostilities in the South Atlantic. The looming conflict between Britain and Argentina over the Falklands (or the Malvinas, according to which side you were on) put a question mark over the whole visit. If war broke out, the Pope wouldn't be able to come, the Cardinal said. Yet by the time John Paul landed at Gatwick Airport on Friday 28 May, British troops had been on the Falklands for seven days, driving the Argentinians off this distant colony by force. That the Pope still came to Britain was a tribute to Cardinal Hume's delicate diplomacy and his international standing among his fellow churchmen. The personal esteem in which John Paul held Basil Hume was crucial.

Although at first the Latin American bishops, and the Argentinian hierarchy in particular, were not totally opposed to the papal visit to Britain going ahead, their attitude hardened considerably when over 300 Argentinians were killed when a Royal Navy warship sank the *General Belgrano* outside the exclusion zone declared by Britain around the Falklands. A week before the papal visit, Archbishop Derek Worlock, engaged alongside the Cardinal in a shuttle diplomacy back and forward to Rome, rated the chances of the trip going ahead at only 50–50.

The Cardinal and his bishops managed to save the day by restyling the visit as a purely pastoral one. There would be no government ministers greeting the Pope and no pressure for him to take sides. And in an impressive Mass for Peace in St Peter's Square on the Saturday before John Paul's scheduled arrival, Cardinal Hume and Archbishop Worlock joined the Pope and their Argentinian counterparts Cardinals Aramburu and Primatesta in a public plea for the two sides to resolve their differences in a peaceful manner. The Pope announced at the Mass that he wanted to go to Argentina – and did so less than two weeks after he left England.

It was Basil Hume who in the end persuaded the Pope to override the objections of the Latin American bishops. The nature of that achievement should not be underestimated. Whatever John Paul's feeling about liberation theology, nearly half the world's Catholics are in Latin America. Only a tiny percentage are in Britain.

The Pope and the former abbot had already been working closely on what should be said on the visit, so as not to offend the English Establishment, Anglicans or indeed English Catholics, with their rebellious tendencies over such subjects as contraception and divorce. The war in the South Atlantic made the task all the more difficult. Many a papal visit has been marred by remarks or occasions that grated, upsetting local sensitivities, as if the host churchmen had put all their energies into crowd control and none into what was to be said to the crowds. No such mistakes were made by Cardinal Hume.

The theme of the six-day tour was the seven sacraments and John Paul spoke on each of these in positive terms. There were none of the lengthy condemnations of birth control or marriage failure that have been a feature of other overseas trips. The history of persecution was touched on, but not in a way to offend. At Westminster Cathedral, John Paul recalled Bishop Richard Challoner, one of the eighteenth-century leaders of the beleaguered Catholic minority. Challoner had promised his flock a better future. That day had now come, said the Pope.

At Buckingham Palace he met the Queen, the head of the Church of England, in an encounter without precedent on English soil, even in pre-Reformation times. It was a courtesy call of one head of state to another, with no political overtones, it was stressed. Yet the two got on well, and emerged smiling. Although the Falklands war didn't come up, the Pope did promise to remember in his prayers Prince Andrew, serving as a helicopter pilot in the South Atlantic.

At Coventry, John Paul again avoided speaking directly about the on-going war but, in a remark that delighted the substantial Christian peace movement, said that 'today the scale and horror of modern warfare – whether nuclear or not – makes it totally unacceptable as a means of settling differences between nations'. At Canterbury, he knelt and prayed with the Archbishop of Canterbury. Together they signed a common declaration committing their two Churches to dialogue. At Liverpool, Britain's showpiece of ecumenism, he spoke of the 'sin of disunity among Christians' and processed along Hope Street, the aptly named thoroughfare which links the city's Catholic and Anglican cathedrals. At Wembley Stadium he took family life and the dangers of sexual permissiveness as his theme. At Manchester's Heaton Park, in an unscripted addition, he remembered in particular the needs of prisoners.

These and other themes John Paul chose for his speeches have also been the themes of Basil Hume's leadership of English Catholicism.

The two men may not see eye-to-eye on subjects like war and peace or unity, but the visit showed them as working to a common agenda. It is to that agenda that we now turn to see how Basil Hume has guided his independently minded flock and, in the process, how he has shaped and defined the Catholic role in English society.

5

Unity in diversity

Dialogue with other churches is not just idle conversation, the airing of what is negotiable. It is getting to know the truth about each other as we search further for truth.

(Cardinal Hume, to the British Council of Churches)

When Basil Hume was a young student at St Benet's Hall in Oxford in the 1940s, he played rugby for the Greyhounds, a scratch fifteen made up of fellow Benedictine students, Jesuit novices from Campion Hall on the other side of the High, and Welsh Methodists from Jesus College on the Turl. Details of the team's success on the field of play are lost in the mists of the Meadows, but as a forerunner of the future Cardinal's ecumenical endeavours the outings have gone into the record books. They'll be keeping a welcome in the Welsh hillsides for their former team-mate.

At the time of that Oxford camaraderie, and indeed for the next two decades, the attitude of Catholics to the Church of England and other Christian Churches in Britain was decidedly stuffy. The dream of Wiseman and Manning that, once the Roman hierarchy was re-established at Westminster, the Anglicans would see the error of their ways and return to the one true faith had been abandoned through lack of public interest. But relations between the two denominations were slow to thaw, even under the more modern Cardinal Heenan. In its dealings with its fellow Christians, the Catholic Church donned the mantle of the lady of the manor welcoming the *nouveaux riches* of the village to the ancestral seat. The Church of England, for its part, tended to look with suspicion at the Pope in Rome, and by association at his followers in England.

The message from many pulpits was not an encouraging one. Catholics were discouraged from attending non-Catholic funerals except in the case of close friends. Catholics were letting the side

81

down if they acted as bridesmaids or best men at the weddings of Anglican friends. Mixed marriages were treated as second class. Even the idea of entering a 'Protestant' church was enough to send eyes heavenwards looking for a thunderbolt. And a synagogue was out of the question.

Cardinal Heenan wrote in his autobiography of the spirit of the age in pre-Vatican II times. 'The word ecumenism was scarcely known outside Protestant theological circles and joint religious services were rare and unpopular. Embarrassment was caused to all parties when Catholic officials were obliged to absent themselves from religious functions. Their custom allowed Catholics to attend weddings and funerals of non-Catholic friends but made no exception for civic or national occasions.' Heenan recognized that the time had come for a change of heart and, as he manoeuvred the Catholic Church out of its fortress, he took his lead from the Second Vatican Council and extended the hand of friendship and co-operation to other Churches. His experiences in the 1930s in Russia made him an enthusiastic backer of the 1965 document *Nostra Aetate*, which abandoned the Catholic Church's habitual disdain for other faiths and pledged closer co-operation with the Jews in particular. Recriminations over the crucifixion were finally to be laid to rest.

It was a mark of the late Cardinal's success at building bridges with the Church of England that the canonization of 40 Catholic martyrs from post-Reformation persecutions – potentially a source of friction with the Anglicans – took place in 1970 without widespread protest on the one side and without triumphalism on the other. Some disquiet about stirring up animosities of the past by the canonizations was expressed before the event by Archbishop Michael Ramsey of Canterbury. But Pope Paul VI moved quickly to deflect any hurt by departing from his text and speaking of two sister Churches embraced in unity, a phrase repeated by Cardinal Hume in his landmark visit to Westminster Abbey on the evening of his consecration in 1976.

Paul VI's sensitivity was a result of both personal inclination and the groundwork done (and well done) by Archbishop Michael Ramsey's historic visit to Rome in March 1966. If Heenan was talking about friendship, the Anglican primate's eyes seemed set on a far horizon – unity. And, for a time at least, he appeared to have Rome on his side. Vatican II seemed to raise the possibility that Anglicans and Catholics might one day reunite. Doors that had remained locked for 400 years were opened by Pope John XXIII and the Council.

Archbishop Geoffrey Fisher recognized the potential for progress with the summoning of the Council and made a historic visit – the first by an Anglican primate – to Rome in 1960. But Fisher, by nature, belonged to the Protestant wing of the Church of England. His successor in 1961, Archbishop Michael Ramsey, was an Anglo-Catholic, a follower in the traditions of the Tractarians and the Oxford Movement of the middle years of the nineteenth century, emphasizing the Catholic heritage of the Church of England but drawing back from the Church of Rome on certain matters of faith and dogma, not least the position of the universal Primate.

Ramsey was the man to exploit the new mood in Rome and his 1966 visit, soon after the end of the Council, was an occasion of great symbolic power. He joined Pope Paul VI in a common act of worship – commonplace today but the first of its kind then – at the ancient basilica of St Paul's-Outside-the-Walls. There the Catholic pontiff gave the Anglican Primate his own episcopal ring, in effect finally at the highest level laying to rest any residual hostility between the two Churches as a result of the post-Reformation excesses. Paul VI was a man for gestures, especially when he sensed that the right form of words could not yet be agreed. In 1966 he could not at a stroke revoke the past hostility between the two Churches or rescind disputed documents like *Apostolicae Curae*, but by the gesture of giving his ring he was saying that the relationship between Catholics and Anglicans would never be quite the same again.

The mood of expectancy that Archbishop Ramsey's visit created was well summed up in a cartoon in the *Catholic Herald* at the time. The Anglican leader was seen at Rome's Trevi Fountain, throwing three coins over his shoulder to make sure, according to the traditional custom, that he would one day return to the Eternal City.

In the immediate aftermath of the visit a theological dialogue was started with five bishops and five theologians from each side meeting at Gazzada in the Alps. The omens were good. On the Anglican side enthusiasm about the prospect of eventual reunion was maintained. Although Michael Ramsey had spent his three coins in vain and did not repeat his visit as Anglican Primate, his successor, Donald Coggan, a man of Protestant leanings, made a memorable – though some said tactless – appeal for inter-communion at St Paul's American Episcopal church in Rome, the day before visiting the Pope in the Vatican. On the Catholic side, however, the momentum quickly weakened. Pope Paul VI had many problems to distract him, not least the fall-out from his 1968 encyclical *Humanae Vitae*, banning artificial contraception.

Practical, grassroots ecumenism did begin to take off, with local Catholic churches playing host to their Anglican neighbours and vice versa. Soon joint action became the norm. Cardinal Heenan made the right noises. Indeed he showed courage when barracked by extreme Protestants led by Ian Paisley during a service at St Paul's Cathedral in London for the recently inaugurated Week of Prayer for Christian Unity. But the Cardinal was all too conscious of the theological barriers to more substantive progress and in his later years he let his fear become paralysing.

Change of gear

With the advent of Basil Hume there was a marked change of pace in Catholic endeavours towards ecumenism. In 1976, the new Cardinal seemed to realize at once the need to cast caution to the wind and make a bold statement of intent to recapture the mood of the heady days of Archbishop Ramsey's visit to Rome a decade earlier. As we have already seen, he did this by going, hours after his installation in Westminster Cathedral, to sing Latin Vespers in Westminster Abbey, formerly a Benedictine house.

It was not an isolated gesture. That effort to give practical expression to the healing of the wounds of England's past religious intolerance has been a feature of his cardinalate. Basil Hume's status as a Benedictine has allowed him to travel to other pre-Reformation abbeys, also once in the keeping of his order but now Anglican cathedrals. In June 1992, for example, he preached the sermon at a Service of Thanksgiving and Dedication in Chester Cathedral, to mark the climax of the celebrations of the 900th anniversary of its foundation as the Benedictine Abbey of St Werburgh. In the congregation were the Prince of Wales, expected to become the next 'supreme governor' of the Church of England, and the Anglican Archbishops of York and Wales and Bishops of Blackburn, Liverpool, Coventry, Wakefield and Manchester. His years at Westminster have seen a series of notable ecumenical firsts. In March 1992, for example, he became the first Cardinal since the seventeenth century to preach before the reigning monarch at the opening of the shared ecumenical church of Christ the Cornerstone in Milton Keynes.

At the heart of Cardinal Hume's vision has been the idea of Churches unloading their historical baggage and freely coming together to build for the future – whether it be in bricks and mortar as at Milton Keynes or in forums where talking enables a shared faith to shine through doctrinal differences. He is not a believer in unity at any price. He has never suggested that the formidable theological gulf that still divides Catholics from their closest cousins the Anglicans and from other more distant relatives in the Christian family will be easily bridged. But he has redefined unity to suit the conditions of his times. He has stressed that unity does not necessitate agreeing on every point, but rather acknowledging and acting on a common faith. At an ecumenical gathering at Chantilly in France, he summed up his philosophy: 'There can be pluralism of doctrine; there cannot be pluralism in faith'. Basil Hume's success has been in putting that particular viewpoint into practice throughout his period in office in an ecumenical climate increasingly chilled by icy winds from Rome. He has sought a practical way ahead while those around him have shown a tendency to flounder on theological differences.

His partnership with Archbishop Runcie on the national stage gave a visible expression to this practical agenda – though their duo was often overshadowed by the Liverpool trio of Archbishop Derek Worlock, Bishop David Sheppard and the local Methodist Moderator of the time. And most significantly Basil Hume decided to boldly go where no Cardinal had been before, and led the Catholic Church into a reformed British Council of Churches. For half a century English Catholicism had stood aloof from this body. But the Cardinal determined that where the Churches could act together they would. The desirable and the possible were blended.

In this as in many other areas, the election of Karol Wojtyła as Pope in 1978 changed decisively what was and is possible for the Catholic Church. For one thing, the new Polish pontiff knew very little about Catholic–Anglican relations. And despite the positive signs given out during his visit to Britain in 1982, increasingly his ecumenical agenda has been dominated by relations with the

Orthodox in his native Eastern Europe – especially after the collapse of the Berlin Wall – and by the beginnings of a troubled dialogue with Islam, fast outstripping Catholicism as the world's largest denomination and a potent force in Middle Eastern and African politics. England has, in ecumenical terms, become a side-show for John Paul. He and his officials have been reluctant to make concessions to the Anglicans that could affect delicate negotiations with other faiths.

This new note of caution, replacing the enthusiasm of Paul VI, has dismayed many. During the by now annual Christian Unity Week celebrations in Rome in January 1992, Lutheran and Baptist representatives pulled out at the last minute from an inter-faith service with John Paul at St Paul's-Outside-the-Walls. Without any progress on the vexed question of inter-communion with the Catholic Church, the event would simply be going through the motions, they argued. They doubted any will on the Catholic side to make real concessions.

Christians in England who have embraced the ecumenical movement with fervour would have recognized the disillusion that wrecked that Roman event. Allaying their discontent, at the same time as coping with the Vatican's policy of retrenchment, has been the task of Cardinal Hume. In it he was helped immeasurably for over a decade by his great friend Robert Runcie, who showed both a boundless patience with Rome's theological objections and a determination, no less strong than the Cardinal's, not to let that once glimpsed goal of unity disappear over the horizon.

How his successor as Archbishop of Canterbury, George Carey, considerably more Protestant than Runcie, will fare remains to be seen. But already the Anglican Primate has taken a more aggressive – and potentially alienating – tone with the Vatican, notably in his attack on its Achilles heel, opposition to birth control, in the run-up to the 1992 Rio Earth Summit.

Personal progress

Basil Hume's own background was an ecumenical one. His father was a Scottish Protestant – though not an agnostic, as has sometimes been claimed. At Ampleforth he encouraged ecumenical links between the Abbey and neighbouring Christians, founding one of the country's earliest local Councils of Churches. An admirer of the Cardinal from those Yorkshire days, and a supporter of his candidacy for Westminster, was Bishop Gordon Wheeler, then of Leeds, who feels that, in his dealings with other Churches, Basil Hume has 'in a deeply personal way . . . exorcised all rivalries and jealousies and prepared the way for greater mutual understanding'.

The new Archbishop followed up his historic visit to Westminster Abbey by becoming the first Catholic leader to address the Church of England General Synod in February 1978. He was given a rapturous reception despite spelling out some unpleasant truths to the delegates. Just by being there, and by his tone, he managed to convey the impression of progress while his words were in fact saying the opposite – and this was, remember, in the days before Pope John Paul II. There would be no inter-communion in the near future until the two denominations could reach agreement on the nature of the Church, he said. And women's ordination would distance any denomination that allowed it from Rome, he added.

Despite this shot across the bows, the honeymoon period – due in no small part to the Cardinal's own enthusiasm – continued well into the 1980s. On the eve of the once-a-decade gathering of the Anglican communion at the Lambeth Conference in the summer of 1978, Basil Hume told Douglas Brown in an interview with the *Church Times* that the 1895 papal bull *Apostolicae Curae*, which deemed Anglican orders null and void, needed 'careful reconsideration'. That rather intemperate document, coming at a time when hopes of converting England back to the one true faith still burned bright in the Vatican, remains, on paper at least, a formidable obstacle to Anglican–Catholic understanding. There is a strong body of opinion that it should be abandoned. The English bishops, though, have to remember Rome and its taste for never admitting it was wrong. Teachings are not changed or abandoned. They develop. As Cardinal Hume remarked to me when discussing this book: 'People are always standing up and saying the Vatican should change this or that. It just doesn't work that way.'

Rather than see inter-Church links suffocate while waiting with bated breath for changes that tend to take decades and centuries rather than days and weeks, the Cardinal and his bishops have worked around the problem. Their relationship with the Anglican hierarchy has been one of pragmatic collegiality – working together, speaking together, being seen together, taking decisions together at a local level where appropriate, in the spirit of Vatican

II's collegial role model for national Catholic bishops' conferences. The two sets of bishops have made a commitment to find their common ground, not to emphasize their differences, a quite remarkable achievement when compared with attitudes prevalent only a century ago at the end of Manning's era.

The best expression of this new spirit has been in Liverpool. Archbishop Derek Worlock always refers to his ecumenical partner as 'Bishop David'. Technically, according to the letter of the law in *Apostolicae Curae*, the Anglican Bishop of Liverpool is not validly ordained, much less a prelate. The Archbishop recalls being questioned on the point on a BBC Radio Two phone-in.

'I replied that this was really part of a wider question which concerned our two Churches. I did not know the particular circumstances of Bishop David's ordination but I did regard the historical basis of Pope Leo XIII's famous "absolutely null and void" judgement as being no longer relevant. There were many issues now involved and our Churches were discussing them. In the meantime I was glad to accept Bishop David's ministry as a Bishop of the Church of England and to work with him in our Christian service of the people. Afterwards the producer said I had ducked the question. Since then the Holy See has made it plain that the issue of orders cannot be seen or judged apart from other matters of belief and practice, especially with regard to the whole sacramental system.'

So, in essence, it is day-to-day business as usual for the English bishops with regard to their Anglican colleagues. They avoid the more technical questions – referring them to a committee. The committee in question developed out of conversations following Michael Ramsey's visit to Rome. From the meeting at Gazzada came the Anglican–Roman Catholic International Preparatory Commission. It produced the Malta Report in 1968. Out of the Malta Report came ARCIC – the Anglican–Roman Catholic International Commission. It laboured for twelve years to prepare a Final Report on three of the theological areas where the two Churches had different ideas: eucharist, with many Anglicans not sharing the Catholics' belief in transubstantiation, that the bread and wine become literally the body and blood of Jesus Christ; ministry, embracing issues such as the *Apostolicae Curae* question; and authority – the place of the Pope and his powers.

Over the last issue in particular, the ecumenical movement has

A game of squash after the opening of the new courts at Romford YMCA, Essex, with YMCA official Dick Martin. Photograph by Brian Smith, © Camera Press Ltd, London.

With the Dalai Lama. Photograph by Carlos Reyes.

Laying the foundations. Photograph by M. M. Franks.

With choristers from Westminster archdiocese. Photograph by Howard Harding, reproduced by kind permission of Howard Harding Associates.

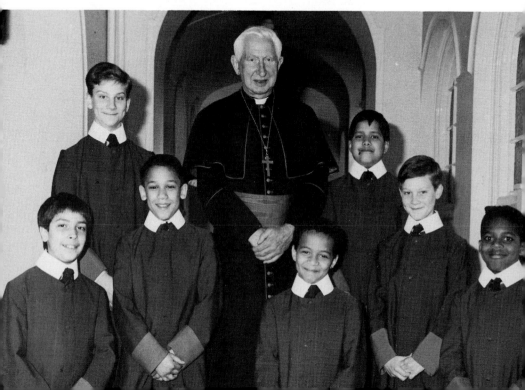

made little progress. John Paul II is never going to concede a reduction in his powers. For him the doctrine of papal infallibility, however discredited in the eyes of individual Catholics, is not an issue for debate. Yet no self-respecting Anglican will ever accept the extent of the authority and jurisdiction that go with the office of Pope. Robert Runcie tried, doggedly and with an admirable determination, in his five meetings with John Paul to find some space for manoeuvre. 'I believe', he said, 'the fabric of Anglican theology and ecclesiology is fundamentally open to the idea of a ministry of unity for the whole Church.' So he could countenance some sort of universal primacy. But his image was more akin to the captain of the cricket team than to an infallible pontiff. 'A universal spokesman . . . to articulate the universal faith of Christians' after due consultation with his fellow bishops was one thing, Dr Runcie said, but 'day to day detailed dictation of the affairs of a particular church from a centralised ecclesiastical bureaucracy' was another.

The latter model is the problem facing Basil Hume in dealing with a stalled ecumenical process. But the Cardinal is above all a practical man. He once described himself as 'academically not quite first division'. Modesty apart, he is not a man for protracted theological debate. As leader of English Catholicism he has attempted to get on with what is possible.

His major achievement in a period when ecumenism appears to be faltering has been to take the Catholic Church within the fold of the British Council of Churches (BCC). He said at his installation as Archbishop of Westminster that his role was 'not to dominate but to animate'. His decision to join the agency of the other Christian Churches in Britain effectively handed the baton to lay Catholics and asked them to see how far they could run with it.

Although there had been involvement in local councils of Churches – such as the Ryedale group that included Ampleforth Abbey – the old fortress mentality kept the Catholic Church out of the BCC when it was set up in 1942. In the early 1980s ecumenists among the bishops' conference, such as Cormac Murphy-O'Connor and Alan Clark, argued for Catholic membership, as indeed had the 1980 National Pastoral Congress. Cardinal Hume sided against them. He saw the BCC as too bureaucratic and wanted a thorough overhaul of its procedures before he would think of joining. However, in 1985 the Churches began a local dialogue – called

'Not Strangers but Pilgrims' – that was so successful that it led Basil Hume at an inter-Church gathering in Swanwick in September 1987 to announce that his Church was going to 'move quite deliberately from a situation of co-operation to one of commitment' in its ecumenical role.

Behind the Cardinal's talk of 'unity in faith' and 'legitimate diversity' lay months of careful negotiations. The BCC was to be disbanded and a new Council of Churches for Britain and Ireland (CCBI) set up with the Catholics as members. The old body was 'dying in the hope of a better resurrection', said its outgoing General Secretary, Dr Philip Morgan.

The launch of the new body took place, appropriately enough, in Liverpool, in September 1990. Absent from the celebrations were the Presbyterian Church of Ireland and the Baptist Union of Scotland. They felt that the clericalism of the Catholic Church and its hierarchical decision-making structure were in conflict with their own traditions of lay leadership and congregations deciding for themselves. Other members of the old BCC shared their fears, but decided to give the new organization a chance. From the Catholic side, there was a determination that the trend in the BCC towards a super-Church would be resisted and that the new CCBI and its regional branches would be at the service of local groups.

How far these different viewpoints have coincided is hard to assess. Joint action through the CCBI over the government's 1992 proposals to cut down the number of overseas political refugees allowed into this country undoubtedly strengthened the Churches' case. Yet the complicated round of consultation necessary to achieve a consensus has made the CCBI bureaucratic and slow to act. And the Catholic Church often prefers to speak out on its own rather than with its new partners.

The CCBI has one big advantage from Cardinal Hume's point of view. It validates and encourages the grassroots inter-Church progress made in the past 25 years that otherwise might have withered in the face of Rome's caution. He has spoken many times about the first step towards unity being Churches praying together. The CCBI puts that idea into a structure. It builds from below rather than waits for progress from above. At Swanwick the Cardinal anticipated this when he said that there could be 'no authentic evolution which does not take place at local level'. In the final analysis, if a great enough head of steam can be built up at local level for inter-Church understanding, whatever Rome says or does will matter little in day-to-day terms. But even at the grassroots level issues like the fact that Anglicans may not go to communion in Catholic churches – while the Church of England is happy to greet Catholics at its altar – show clearly the doctrinal difficulties that have caused the dream of reunion from the Ramsey era to be traded in for something altogether more modest.

The problems

The worldwide fruits of the Second Vatican Council's decision to start a new chapter in relations with other Churches are deceptively hard to assess. In one sense they are all too easy to see. The Pope greets religious leaders from around the world, both at the Vatican and on his travels. In 1982 he was pictured in Canterbury Cathedral with Robert Runcie. In 1986 he held a gathering of all the world's faiths at Assisi, his white robes vying for attention with Red Indian head-dresses and the saffron of Buddhists. Everywhere there are smiles and mutual congratulations. But behind the photo opportunities, how much is being achieved in concrete terms?

Old suspicions are being laid to rest, new friendships forged. But unity among the Churches, even those of like mind, still seems a long way distant. The only successful mergers of recent times have been of two small – on a global scale – Christian Churches in India, and of the English Congregationalists and Presbyterians in the United Reformed Church.

Despite Cardinal Hume's record of practical ecumenism, during his leadership the Catholic and Anglican Churches as institutions have moved further apart. At grassroots level it is another story, as we have seen. But hopes of eventual unity have receded rather than progressed, for all the Cardinal's sterling record of acting in unison with his Anglican counterparts.

The main stumbling-block has been the issue of women priests, referred to by the Cardinal at the General Synod in 1978. Histori-cally, both the Anglican and Roman Catholic communions have almost entirely excluded women from the ordained ministry, although in the early centuries of the Christian Church there is disputed evidence of women priests. (The ninth century is even reputed to have witnessed a woman Pope, Joan, who admittedly

91

did have to dress up as a man, so the legend goes, to fool the men into electing her to the throne of St Peter.)

The second half of the twentieth century has seen a decisive break with tradition in Anglican circles. In Hong Kong at the height of the Second World War women were ordained to the priestly ministry. At first much was made of the one-off nature of these decisions, forced on the local Church by an acute shortage of male ordinands. Yet by the onset of the final decade of the century there were well over a thousand women priests in various provinces of the Anglican communion and a couple of women bishops.

The attitude of the Church of England was initially hostile. Archbishop Michael Ramsey was a firm opponent – one factor in this no doubt being a realization that any move in the direction of women priests would damage the relations he was fostering with Rome. Robert Runcie was reluctant, if equivocal, for much the same reason. George Carey, though, had been a long-time supporter of the Movement for the Ordination of Women and is not a man to trim his attitude to what is acceptable to Rome. In November 1992, after 20 years of debate, the General Synod of the Church of England gave its backing to women priests. Cardinal Hume and the Vatican both responded with expressions of regret, describing the vote as a 'grave obstacle' to unity talks.

All this has made for difficult times for inter-Church understanding. Although the Church of England is but one province of the Anglican Communion, the symbolic value of its actions in the eyes of the Vatican – as the mother Church and as the seat of the Anglican primate – is immense. Robert Runcie, conscious of this and anxious to hasten the day of eventual reunion between Anglicans and Catholics, was accused by his own side of formulating his policy with one eye on what Rome thought. And the Vatican left him in little doubt about its opinions.

In a correspondence between December 1984 and June 1986, the Pope told Dr Runcie that the ordination of women would introduce 'an element of grave difficulty' into unity discussions. The gap between the two Churches became yet more apparent in 1988 with the publication of *Mulieris Dignitatem*, John Paul's apostolic letter which once more emphatically rejected the possibility of women's ordination. At the Last Supper Jesus was seen to be surrounded by his male disciples, neatly laid out like apostle teaspoons. What was good enough for Christ was good enough for the ministry of the Catholic Church, the Pope said.

Cardinal Hume felt as trapped by the situation as Robert Runcie. He made it plain that he personally was not opposed to the ordination of women, but had to follow Rome. In a BBC World Service phone-in he once remarked: 'I personally, if the authorities of my Church agreed to the ordination of women, would have no problem about it'. Indeed one way in which the Cardinal has attempted to review and renew English Catholicism has been by giving women more of a role and a voice in their Church. No longer can a woman serve the Church only by arranging flowers and cooking the priest's Sunday roast. In his own Westminster diocese the Cardinal has led by example by employing a woman, Kathleen O'Gorman, as head of the education office, despite the vocal opposition of several of his priests. And in 1991 a sub-group of the bishops' conference began discussions with representatives of the National Board of Catholic Women following the publication of the latter's mildly critical report *Women – Status and Role, Life and Mission.*

Such small steps have little bearing on the broader impasse over women priests. Even the time-honoured recourse of referring the question to ARCIC, or to ARCIC II, which was set up in the wake of the Pope's 1982 visit and the visible show of togetherness at Canterbury Cathedral, is no longer effective. *Mulieris Dignitatem* has closed that avenue. In 1982 quiet grumblings were emanating from the Congregation for the Doctrine of the Faith about ARCIC I and its final report. Talk among English churchpeople of 'substantial agreement' was given short shrift in Rome.

The wheels of the Catholic Church move notoriously slowly. It took the Vatican a whole decade to say what it really thought about ARCIC. At least it did the commission the honour of studying its conclusions carefully, but the verdict came as a profound disappointment to many English bishops, Roman Catholic and Anglican. The Vatican's concern, as revealed in its December 1991 statement, was with the phrase 'substantial agreement'. While it did not deny that ARCIC had found much common ground between the two Churches, it saw substantial agreement as implying that everything that mattered had been sewn up. And Rome felt that ARCIC, in its twelve years of discussions, had not found an acceptable formula for such central issues as eucharist and ministry. While uttering praise of ARCIC's common affirmation of the 'sacramental sacrifice' involved in the eucharist, Rome went on: 'the Catholic Church looks for certain clarifications which will assure that these affirmations are understood in a way that conforms to Catholic doctrine'. On issues like the elevated status of Christ's mother in Catholic doctrine and papal infallibility the Vatican said that it found little by way of convergence in the ARCIC report.

For the English churchpeople involved in ARCIC, Rome's narrow and somewhat negative definition of 'substantial agreement' went against the whole method that they had developed in their discussions. They had aimed not to achieve verbatim acceptance of the different dogmas of both Churches by each other, but rather to uncover a common substance of faith – as they had been asked to do by Pope John Paul II at Canterbury Cathedral. Having achieved that broader task, they were angry at being criticized for not dotting the *i*s and crossing the *t*s.

The Anglican co-chairman of ARCIC II, Bishop Mark Santer of Birmingham, summed up the despondency of many involved in the dialogue. 'The authorities in Rome seem to be asking not so much for agreement on essential matters of faith which is necessary and must be possible but for identity of formulation with current Roman Catholic teaching which is neither necessary nor possible.' It is a measure of how close the Roman Catholic and Anglican Churches in Britain have grown in their domestic vision of unity that Bishop Santer's remarks could have been made by Cardinal Hume – except of course that the Cardinal would be more moderate in his expression.

Stronger criticism was left to one of the men who might have been given the Westminster job in 1976, Bishop Alan Clark of East Anglia, the Catholic co-chairman of ARCIC I. He accused the Vatican of having no interest in or understanding of what the commission had been working towards for twelve years. 'It's going to make life difficult for us in the future but I don't think any of us will give up.' This typically English attitude of 'chin up and carry on fighting' hides a great deal of despair at the evaporation of the high hopes of the late 1960s. Cardinal Hume, like many in his flock, is downhearted. Sometimes at ecumenical events one has the sense that he is going through the motions, that the genuine excitement of his trip to Westminster Abbey in 1976 is no longer there.

'It's very sad. . . . There is no doubt that the issue of women's ordination is a major obstacle to Christian unity', he said in a 1991 interview. 'It has always seemed to me so clear that Christ prayed for Christian unity.'

6

Her Majesty's Loyal Opposition?

It is not for the church as a whole to advocate this or that
political constitution. It is not for her spiritual leaders to
pronounce on the best monetary policy or economic system.
Instead she is concerned with something deeper and more far-
reaching. She is the guardian of a priceless treasure, since
she is primarily engaged with the 'truth concerning man'.

(Basil Hume, *To Be a Pilgrim*)

The young George Hume grew up in relative affluence in Newcastle
in the 1920s. He, his brother and his sisters lived in a big house, were
looked after by a nurse, went for riding lessons. It was a well-heeled
life in a city hard hit by the Depression. For this was the age when
Britain's traditional heavy industries began to feel the pinch of competition from around the world. Just six miles east of the Hume home
in Newcastle was the shipbuilding town of Jarrow, starting-point for
the famous 1930s protest march to London by the unemployed.

The future Cardinal did not live in an ivory tower. He was aware
from an early age of the poverty that was abroad in his home city.
There was his surgeon father's work at the local hospitals. The
Hume children would occasionally visit the wards for Christmas
parties and glimpse how the other half lived. More significantly, as
he recalled many years later in a presidential address to the housing
charity, Shelter, he saw shoeless and stockingless children in the
streets, and women in church wearing their husbands' caps for
head-covering. As a boy he would accompany a Dominican friend
of his mother's to the other side of the tracks. With Fr Alfred
Pike, he met families who lived twelve to a room. 'I was forced to
compare my own good fortune with theirs', he told his audience. 'I
think that childhood experience determined my way of life – oddly
to become a monk.'

At first he thought of being a Dominican, working among the poor. Schooldays at Ampleforth changed his allegiance to the Benedictines, but did nothing to dim his commitment to a ministry alongside those in need. Despite the wealthy trappings of the abbey and its exclusive private school, the community also ran working-class parishes in several northern cities.

The young Father Basil – he followed the tradition of his order and took a saint's name on ordination – hoped to be sent to one such outpost in Liverpool, but instead was put to work teaching modern languages to the boys and dogmatic theology to junior monks. First as a housemaster, struggling to read Aquinas while 40 boys crowded into his room to watch *Juke Box Jury*, and then as abbot, his attentions were channelled elsewhere.

When he arrived at Westminster, many feared that he would find the transformation from running a well-cushioned rural abbey to heading a capital city diocese, with every variety of social problem within its boundaries, a painful one. The new Cardinal, some of the long-serving Westminster priests pointed out, had no parish experience, save for a very brief spell helping out at Ampleforth's local church. And in the hills of north Yorkshire, they speculated, he had been removed from the type of acute social needs witnessed every day in the streets around Westminster Cathedral.

Such apprehensions had failed to take into account Basil Hume's formative experiences with Fr Pike in the slums of Newcastle. The new Cardinal moved swiftly to demonstrate that his youthful enthusiasms had not deserted him during his long years as abbot. While he did not claim to bring a suitcase full of easy answers, Basil Hume at once set the tone for his stewardship – a preference for practical gestures, geared towards individual needs, over political posturing and ideological stances. The Cardinal is a doer and an enabler, not a philosopher.

He recognized immediately that the needs around his cathedral were as acute as anything he had witnessed all those years ago in the narrow streets around the Tyneside shipyards. The open piazza in front of the cathedral, for example, is a favourite resting place for the homeless. The cathedral and the adjoining clergy house act as a magnet for those in need. The front doorbell is forever being rung by a stream of people seeking advice, food and shelter. Young Irish immigrants, following in the footsteps of those early recruits to

English Catholicism who crossed to Liverpool to avoid the famine, are a significant group among those turning to the Church in their hour of need.

The Cardinal's response to what he found on his doorstep was to create a model community around the cathedral, offering practical support and leading others with bigger budgets – principally the government – to the path of righteousness by showing them an example of what can be done. Dotted around the maze of streets in the shadow of Archbishop's House – once described by the late Patrick O'Donovan as resembling 'a nursing home for upper-class alcoholics' – there is a network of Catholic organizations offering not only the spiritual guidance that has traditionally been the remit of the Church but also a roof, a bed and a hot meal.

Just as Prince Charles has put his pet architectural and environmental theories into practice by building working model villages on the land of his Duchy of Cornwall, to show ministers where he thinks they are going wrong, so the Cardinal has earmarked the property and resources of his office to demonstrate that the Church's concern for those in need is more than words.

The Cardinal Hume Centre has the specific brief of looking after young people at risk. It includes a hostel for 16–20-year-olds – always high on the former housemaster's list of concerns – who would otherwise be on the streets, prey to drugs and crime. There is a medical service for those whose lack of an address means they cannot go to a GP for treatment. And plans are afoot to build a place where youngsters who are hooked on glue sniffing and other substance abuse can be helped. Then there is the Cathedral Night Shelter, run every evening in the gloomy but spacious Cathedral Hall. By day it is the venue for gatherings of worthy Catholic organizations but by night it is home to 40 men and women who would otherwise be sleeping rough. Linked to the cathedral social services network is The Passage, a day centre for down-and-outs that also offers alcohol and probation counselling and some resettlement accommodation. And there is St Louise's Hostel, catering for 125 girls newly arrived in London looking for work, and the St Vincent's Centre, a welfare hostel for young women between 16 and 25, open to pregnant women of all ages. These first-stop shelters feed into a network of halfway houses, warden-supervised stepping-stones between the hostels and independent living in the community. The De Paul Trust, closely linked with the cathedral, has a series of shared houses where people can get used to coping for themselves in a supportive environment.

It all adds up to an impressive demonstration that the Cardinal practises what he preaches. By putting his faith in bricks and mortar, he can stand up and challenge the government on the inadequacies of its social services provision. And his case is then all the harder to refute.

The policy has worked. The cathedral network has so impressed Whitehall that the Department of the Environment, among others, has stumped up considerable sums of money to support the work of The Passage, the Cardinal Hume Centre and the night shelter. And Cardinal Hume, though leaving the day-to-day details to staff at each of the venues, has kept a close eye on what goes on and a ready ear for the problems that arise. His is a pastor's concern. 'One of the things that really meant a great deal to me was when, organized by Mother Teresa's nuns, I gave a half-day recollection with the ladies and gentlemen who would have been sleeping rough that night in Westminster', he once told me. 'We wandered around the cathedral together, doing the stations of the cross. I think what's wonderful about being a bishop is that you can chat with anyone. You can chat with guys who are drinking on the piazza. I don't find any difficulty there. I find myself at home in that world. The most marvellous thing about being a bishop is that small gestures can go a long, long way.'

The link between his work with the homeless and his lifelong concern for young people is highlighted by a dream the Cardinal revealed to me. 'If I weren't in this job, and if I weren't a monk, I should like to do something like run Centrepoint [a central London hostel for the homeless]. I feel very deeply about young people pouring into London at risk. I say constantly this is where the Church should be, this is our job. Where would St Vincent de Paul have been today? Round Centrepoint.'

While he goes about his public duties with dedication and with a boundless charm, the reluctant Cardinal comes alive when in the company of young people. His housemaster's training has stood him in good stead. He goes every year with a group of young adults on a pilgrimage to Lourdes, not presiding over the party, standing on his dignity, but mucking in. And he likes a rogue, as he once told *The Sunday Times*. 'What appeals to me is their humility. You never meet a conceited rogue.' He is occasionally in the habit of abandoning the formalities that linger on in Archbishop's House and inviting whole groups of youngsters over for sandwiches and a chat.

It is his humanity, his ability to be the simple monk, that puts people at their ease. When he speaks, even from the pulpit, he has a knack for establishing a direct rapport. His sermons and his broadcasts at Easter and Christmas never take refuge in religious rhetoric or cloudy phraseology. It is his accessibility that makes the Cardinal such a powerful advocate for disadvantaged groups like the homeless. Rather than make a speech slamming the government, he makes his point by being seen in action. And it is not just a question of floating in for a photo call, like a visiting royal, to be seen to care.

The Cardinal himself seems honestly unaware of the 'Hume effect'. It is not an acquired affectation or skill. But it explains why the marginalized, the Catholic community, ministers and the general public have grown to trust him and to listen attentively to his concerns. Soon after his elevation a 'vox pop' camera team was sent out by a TV news programme to expose the public's ignorance of current affairs. Five out of six passers-by could not name the Archbishop of Canterbury but the sixth, the proverbial little old lady so beloved of Esther Rantzen's excursions on the streets, was sure she knew: 'It's that nice Cardinal Hume'.

Balancing the books

Cardinal Hume has tried, wherever possible, to lead English Catholicism by consensus, balancing the demands of different factions. And within his diocese he has likewise had to weigh the expectations of different groups: those priests and advisers who want to see a radical social programme in response to the needs in the cathedral's own backyard, and those voices who feel the Church's role is not first and foremost to take the place of social workers. To head off any criticisms from this latter camp, the Cardinal has insisted that the cathedral itself remains first and foremost a house of prayer. None of the social work developments has been allowed to encroach upon the daily round of Masses, confessions and services. The temptation to make John Bentley's Byzantine masterpiece into a tourist trap has been resisted, with a noticeable absence of the commercialism and cash registers to be seen further down Victoria Street at Westminster Abbey.

In championing the liturgical excellence of the cathedral, Basil Hume has worked tirelessly to save its Choir School, threatened with closure when he arrived at Westminster because of lack of funds. Thanks to a successful appeal, its future is decidedly rosier, with the services in the cathedral benefiting musically as a consequence. For the Cardinal the proximity of the Choir School, joined by a short corridor to Archbishop's House, has another benefit. The choristers serve Mass in his private chapel when he is in residence and, in his quieter moments, Basil Hume has been known to drop in on evening prep to chat with the pupils. Once a housemaster. . . .

Set against the development of a model community around Westminster Cathedral has been Basil Hume's inability to get a grip on the finances of the diocese as they have plunged deeper and deeper into the red. Westminster is not alone in having trouble with its bank manager. It is an endemic problem in the Catholic Church. The Vatican is running an annual budget deficit of around £50 million. Even the prosperous if geographically scattered north-western diocese of Shrewsbury recently revealed a hole of £3 million in its bank account.

In a Britain where monetary disciplines have cut back on public spending on social services throughout the 1980s and early 1990s, the Church has felt itself called to take on an increased burden. Yet at the same time, with ever declining Mass attendances and a portfolio of ageing Victorian properties in need of repair, its funding base is steadily being eroded.

Westminster was running a deficit of several million pounds each year when Basil Hume arrived in 1976. There were strenuous efforts at reduction, selling off some of the treasures of Archbishop's House, scaling down the pomp and circumstance so beloved of his predecessors. (For the first few weeks in Archbishop's House Cardinal Hume was puzzled by one of the buttons on the internal telephone system. It was marked 'HE' and he couldn't think what the letters stood for. Eventually his secretary had to enlighten him. It was his own line – HE being short for His Eminence.) The Cardinal also decided that some of the investments made by the diocese in previous years had been unwise or, more to the point, unethical. Shares in companies in South Africa were sold off on his orders.

The deficit stood at £4.9 million in March 1985, when Basil Hume took the unprecedented step of publishing accounts. His openness was greeted with approval by the laity in the parishes, who were continually being asked to dig deeper into their pockets to ease the shortfall. Yet there was concern at the broadcasting of such statistics among many of the old guard among the diocesan clergy, used to the more autocratic regime of Cardinal Heenan. Diocesan finances had traditionally been a matter for the bishop, his close clerical advisers and a carefully selected 'Catholic accountant'. Throwing the books open to the laity did not meet with universal approval. Equally there was some criticism of their new leader's commitment to building up the social services network round the cathedral at a time when Westminster was short of cash. Comments were also made about the much-expanded use of lay advisers.

The Cardinal's personal staff remains tiny in comparison with that of other Church leaders. The Archbishop of Canterbury, for example, has a professional office team at Lambeth Palace running into double figures, with specialist press officers, ecumenical advisers, roving ambassadors and so on. Basil Hume, by contrast, makes do with just three people in his public affairs office (though to have such a body would have been unthinkable in Cardinal Heenan's day): the always diplomatic Charles Wookey, a former clerk in the Houses of Parliament; Major Patrick Victory, who does a lot of the detailed research that underpins the Cardinal's campaigns; and a secretary.

One development resented in particular by some of the Westminster clergy was the establishment in 1979 of the Social and Pastoral Action agency. Charged with expanding the pastoral strategy seen around Victoria to a diocese-wide constituency, its largely lay team took as their brief not only the 500,000 Catholics in that area, but the whole population of four million.

Despite deciding early in his time at Westminster to sub-divide his diocese into five pastoral areas, each with its own auxiliary bishop, Basil Hume has not limited his social concern to the immediate vicinity of his cathedral. He works closely with his auxiliaries, meeting them each week to discuss the problems they are dealing with, whether they be in Bishop Victor Guazzelli's run-down East End pastoral area or Bishop James O'Brien's affluent Hertfordshire. The Cardinal's travels around the diocese are not only for traditional Sunday visitations to parishes and confirmations. Soon after his arrival at Archbishop's House, riots erupted during the annual Notting Hill Carnival in west London. The local parish priest was told on the phone the next morning that the Cardinal was coming over to meet police and local community leaders and see for himself what had happened.

With so many calls on resources and such a wide-ranging strategy, the harmonization of income with expenditure is still a long way off for the Westminster diocese. Those who judge the Church and its leaders by the state of their bank balances will not give Cardinal Hume unqualified approval. But for the majority who want to see the Church act, the financial headaches will be a price well worth paying. Cardinal Hume has made sure that the old adage of G. K. Chesterton cannot be applied to his leadership: 'the trouble with Christianity is not that it has been tried and found wanting but that it has been found difficult and never tried'.

Best-kept secret

The Catholic Church's social teaching is often called its best-kept secret. Pope John Paul II has produced two powerfully worded encyclicals on injustice and oppression within the capitalist and socialist systems: *Sollicitudo Rei Socialis* (1987) and *Centesimus Annus* (1990). While commending traditional notions of charity – giving the poor food to eat – both make plain that the Church's prime concern is for justice and human rights – asking why the poor have nothing to eat. Both documents are eloquent statements in a long tradition of Church teaching siding with the marginalized against their oppressors that can be traced, falteringly at times, back to Jesus' Sermon on the Mount: Blessed are the poor. Yet the social gospel of the Catholic Church has too often been overshadowed by its sexual code, especially in pronouncements from Rome, as was discussed earlier.

With Basil Hume, however, the often overlooked social teaching of the Church has received more emphasis. This is partly to do with the prevailing attitudes in English Catholicism and society at large. People want to be free to make up their own decisions about sexuality, as Michael Hornsby-Smith's sociological research has so convincingly revealed. Just as important is the fact that the Cardinal is reluctant to lecture on sexual matters. He doesn't preach against the pill and only enters the public debate to talk about moral standards when a specific issue – the fight for abortion law reform, the national debate on embryo experimentation – demands his attention.

In his day-to-day work, the Cardinal prefers to concentrate on people and social needs, areas where Church teaching has a practical contribution to make. His role in developing the Westminster Cathedral network has been symptomatic of a more general approach in making Catholicism relevant to the society around it by what it does rather than by what it says, by the positive benefits it can offer rather than the things it rules out. What the Cardinal has struggled to build in his diocese cannot be seen in isolation from his contribution on the national stage. If people listen to what he has to say about housing, they do so in the knowledge that he has got his hands dirty and knows what he is talking about.

Basil Hume has been patron since soon after he travelled south from Ampleforth of the campaigning and decidedly un-churchy housing charity Shelter, started in the 1960s in the wake of the celebrated TV play *Cathy Come Home*. Although several priests were prominent in the setting-up of Shelter, it is a secular organization. Basil Hume's involvement with this charity reflects both the weight he carries in the public conscience on social issues and his own determination to step outside the narrow confines of the Catholic community on issues of public policy that he feels concern everyone, regardless of creed.

Although he also heads the smaller Catholic Housing Aid Society (CHAS), the Cardinal's role as the public face of Shelter is another indicator of his determination to brush away the old fortress mentality of those who wish to confirm their attention to Catholic charities serving only the Catholic community, mirroring and to some extent duplicating the work done in the secular sphere by other organizations. He has bridged the gulf. The Church is now to work in partnership, where appropriate, with campaigning agencies. (Occasionally that more open policy can create problems, as was the case in January 1986 when Cardinal Hume resigned as a patron of Mencap because that charity's public endorsement of experimentation on embryos went against Catholic teaching.) While long-standing Catholic bodies are treated with respect, the Cardinal makes more of an impact when his credentials are not simply as leader of the Catholic community, working with organizations that, in the public mind, are run by Catholics for Catholics.

CHAS itself, it should be pointed out, serves people regardless of denomination and has a record to rival Shelter in critical analysis of

Whitehall policies. But the age of the Catholic charity that confines its help to Catholics, or at least the charity that has the word Catholic in its title, is passing. Even CHAS prefers to be known by its acronym rather than its full title. A more socially mobile Catholic community no longer restricts its attention and its donations to demonstrably Catholic organizations. Sometimes, in order to stress their liberation from the fortress mentality, they deliberately support secular alternatives.

The Cardinal has broken with the traditions of his predecessors and has taken on, alongside his role as the leader and nurturer of English Catholicism, a brief to speak to the broadest possible audience on questions of public policy where he sees fundamental moral principles as being involved.

Priests and politics

Such a development has, inevitably, left him open to charges of interfering in politics. The argument about priests and their involvement in politics is an old one. In the 1980s, however, it was given particular resonance by the repeated clashes between the iconoclastic governments of Margaret Thatcher and leading churchmen. The Iron Lady broke the mould of the consensus politics of post-war Britain and for much of her period in office faced an ineffectual and divided Opposition that stumbled to three successive election defeats. Several senior churchmen, led by the urban bishops in the Anglican Church, clearly felt that in the absence of anyone else they should, in the national interest, assume the mantle of Her Majesty's Loyal Opposition.

Faith in the City, the 1985 report from the Archbishop of Canterbury's commission on urban priority areas, caused a considerable storm because of its criticisms of government policy. One cabinet minister labelled the report Marxist. David Jenkins, the Bishop of Durham, lectured the government on a whole variety of subjects from the error of its ways in the long-running and bitter miners' strike of the mid-1980s to the wrong-headedness of deregulating bus services. He defended himself against the repeated onslaughts of politicians and journalists by saying that the Thatcher years were times of upheaval in the economic and social spheres and that people therefore looked for guidance to the Church as an institution that was more stable and enduring, part of the national framework. 'The Thatcherite modification, whereby consensus has been thrown out and conviction is the thing, has in many ways carried all before it', he told me at the time. 'This thrusts the Church, especially the Established Church, though with others assisting, into the centre not of straightforward political opposition, but of speaking up for issues that are being ignored, overridden or for the moment settled in a way that up to now would not have been thought of as the right way.' He had little time for bishops who were 'generally speaking, generally speaking'.

Cardinal Hume would have a great deal of sympathy with Dr Jenkins's thesis that the Church should be a voice for the voiceless. But their respective ways of putting that idea into practice couldn't be more different. Where the Anglican bishop rapidly made himself a figure of derision in government circles and was thereby dismissed as irrelevant, even meriting a *Spitting Image* puppet complete with miner's lamp attached to his mitre, the Catholic cardinal has a remarkable record in commanding the respect of both ministers and journalists. He has never suffered either satire in latex or a bad press and is listened to with courtesy in Whitehall, where his concerns have on several notable occasions (as will be discussed) been taken on board.

It is part of the pastoral role of bishops, the Cardinal feels, to bring to notice issues and, more importantly, those of their flock whose needs are being overlooked. 'When you come to caring for the flock, then you've got to have a special concern for the disadvantaged, for the poor, for those who are not able to care for themselves', he told me. 'Once you begin to make the flock your special concern, then of course how they fare in the world, their condition, becomes a matter of rather considerable importance. Anything that is a denial of respect for their persons, or any injustice in their situation, that will call for the involvement of the pastor . . . so it is in that way that we can also get involved in matters which are the concern of the politician.' The cautious choice of words has been reflected in a cautious policy. The capacity of Church leaders to command the attention of ministers and public is a privilege, especially when it comes to questions that are not *prima facie* 'religious'. And Basil Hume has been anxious, over-anxious some would say, not to abuse that privilege lest it be rescinded.

When it comes to translating the practical concern he has shown in his own diocese into the language of government policy, the

Cardinal's starting-point is always to make sure he is in full command of all the facts. Having day-to-day experience in the cathedral social services network of the issue in question is definitely an asset. But he can take quite some persuading before he acts.

The next step is a private approach to ministers. The Cardinal has never been a man for jumping on to his soap box lightly. 'I had a very interesting case', he recalled, 'when a very able woman who works at The Passage was very upset at new DSS regulations and how they stopped people at the centre getting money. Well, I set up a meeting for her with the Minister. He came here to Archbishop's House and met the woman from The Passage and I was present.' The image is an intriguing one. Ministers answer an invitation to come and discuss in private a matter of concern with the Cardinal. Obviously his office carries a certain cachet. But there is also the fact that he has a reputation in Whitehall for being reasonable, a man from the same background as ministers with whom they can talk as an equal over an informal drink.

Basil Hume's approaches to ministers are very often made because of concern over individuals. When he hears of an injustice against people, he is not afraid to go to those in power with specific cases in mind. In this willingness to be particular he is the antithesis of politicians and bureaucrats, whose tendency is to steer clear of individual cases and stick to generalizations and broader principles. Nowhere was the Cardinal's penchant for starting with one person's plight and ending up making a major political point better demonstrated than in his campaign for the Guildford Four. It began with a meeting with Gerard Conlon, one of the four people convicted of being IRA bombers, and developed into the Cardinal criticizing the entire criminal justice system (of which more later).

If the Irish justice cases are left to one side, it is hard to assess the effectiveness of the Cardinal's approach of private and largely unreported pressure in wringing concessions out of the government. The willingness of Whitehall chiefs to go and listen to Basil Hume's concern on technical details of legislation is a testament to the respect he commands in the corridors of power. 'I think it is true that if I ask to see somebody, then they treat us very well. I've never been refused, though I'm careful not to overplay my hand. I do get treated with enormous understanding and courtesy.'

It is only when such discreet approaches fail to bear fruit that the Cardinal contemplates making his worries public. And even then, as one of his former advisers remarked, the brief is to draft something that is 'clear, incisive, challenging, yet non-controversial'. A balanced tone is the order of the day, to the frustration of some of those around Basil Hume.

Over housing in particular, he has shown a marked reluctance to make public statements. In the early 1980s he issued a joint pastoral letter with the Anglican Bishop of London on homelessness, to be read in the capital's churches. And on several occasions he has gone on the record – particularly in his contributions to Shelter campaigns – to make plain his view that housing is a moral issue not just for the Churches but for the well-being of our society. But major interventions by him are few and far between.

There is an important point here. Part of his caution about overplaying his hand is a reluctance to stand up on a public platform and talk in technical detail about an issue where he doesn't have firsthand experience. For all the backing he has given to the various projects around his cathedral, the many calls on Basil Hume's time do not allow him to develop a day-to-day familiarity with social security regulations and the finer points of such processes as tenant transfers. If he were to make a speech on such matters, it would have to be written by his team of advisers, with input from Church experts like Robina Rafferty of the Catholic Housing Aid Society. And the Cardinal clearly feels that to read out someone else's thoughts, no matter how much he agrees with them, would weaken his impact and leave him exposed. It is only on matters where he has intimate knowledge of his subject – like education – that the Cardinal is prepared to slog it out over technical points in public. On housing policy, it has tended to be Archbishop Derek Worlock of Liverpool who has done the talking to specialist bodies like the Institute of Housing.

Where Basil Hume prefers people to detailed research, making decisions instinctively, Archbishop Worlock likes to work through the facts of the argument beforehand. He has an encyclopaedic knowledge of the Church and its teachings since the 1950s, when he was secretary to Cardinals Griffin and Godfrey, and is not afraid to debate with the experts on specific matters. He has shown himself ready and willing to criticize the government publicly over homelessness, for example. In the summer of 1989 the Archbishop addressed the Institute of Housing's annual conference at Harrogate.

He began on common ground with Cardinal Hume – the general

point that housing is a moral issue. But he went on to develop the argument in detail and attacked as guilty of double standards those ministers who criticize the Churches' involvement in social issues. 'We are being asked to indulge in selective morality: to condemn sexual immorality, the laziness of those reluctant to move home to find a job, and of course violence and football hooliganism. But lay off issues of social and economic justice, or you will be branded as an ecclesiastical politician or a political ecclesiastic, suffering from a bad attack of "Durhamitis".'

The Archbishop cast his mind back to a 1985 statement from the Catholic bishops, *Housing Is a Moral Issue*: 'The then Minister for Housing replied that "if housing is a moral issue then so too are health and personal social services, social security and education". Frankly he took the words right out of my mouth.' Building on statistics and observations from his own involvement in urban regeneration programmes in a Liverpool still blighted by the after-effects of wartime bombing and ill-conceived redevelopment policies of the 1950s and 1960s, he effectively pulled the rug from under the government's feet on their economic strategy. 'If we are dealing with justice and not with charity, then attention must be given to the distribution of wealth as well as wealth creation; and through taxes and rates, benefits and resources have to be increased to the less fortunate and the poor. . . . One does not have to be a collectivist to judge justice in society by the condition of the disadvantaged, as well as the number of millionaires.'

Archbishop Worlock has taken the sort of campaigning and confrontational stance on social matters that Cardinal Hume has adopted on schools. In their respective areas of expertise, the two often complement each other. Whether Archbishop Worlock's position is because of the acute plight of his city, personal inclination or his close relationship with his Anglican counterpart, Bishop David Sheppard, is hard to decide.

The contrast between English Catholicism's two leading lights, who work so closely on so many matters, could be seen when Archbishop Worlock joined Bishop Sheppard to challenge the government on specific technical details, like the cherished 'trickle down' theory that continues to be an axiom behind Conservative economic policy. This holds that if the rich get richer the poor will inevitably benefit in the end, and see an improvement in their living standards. 'Nonsense', said the two in their book *Better Together*, and they went on to use the language of financiers to debunk the argument.

Derek Worlock has, it would be fair to say, engaged in some of the behind-the-scenes lobbying with government ministers that Basil Hume has made his hallmark. In the aftermath of the Liverpool riots of the early 1980s, he frequently travelled to London to meet the Minister for Merseyside, Michael Heseltine. But the Archbishop's chosen role was that of go-between, the confidant of government, local council and the people of Liverpool. Where the Cardinal will sit down quietly with ministers and urge them to change their minds over some issue or other, Archbishop Worlock, who is not by birth as at ease with the ruling classes as Basil Hume, tends to act as a kind of one-man ACAS, avoiding negotiation lest it compromise his position.

Primus inter pares

Cardinal Hume is not the Primate of England and Wales. He is the only Cardinal among the English hierarchy but his authority derives from the fact that he is president of the bishops' conference, the first among equals.

The distinction between when he is speaking on behalf of all the bishops and when he is speaking off his own bat can be a hard one to draw. The press, of course, want to hear the Cardinal's comments on every matter. For the media he *is* Catholicism. They do not want to be diverted to one of the other bishops. Aside from Archbishop Worlock none of the hierarchy has a very high public profile. Yet good Vatican II man that he is, Basil Hume believes in the idea of collegiality, fellow bishops acting together wherever possible to bring their collective weight and *gravitas* to bear on particular subjects. On social concerns he has tried to spread the burden of enunciating Catholicism's case among his fellow prelates.

One of the features of collegiality that earlier cardinals like Wiseman, Manning and Bourne would have found intolerable is that it means you sometimes have to walk because your fellow bishops do not want to jog with you. But for Cardinal Hume, the abbot who followed St Benedict's dictum that he should 'so arrange everything so that the strong have something to yearn for and the weak nothing to run from', collective responsibility has often seemed more attractive taking an outspoken personal stand. He has led the bishops' conference, as in other areas of his work, by consensus, finding the middle way.

One of the reforms in the upper echelons of the Catholic Church ushered in during Cardinal Hume's leadership has made the bishops' conference more professional and more structured than ever before. Archbishop Worlock oversaw the changes, bringing his characteristic attention to detail to bear on an essentially technical matter. Where in the 1970s there was a commission, in the 1980s there was a general secretariat, based in central London, co-ordinating activities and fielding questions from the media. The old commission had been set up in the wake of the Second Vatican Council but many grew to see it as too narrow in focus and unable to match the increasing horizons of the Church in its involvement in all manner of social concerns. The proposal document for reform from commission to secretariat was titled 'In the house of the living God'. Those who had despaired of the limitations of the commission dubbed it 'In the house of the living dead'. Under the new set-up, different departments oversee different areas of the life of the Church and nation. Individual bishops take responsibility for different subjects and in theory relieve the Cardinal and to a lesser extent Archbishop Worlock of the limelight.

It was through the revised structures of the hierarchy that in 1990 the Department for Citizenship and Social Responsibility – the Church as it modernizes has yet to get its tongue round catchy names, but give it time – produced its report *Homelessness: a Fact and a Scandal*, which attracted national headlines. It contained just the sort of specific, technical, item-by-item criticisms that Cardinal Hume likes to avoid in his speeches. But the auspices of the bishops' conference allowed space for detailed research. Government policies – the sale of council houses, incentives to first-time buyers – were put under the microscope and shown to have 'failed completely to ensure an adequate supply of houses'.

There have been other bishops' conference reports looking at the national social and political implications of the social concerns that the Cardinal has embraced in a personal way on his own doorstep, such as drug abuse among the young, a subject tackled in an August 1986 report from the Social Welfare Commission of the Bishops' Conference. All in all the general secretariat has taken the first steps towards providing the bishops with a research department, a think-tank able to harness the expertise on different issues that exists in the Catholic community.

Another new avenue for making the Church's concern felt, without the burden falling on the Cardinal to take to his soap box, has been opened up by Catholic membership of the Council of Churches for Britain and Ireland. Fears that there were racist overtones and a deprivation of human rights in proposed government legislation on immigration were tackled both in public statements and in delegations to the Home Office by a CCBI team including a Catholic auxiliary bishop.

Trial and error

One of Cardinal Hume's most significant and most public successes was in getting the cases of the Guildford Four put again before the Court of Appeal in October 1989. The story of his involvement is a classic Cardinal Hume campaign, starting out from personal contact, working through private meetings with ministers, and eventually going public in pursuit of his goal.

Gerard Conlon, Paul Hill, Paddy Armstrong and Carole Richardson had been found guilty in October 1975 of planting bombs a year earlier at two Guildford pubs, the Horse and Groom and the Seven Stars, killing five people and maiming many more. They were sentenced to life imprisonment. Their appeal in 1977 was turned down but by the late 1970s influential voices were being raised to say that there had been a miscarriage of justice. Prominent among those early campaigners for the Four were Church figures like Belfast priests Fathers Denis Faul and Raymond Murray and Sister Sarah Clarke. Their interest and that of his prison chaplains brought Cardinal Hume along to meet the men and as a result of that he began in the late 1970s to ask that their convictions be looked at again.

His involvement in the Guildford Four's case, however, began with his concern for another prisoner, Guiseppe Conlon, father of Gerard. In the wake of the Guildford convictions, Gerard Conlon's aunt and uncle, Anne and Patrick Maguire, their teenage sons Vincent and Patrick, his father Guiseppe and two others were charged and found guilty of running a bomb-making factory at their north London home. The Maguire Seven, as they became known, were alleged to have supplied the bombs for the Guildford outrage.

Guiseppe Conlon, a devout Catholic, suffered from breathing

problems, which prison life did nothing to improve. When his parole applications were rejected, concern about his plight reached Cardinal Hume. In his book, *Proved Innocent*, Gerard Conlon recalls the first meeting. He had been called in from a football match. 'All of a sudden, I saw this tall, thin grey-haired figure waiting for me, wearing a black cape and a red skull-cap, and my first impression was, here was Batman come to see me. Then I heard this screw saying to him, "Your eminence, this is Conlon".

'And the caped figure came up to me and just put his arms round me and said "I'm Cardinal Hume. Will you take me to see your father?" It's very unusual to get a visit in the cells, but we walked over to my father's cell, other prisoners gawping openly at us and me feeling very nervous and tongue-tied.

'We went into the cell and I said "Dad, Cardinal Hume's come to see you". Then I felt better because I knew my father's quality. I knew there was now no way Cardinal Hume would not go away convinced that innocent people were in prison. I couldn't have done it but I knew my father could. And he did, because when Cardinal Hume left he said to the screws "Make sure you treat these men well because there may have been a miscarriage of justice".'

The Cardinal returned to Wormwood Scrubs on several occasions and pressed the Home Office to release Guiseppe Conlon on the grounds of ill-health. It was to no avail. He died in a prison hospital on 18 January 1980. The next day his wife received a letter from William Whitelaw, the Home Secretary, saying that her husband was to be released into her custody on compassionate grounds. The Cardinal's interest had, however, been engaged. On his visits to Guiseppe Conlon he began to question the convictions of the Maguire Seven and by association of the Guildford Four.

'It started before the Conservatives got in in 1979', he told me. 'I remember talking to the Labour Home Secretary, Merlyn Rees, and his number two, Brynmor John. I'd seen Guiseppe Conlon and realized that something had gone wrong. They were prepared to listen. When Margaret Thatcher came to Downing Street I wrote to her and asked to come to speak to her about Ireland. So I went round there. I spoke about Ireland and then I brought up these cases. "Are you saying that there are people in our prisons who are innocent?" she said. "That's terrible, terrible." But I said "I can't prove it". So then that started off and I went to see the Home Secretary and got nowhere.'

Simultaneously, the Cardinal had also been contacted by those who felt another group of Irishmen had been wrongly convicted of a terrorist outrage. John Walker, Gerry Hunter, Billy Power, Hughie Callaghan, Richard McIlkenny and Paddy Hill – collectively the Birmingham Six – were found guilty in 1975 of pub bombings in the Midlands city that left 21 people dead.

'I was, in fact, mentioning the Birmingham case before the Guildford one. I was amazed when I discovered this recently looking back through my letters. It was because I'd met two of them in prison. My first interest was Guiseppe Conlon and then I met two of the Six in prison. I was in Wormwood Scrubs and not long before I'd said something against the IRA and as a result a whole group walked out when I appeared. I was wandering around the prison and someone – one of the category "A" IRA prisoners – cornered me and said those men over there – pointing to the two Birmingham men – are innocent.'

Despite the Cardinal's lobbying behind the scenes, little progress was made in getting the cases back to the Court of Appeal. For the Home Secretary to make such a referral there has to be new evidence. The decisive moment, according to Cardinal Hume, came in 1986 with the publication of Robert Kee's book *Trial and Error*. Not only did it begin to bring out the short-comings in the scientific evidence against the Four and the fact that their 'confessions' had effectively been beaten out of them, with police notes altered subsequently, but the book also acted as a catalyst in the formation of what became known as the Cardinal's Delegation.

Two former Labour Home Secretaries – Lord Jenkins (1965–67 and 1974–76) and Merlyn Rees (1976–79) – were joined by two former Law Lords, Jesuit-educated Lord Devlin and Lord Scarman, in the delegation. The significance of the fact that Cardinal Hume led this distinguished group is a pointer to his standing and influence in the corridors of power. The Cardinal himself is much more modest about his role: 'I hadn't been the Home Secretary or a Law Lord. I was the joker in the pack. Because we met at Archbishop's House it became known as the Cardinal's Delegation. And at that same time I got myself organized with Paddy Victory [of his public affairs office], gathering the facts. Without him we couldn't have got as far as we did. And, of course, it wasn't just us. All sorts of other people were involved.'

The group visited Douglas Hurd at the Home Office on several occasions, taking items of new evidence they had uncovered with Robert Kee's assistance. Although the details of the meetings remained private, the Delegation was photographed outside the ministry, willing for their activities to be reported.

In 1989 their efforts bore fruit. Under pressure from all directions – including a plea by the Archbishop of Canterbury – Douglas Hurd referred the case back to the Court of Appeal. In October of that year the Director of Public Prosecutions announced that the 1975 convictions could not be sustained in the face of the new evidence and the Four were released.

Gerard Conlon was quick to pay tribute to Basil Hume's role in getting them freed. 'The Cardinal was working on our behalf in his own way which was quiet, serious and enormously influential. I always believed that to win we had somehow to find our own members of the Establishment to fight our corner against the majority that would be automatically against us. I knew that there would be people with the right background and connections who had the capacity to think for themselves, and it is just a matter of finding them.'

One of the first demands that the Guildford Four made on their release was that the case of the Birmingham Six be reconsidered. The Appeal Court had considered it on the instructions of Douglas Hurd in 1987 but had confirmed the convictions. Cardinal Hume had always been less involved in their fight but the momentum of his success in winning freedom for one group led him inevitably to take up the case of the other. 'I knew a great deal about the Guildford case. The reason I was always more silent on the Birmingham case was that I didn't know it so well.' In October 1987, in welcoming Douglas Hurd's decision to refer the Birmingham Six's convictions back to the Appeal Court, the Cardinal had stated his 'grave doubts. I have spoken to two of them and I would put a question mark beside their guilt.'

The Cardinal began to apply the same sort of pressure in 1989 and 1990 that had proved so effective over the Guildford Four. Again he built his case on the question of new evidence and in March 1991 the approach again bore fruit. The case was referred back to the Court of Appeal by the Home Office and this time the Director of Public Prosecutions said that the Crown could no longer rely on either the forensic evidence or the 'confessions' of the men. When the Six walked free on 22 March they paid tribute to the Cardinal, but his more limited role in their case was reflected by their praise for the support of a whole range of Church figures.

The release of the Six was followed by the announcement that a Royal Commission was to investigate the whole area of criminal justice and what had gone wrong with the system in the two Irish bombing cases. However, before turning his attention – along with the rest of his Delegation – to the evidence they should present to the Commission, the Cardinal had one outstanding injustice to clear up. It was the case of Guiseppe Conlon that had first drawn him into this whole area, and it was not until the autumn of 1991 that the convictions of the Maguire Seven were finally quashed. The forensic evidence that had been the only 'proof' of their activities was thoroughly discredited.

The Cardinal's involvement had begun on a human level with his concern for a sick prisoner. In December 1991, it led him to put his name to a submission to the Royal Commission on criminal justice that made detailed criticisms of the appeals system in British courts. 'We can now see that a major casualty of the IRA "mainland" bombing campaign of 1974–5 was the English criminal justice system', he and his Delegation of two former Home Secretaries and two former Law Lords told the Commission. It was not just police dishonesty and scientific error that were to blame, they went on, but a failure of the courts. In specific terms, the Delegation recommended that convictions should not be made on the basis of uncorroborated evidence, that an independent forensic science service should be made available to the courts, and that a new Court of Review should be set up to investigate miscarriages of justice without a reference from the Home Secretary.

This was one of the few occasions on which the Cardinal was involved in such a specific, detailed set of proposals for reform, and shows his strength of feeling about the injustices suffered by the 17 people involved in the various cases, not to mention their families. The sight of the leader of English Catholicism at the forefront of such a crusade was unprecedented. Yet it was very much characteristic of Cardinal Hume's work in social matters that he picked up on the case of an individual and pursued it with such vigour that all sorts of other questions were raised. Some ascribed his interest to the Irish roots of the accused. After all, it was pointed out, there is a sizeable proportion of English Catholics who can trace their roots back to Ireland. That was certainly a part of it, the Cardinal acknowledges. But just as important was for the Church to stand up for justice in the face of a shameful injustice.

The interconnection between law and morals in Cardinal Hume's mind is one we will explore at greater length in the context of his public policy contributions on issues of sexual morality. But speaking in 1985 to the Thomas More Society, a club of distinguished lawyers, Cardinal Hume outlined the moral role of their profession: 'For Christians professional integrity must go beyond professional conventions. You are required to reflect deeply on what you are about as practitioners of the law. You have to think about what the law is for and the philosophy which lies behind it.' For the Church, he went on, it was a question of giving 'witness to the principles which true law should not transgress'. Such a definition could just as well be applied to the Cardinal's intervention in the Guildford, Maguire and Birmingham cases as it could to his contributions on abortion and embryology. It is his gift to be able to see Catholicism in broad terms never envisaged by his predecessors.

The message that the Cardinal is the man to go to when you've been wrongly accused has evidently got through to the public. Basil Hume reports an increase in the number of appeals against wrongful conviction in his postbag. But he is fighting shy of becoming a latter-day Lord Longford. 'I won't take up these cases unless I can prove to myself that something has gone wrong – you can't just take things up. I start with instinct but you have to learn about the case.' It was instinct that day in Wormwood Scrubs in 1979 that made Basil Hume feel Guiseppe Conlon was unjustly convicted. As Gerard recalls, the Cardinal 'has continued to say ever since that that meeting was enough to convince him we were innocent, even before he'd seen the evidence'.

Because he engages at a personal level, his support carries on after release. In the case of Patrick Maguire, arrested, beaten by policemen and finally convicted along with his mother Anne of bomb-making charges even though he was only 14, Basil Hume has played the role of a father figure. When Patrick had served his sentence he was still a teenager. His mother, father and brother were still in prison. He went off the rails, became involved with drugs and found it hard to settle down to a job. But Cardinal Hume has tried to give him support and a focus in life. Patrick began accompanying the Cardinal on the Westminster diocesan young adults' pilgrimage to Lourdes. It was an experience that gave him a new direction in life, talking about his experiences and encouraging other young people not to get sucked into a life of drugs and crime.

Such a commitment to helping other young people has won the Cardinal's backing – as we would expect since one of the major areas of Basil Hume's activity as leader of English Catholicism has been concerned with schools and what is taught in them. It is to that campaign that we now turn.

7

Faith in bricks and mortar

Do not rest until you see this want supplied: prefer the establishment of good schools to every other work. Indeed, wherever there may seem to be an opening for a new mission, we should prefer the erection of a school, so arranged to serve temporally as a chapel, to that of a church without one.

(First Synod of the restored English hierarchy, 1852)

Cardinal Basil Hume read the lesson at the memorial service in Westminster Abbey for Lord Butler of Saffron Walden in April 1982, a sign, the Tory statesman's widow said, of her late husband's respect for the Catholic Church.

Some education experts might have found the Cardinal's role in the memorial service puzzling, even contradictory. They had been arguing for years that as pilot of the 1944 Education Act, R. A. Butler had been frustrated by the Catholic Church in his wish to set up a single, unified secondary school system controlled by Whitehall. His great piece of legislation, his monument, was, according to this theory, compromised by the bishops' stubborn determination to retain control of their schools. Yet here was the Cardinal Archbishop of Westminster at the lectern at Butler's final farewell to friends.

After the event Cardinal Hume feels confident in dismissing any lingering suggestion that Butler had a lasting grudge against the Church – or indeed a master plan to dismantle the separate Catholic schools' sector. He told me: 'I was invited to read the lesson, Lady Butler said, because her husband had so much respect for the Catholic Church. I was very touched at the time because I had a great admiration for Butler and I remember that summer I made a special pilgrimage to Saffron Walden to pray over his tomb.' And the Cardinal takes Butler's attitude as a sign of the view still prevalent in Whitehall about the separate Catholic school system. The odd rumbling may come from some obscure Carlton Club education committee every now and again about the need for a new broom and an end to ecclesiastical privileges, but – contrary to the fears that have haunted the Catholic community for years – Basil Hume is confident that there is no time-bomb scheme to compromise the Church's independence ticking away in a minister's filing cabinet.

'I don't look at things that way. I think it's terribly neurotic. It would be true to say that they [the Department For Education] have always seen us as awkward. And equally there may be negative effects from what the Conservative government is trying to do positively. All this business of parental choice and getting rid of local authorities obviously makes us as Church people alert to the dangers. But in broad terms I had a very good letter from Margaret Thatcher when she was Prime Minister. I wrote to her and asked was she behind Catholic schools and got a very positive letter back.'

The bottom line, then, according to the Cardinal, is that the dual system of Church–State partnership, established at the start of the century and set in stone by Butler, is going to run and run. And that is still what Whitehall is saying. One of the most combative Education Secretaries of recent times, Kenneth Clarke, confirmed in an interview in 1991 with the *Catholic Herald* that in his opinion 'the basic settlement of 1944 is healthy and intact'.

Butler's reforms, which, *pace* Kenneth Baker's actions in 1988 and John Patten's in 1992, represent the most fundamental shake-up of the British education system this century, provided secondary education for every boy and girl up to the age of 15. The Butler Act also brought the hitherto fiercely independent and administratively semi-detached Catholic sector into the state fold. Its funding was set on a firm base thanks to the taxpayer. But after much protracted debate the Church was left with substantial freedom as to what was written on the blackboard.

Butler's wisdom in erecting a dual system can be seen with hindsight. Although there are still experts and voters who argue that giving taxpayers' money to Catholic schools is like the state funding private hospitals when it already has the NHS, they are a dwindling bunch. Catholic schools, by their success in exams and in turning out well-balanced young men and women rather than

With Bruce Kent. Photograph by Carlos Reyes.

With Archbishop Coggan on the historic occasion of an address by the Cardinal to the Church of England's General Synod in February 1978. © *Central Press Photos.*

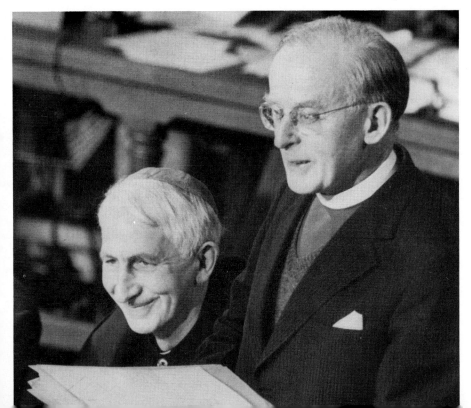

Touring a camp in Makala, Ethiopia, 1984. Photograph by NC from KNA.

With Ken Livingstone, after opening The Passage. Photograph by Liam White.

papal storm troopers, have become part of the British landscape, awkward administratively perhaps, but no more so than many other anomalies we live with in the name of tradition.

Part of Cardinal Hume's task as Catholic leader has been to remain vigilant that the Church's freedoms in education are not lost. Yet unlike his predecessors, for him vigilance has not become an obsession when he deals with the DFE. In this field, as i many others, he has pursued a new, more confident and outspoken strategy, symbolic of a new assertiveness, a cohesiveness with the rest of society felt in the Catholic community.

Because of the long history of persecution of attempts to establish a separate Catholic school network in centuries gone by, the dogmatic importance the Church attaches to the right to educate its own, and the slow acceptance by the British government of its responsibility to provide funds to make that right a reality, the Catholic hierarchy has treated successive education ministe s with suspicion throughout the twentieth century. Cardinal Hume has swept such a constrictive legacy away. While the fortress Church of old guarded the freedoms it subsequently won to run schools with a passion that would make Teresa of Avila look pale and equivocal, the former housemaster at Ampleforth has moved outwards to make an eye-catching and often controversial contribution to the national education debate. In an age when he feels secularism has taken away any consensus on public morality, Cardinal Hume has focused on the need to give all young people – Catholic or not – a basic code of non-negotiable values.

The Catholic community no longer needs to feel so protective and defensive about its schools' system, he says. Its success speaks for itself. If Mrs Thatcher wrote favourably to Cardinal Hume of Catholic schools, then her reasons are not hard to discern. In return for being allowed a bit of leeway, many turn in substantially better results than their secular counterparts. For example, in the days of the Inner London Education Authority, regularly topping the charts of best exam performances were a host of Catholic establishments, led by the London Oratory and the Cardinal Vaughan School. And market forces, freedom to choose, those buzz-words of the Thatcherite reforming zeal of the 1980s, vindicated Catholic schools. A large number of neighbourhood Catholic comprehensives are over-subscribed at the expense of their secular counterparts, often by parents who are not of the faith but who admire the end results of the Catholic system. For many such colleges have a reputation for firm discipline and a sceptical approach to some of the more avant-garde educational techniques. Or, as the proverbial London cabbie once put it to me, 'they've got nice uniforms and the brothers keep the kids in check'.

While the reality may belie this stereotype – the exodus of religious orders from schools has been a feature of recent years, as congregations redefine their aims and cope with a shortage of vocations – the public image of Catholic schools has never been better, in marked contrast to the widely held suspicion, still around when Butler contemplated his reforms, that they were hotbeds of proselytization and popish plots to win back Mary's Dowry. Today, the link between the Catholic school and authority figures like the parish priest is attractive to parents. Equally, the ties between parish and school, in terms of parental concern and input, undoubtedly contribute to an atmosphere of motivation and support.

This popularity outside the confines of the Catholic community has, however, confronted the Church with a new set of dilemmas. It has become a victim of its own success and finds itself having to take tough decisions about who to turn away if the essential 'Catholic ethos' of the school is to be maintained. And that Catholic ethos is after all the reason for the dual system under which the government dips into the taxpayers' pockets to fund the Church's schools. This broader argument about what it is that distinguishes a Catholic school has been around since the first foundation stones were laid in the mid-nineteenth century. However, in Cardinal Hume's era it has become more heated because of the demand for places from outside the Catholic community and more importantly because of the need to respond to the tidal wave of reforms introduced from 1986 onwards by the Conservatives, bringing with them, the bishops allege, a 'mechanistic' approach to education.

Innovations like City Technology Colleges, a National Curriculum designed to prepare young people for jobs, and the involvement of industry and commerce in the classroom have all been features of Tory reforms. None has won unqualified approval from the Cardinal. In a series of widely reported speeches to various educational gatherings, he has attacked what he sees as a 'value-free' philosophy that in practical terms can stop schools creating rounded human beings.

Against the Conservative philosophy of schools fashioning round pegs for the round slots that need filling in the world of work he has set out a wholly different vision of education that nurtures both body and spirit. The tension between humanist, secular ideals in education and the Catholic ethos is an old one, but it has been brought into sharp focus by recent reforms. In the past the Catholic response as an introspective minority community in an officially Anglican state would have been to keep their heads down and get on with running Church schools without challenging government ideas on a national stage.

For Cardinal Hume there has been no such coyness. In place of rallying the troops as of old to raise money for bricks and mortar for Catholic schools, he has adopted a more exposed, more questioning stance on a wide range of issues. He addressed headteachers in 1991 on the role of religious education in secular schools and questioned the general training teachers receive. For the North of England Education Conference in 1990 he unpicked the ideas holding together the government's provision for 16–18-year-olds, and went on to attack its student loans scheme.

The symbolism of this high profile for English Catholicism is obvious. No longer is it humbly thanking Whitehall for its generosity in funding Catholic schools and keeping mum as recompense. It is more assertive, more confident, ready to take its place in society and in the national debate on an issue where it and its leader have considerable expertise.

There has been a price to pay, however, for the Cardinal's willingness to debate. He has earned the personal animosity of some education ministers. Kenneth Baker, pilot of the 1988 Education Reform Act, was known to keep the Cardinal at arms' length and resolutely refused to compromise over Church concerns about his opting out plans. Kenneth Clarke accused Basil Hume of being in the pocket of trade unions because he defended the right of local authorities to run schools. And in response to a more assertive Church in effect redefining the old dual system of partnership in education – demanding to be taken seriously as a full and equal partner – the challenge has come back from Whitehall to the bishops to set out clearly what it is that makes Catholic schools special, the Catholic 'ethos'.

Under siege

Before finding out why Catholic schools mean so much to the Church universal, we must first understand why schools have meant so much to the Catholic community in England. From the post-Reformation period onwards, the very notion of Catholic education was alien and proscribed in these islands. Schools were seen by the Protestant authorities as an effective way of extinguishing the last flames of the Catholic faith. In the late sixteenth century the idea was put forward that children should be removed from their Catholic parents and educated in a Protestant environment to purge them of popish tendencies.

By the end of Elizabeth I's reign all teachers were required to take the Oath of Supremacy. Penalties against secret Catholic schools were on the statute book and at times of mortal peril to the nation and the national Church – the Spanish Armada, the Gunpowder Plot, the Jacobite invasions – these were trotted out by monarchs and ministers and used as a clarion call to patriotism and anti-Catholic prejudice.

It was only with the final removal of legal barriers and penalties for Catholics in the opening years of the nineteenth century that schools could set up their blackboards openly. But even then, given the still fresh memories of persecution, there was a good deal of hesitancy. This was reflected in the lack of a clear notion as to how the schools were to operate and a desire not to prompt anti-Catholic hysteria in the population at large. Bishop Briggs, Vicar Apostolic of the Northern District, therefore wrote in 1840: 'Let not your schools be exclusive, but open to children of all religious denominations, and when Protestant children attend let them not share in the duties of prayer or religious instruction unless at their own desire, expressly sanctioned by their parents or guardian'.

Yet the core idea of a segregated school system soon took hold despite such woollyheadedness (and indeed, given the suspicion with which Catholics were viewed in the 1840s, it is unlikely that many Protestant parents took Bishop Briggs up on his offer to educate their offspring). The setting up of a separate Catholic educational network was driven by fear – that the minds and spirits of Catholic youth would be best nurtured in a Catholic environment and not tainted and twisted in Anglican or secular schools.

It is interesting to reflect, looking around the world, that the

124

most active and dynamic Catholic school networks were built in countries – Australia, New Zealand, Canada – where Catholics are not in the majority. The system thrived on the defensive. And it was certainly that fortress model, as Cardinal Hume once dubbed it, that determined the character of Catholic schools for the first three-quarters of this century. Education became the keep of the fortress, with schools in the front bailey.

After restoration of the hierarchy in 1850 the bishops decided to make schools their main priority. In one of their first joint pastoral letters they urged that every parish must have its school and that in new parishes the building of a classroom was more important than that of a church. 'Do not rest until you see this want supplied: prefer the establishment of good schools to every other work. Indeed, wherever there may seem to be an opening for a new mission, we should prefer the erection of a school, so arranged to serve temporally as a chapel, to that of a church without one.' The bishops went on: 'the building of living and chosen stones, the spiritual sanctuary of the Church, is of far greater importance than the temple made with hands'.

The message was reinforced at the 1852 Synod of the English bishops. 'The first necessity, therefore, is a sufficient provision of education adequate to the wants of our poor. It must be universal . . . prefer the establishment of good schools to every other work.' The deep-rooted fear of Protestants and others polluting young Catholic minds comes through loud and clear in the Synod's statement: 'We turn our thoughts towards the education in sound faith and virtuous morals of our poorest children – often their faith is exposed to serious trials'.

The bishops' schemes received their first official boost with Forster's 1870 Education Act, legislation that hinted at a partnership to come between Church and State over schools. It was with Balfour's 1902 Act, however, that the dual system can be said to have made its debut. This allowed sizeable amounts of taxpayers' money to go towards Catholic schools, and was reinforced in 1936. Throughout this period, however, isolation and protectionism were the order of the day. If it wasn't Anglicanism that would harm young Catholic minds, it was the secular values of the State. Cardinal Wiseman's warning of the 'swamping' of religion by secular knowledge remained a constant theme in Catholic teaching and in Church dealings with government. The offspring of the faithful had to be ringfenced, lest they got infected by worldly contagions.

Wiseman's successor Cardinal Manning, a man so committed to education that he put off building a new cathedral in Westminster so as to be able to provide schools for the poor, developed this theme in a pastoral letter, arguing that the Catholic ethos must be all pervasive. 'Christian training – education in its truest form . . . may not be taken in doses once a week, nor even once a day, but like the salt that seasons our food it must be in the food at every meal. . . . It must be in history, geography, reading lessons; in the manners and examples of the teachers – in his or her very eyes.'

The creation and maintenance of this sacred atmosphere where even domestic science and woodwork have a spiritual significance has been a central plank of Catholic efforts and remains so under Cardinal Hume. But the nuances have changed. In the past Archbishops of Westminster seemed to be saying that a Catholic education was implicitly superior to anything offered on the outside of the fortress. Today Cardinal Hume contents himself with arguing that it is different. Yet the core theme of many of his attacks on recent government education reforms echoes the themes of the past. Cardinal Bourne at the end of the First World War said that 'education should not aim merely at making them [pupils] better instruments of production'. Cardinal Hume at the end of the 1980s disputed the 'mechanistic model' that underpinned Conservative innovations and upheld Catholic schools' duty to 'fill the spiritual void that is a feature of our education'.

The fortress Church with its segregated schools derived great strength and encouragement from the Vatican. As early as 1864 the apostolic letter *Quum non sine* was condemning secularism in education. 'An education whose sole interest lies in knowledge of natural things and in the aims of human society . . . inevitably falls under the yoke of error and falsehood.' In 1929 Pope Pius XI wrote in his encyclical letter *Divini Illius Magistri*: 'nor can the Church tolerate the type of mixed school . . . in which Catholics, although receiving religious instruction apart, are taught other subjects in common with non-Catholics'.

By the outbreak of the Second World War, 7 per cent of the elementary school population was being educated in 1,266 Catholic assisted schools. Butler's 1944 Act consolidated on and continued that growth. The overhaul of the national education system

126

was part of the wartime efforts to build a land fit for heroes. In drawing up his plans Butler worked especially closely with Bishop George Beck, Cardinal Hinsley being preoccupied with the war. Yet the negotiations were never easy.

In 1944 Butler had hoped to bring the Catholic schools – and indeed their Anglican counterparts – under complete Whitehall control. In his memoirs for the time he wrote: 'I realised that no single step would have made the education service simpler or tidier than to transfer the voluntary schools to the ownership and total control of the state or local authorities'. Such an aim inevitably meant that on the Catholic side suspicion and defensiveness remained near the surface. When he wasn't getting his own way with the government, Bishop Beck roused the Catholic community. 'Against the menace of the Total State Catholics are at present waging their defensive war. Secularism and undenomina- tionalism inevitably open the door to totalitarianism. The Catholic view of life and education, with its defence of the super-natural and its emphasis on the independence of the spirit, is a view which is antagonistic to totalitarianism.'

Meanwhile the minister had always to keep in mind that what- ever his respect for Catholicism and its schools, the general public might not welcome too handsome a contribution from state coffers to a minority community that still aroused some hostility. Butler's initial suggestion that all Church – or voluntary, to use the administrative term – schools should opt for 'controlled' status wasn't well received. It would have meant that all day-to-day and capital costs would be met from the public purse. The price was that the local education authority appointed the majority of the governors. Denominational teaching by 'reserved' teachers appointed by the governors for that purpose was part of the scheme of things in controlled schools, but the loss of power was more than the Catholic authorities could stomach.

Cardinal Hinsley in 1943 effectively ended Butler's hopes of any immediate introduction of his Bill in that session of Parliament because voluntary controlled status was not good enough. In a let- ter to *The Times* in October of that year, Hinsley argued that freedom of conscience must be respected, that Catholicism was committed to the progress of education and that 'Catholic parents have a special claim for fair play, especially from any and every party or group that professes to uphold the just claims of the

workers and the rights of minorities'. Butler could not risk upsetting the coalition government over the schools issue, as Churchill
realized on reading Hinsley's letter. The Prime Minister sent
Butler a note, accompanying a copy of the letter stuck on a piece of
cardboard: 'There you are, fixed, old cock'.

Butler was forced to compromise. Church schools could opt for
voluntary 'aided' status. This meant that the foundation governors
of the school, appointed by the trustee (either the local bishop or
the religious order running the school), were in the majority, but
50 per cent of any capital expenditure had to be raised by the
Church (this was reduced by stages to 15 per cent in 1959). Effective control was therefore in the hands of the governors, who had
substantial powers over the hiring and firing of teachers. All
Catholic schools took that option and around two-thirds of the
Church of England schools followed suit. The long-term benefits
of Hinsley's victory – which he did not live to see, dying at the end
of 1943 – were substantial. Catholic schools made up 5 per cent of
the system at the turn of the century, growing to 7 per cent in
1938, and again to a little under 10 per cent today.

Butler had carried off quite a coup. He set a hurdle for financial
contributions to the capital costs of the schools, in return for which
the Church authorities would retain a large measure of independence, that was too high for a large number of Anglican schools
but low enough for all the Catholics to clear after a couple of
refusals. And to the public the minister did not appear over-
generous to the Catholic community.

Butler's Act ushered in a period of peace and prosperity in
schools. For the Catholic community bricks and mortar were the
rallying cries, the modern crusade. The number of Catholic schools
grew from just over 1,000 to nearer 3,000. Parishes organized fairs,
tombolas and sponsored walks to raise the Church's contribution
to capital costs. While diocesan bank balances fell heavily into the
red, expanding rolls maintained the momentum to build.

It was only in the 1970s that the clouds began to gather. The
baby boom abated, not only because of social trends in an increasingly prosperous Britain but also because of a more articulate and
thoughtful Catholic laity's willingness to defy the Pope and use
the pill. No longer was it a question of building schools but of
choosing which ones with empty desks to close or amalgamate,
with all the attendant stresses and strains of parental campaigns.

The introduction of the comprehensive system in the 1970s was a difficult period. Religious orders were often to be found running the old-style grammar schools. Many were reluctant to throw their lot in with the neighbourhood Catholic secondary modern and instead chose to go private, or simply packed their bags. Orders like the Faithful Companions of Jesus, who had almost single-handedly built up the network of girls' schools in inner-city Liverpool, had since the reforms of the Second Vatican Council begun to look outside education for their mission. The advent of the comprehensive system merely accelerated that process. Many of the old convent grammar schools were in any case too small to stand alone as comprehensives. In the ensuing amalgamations, many orders withdrew on an institutional level from education, though individual brothers and nuns continued to work in the schools. The 1970s saw the laity replace the religious who had educated them as the personnel running Catholic schools.

The orders that did remain often opted for fee-paying status, swelling the ranks of Catholic private schools, which had been dwindling during the bricks and mortar boom of the 1950s and 1960s. This switch away from the state sector brought the wider debate about private schools into the Catholic domain. Whereas previously there had been only a handful of fee-paying colleges, like Ampleforth, Stonyhurst and Downside, run by Catholic orders, the 1970s saw large numbers of day schools join the ranks.

For these independent schools, the advent of a Conservative government in 1979 was to bring many blessings. The assisted places scheme allowed a privileged stream of grammar-equivalent children to go to private schools at the taxpayers' expense. It was a concession promoted with great gusto in the Catholic community. Yet if there were benefits for the Church, from the mid-1980s onwards the drive to shake up the education system, principally under Kenneth Baker, was to present the Church with its biggest challenge since 1944. Underpinning the Catholic attitude to the changes was the view that the ethos of its schools was special and distinct. Mr Baker, in effect, challenged the bishops to define that ethos.

A Catholic ethos

It is no easy matter to discover the existence of a specifically Christian doctrine of education or any modern systematic theology of Catholic education. The emphasis has, in Britain at least, been a practical one. The Catholic community, for historical reasons largely connected with its fear of persecution, wanted its own schools. The government agreed, and the schools were built. They exist. That is the ethos.

In the turbulent times of the Thatcherite revolution, arguing from the position that if something exists therefore it must carry on existing was never good enough. The challenge for Cardinal Hume and his bishops, both in defending the Catholic system and in contributing to a national debate on education, was to say what was distinct about the Church's way of doing things. Did it mean more than the presence of a handful of nuns and priests in the classrooms, a greater part of the timetable given over to religious education, and devotional statues next to the blackboard?

The Second Vatican Council defined a Catholic school in its Declaration on Christian Education: 'The Catholic school pursues cultural goals and the natural development of youth to the same degree as any other school. What makes the Catholic school distinctive is its attempt to generate a community climate in the school that is permeated by the gospel spirit of freedom and love. It tries to guide the adolescents in such a way that personality development goes hand in hand with the development of the ''new creature'' that each one has become through baptism. It tries to relate all of human culture to the good news of salvation so that the light of faith will illuminate everything that the students will gradually come to learn about the world, about life and about the human person.'

The post-Reformation period saw the development of two bases on which to think about education: the humanist, acquiring knowledge and skills for life; and the religious, repeated down the centuries up to and including the Vatican II document. This division has never been repaired in the modern mind and it is why the Church on a worldwide scale has insisted on having its own schools, to integrate both secular and revealed knowledge, to transmit the faith. Catholic education is therefore something of a cocktail, and if it is to be imbibed deeply it has to consist of the right measures of gin *and* vermouth.

While for the secular humanists life on earth is the be-all and end-all, and hence the pupil must be equipped to deal effectively with that life, for the Christian our time on this planet is but a passing phase. So denominational schools should be preparing for the immediate future, but without losing sight of the life after death that is central to the faith. Pope Pius XI wrote that there can be no education that is not wholly directed to man's last end. Formation in the faith (catechesis) and spreading the good news of faith (evangelization) are elements in Christian education that play no part in the secular curriculum.

The Catholic Church strives in its schools not just for good results and a good job – though that may be part of it – but for moral excellence and ultimately for salvation. The nurturing of body and soul is combined. The American bishops wrote in 1933: 'the unchangeable element of education and its real purpose – to fit men for life in eternity as well as in time; to teach men to think rightly and to live rightly, to instil sound principle in our youth, principles not only of civic righteousness, but of Catholic faith and morality, to educate groups, according to their capacity, so as to make them the best men and the best women of our country – and all this with a thorough training in the secular branches of knowledge'.

The promotion of the 'earthly city' as well as 'advancing the reign of God' was a key concept in the Vatican II view of the role of Catholic schools. It shifted the emphasis to the school coexisting with and indeed thriving in the environment and community. What to do when the values of the community and of the government were at odds with the values of the Church was the dilemma that confronted Cardinal Hume when Margaret Thatcher's administrations turned their reforming and rationalizing gaze on to the educational system.

Three-pronged campaign

The Conservative vision for education was a radical variation on the humanist theme. Its emphasis was towards future employment, its goal jobs for the boys and girls. Once they had taken on board the true nature of the vision – and it was to some extent disguised in the Education Reform Act of 1988 by empty talk of spiritual values – the Cardinal and his Church had several choices: put up, shut up and make sure the poison didn't get into the Catholic system, in effect a variation on the theme of the old fortress; or stand up and fight for the Catholic approach in Catholic schools; or, the most challenging option, expound a different view of education to be practised in all schools in the belief that such a strategy would be for the benefit of the moral well-being of the whole nation.

It is symptomatic of the confidence of the Church that Cardinal Hume chose the last of these three, commanding a national stage and – more so than he has on any other issue – publicly castigating the government over its policies. For in education, and the way in which we as a society bring up our young people, Cardinal Hume sees the seeds of the decline into secularism, the value-free individualism that he fears is corrupting the Western world. And, by association, in standing up over schools for a vision of a society with collective responsibilities, a duty to nurture weaker members, Cardinal Hume was also launching a more wide-ranging critique of the sort of 'survival of the fittest' nation that the Conservative governments of the 1980s seemed to want to create.

Unlike 1944, when the Catholic Church mobilized its resources in advance to shape Butler's legislation, in 1988 the Education Reform Act seemed to catch it unaware of the true implications of the changes. There was little concerted campaigning before Parliament gave its approval, although individual items were raised with ministers with varying degrees of success. The broader approach appeared to be a wait-and-see policy.

By 1989, after a bruising clash over the fate of a school in his diocese to which we must return later, Cardinal Hume had seen enough of the reforms to know that he didn't like them at all. In a series of major addresses that made national headlines, he outlined what he perceived as the underlying philosophy of the government reforms, and in exposing the flaws of this vision he simultaneously presented an alternative scenario, informed but not dominated by the Christian view of a society with collective moral values.

In these landmark public interventions on the 1988 reforms, the Cardinal habitually began by quoting the very first statement in the Act on the purpose of education. The curriculum should promote 'the spiritual, moral, cultural, mental and physical development of pupils at the school and of society and prepare such pupils for the opportunities, responsibilities and experiences of adult life'. These fine words had at the time of the passage of the Act through Parliament calmed Catholic nerves as to the true nature of the reform. But soon the elegant phrases began to ring hollow.

In a philosophical sense, as Cardinal Hume made clear to the North of England Education Conference in January 1990, the Act was by definition in the humanist model rather than the Christian one. Commenting on its attempt to prepare youngsters for adult life and its challenges, he asked: 'Might it not be sobering but revealing to reflect occasionally on the wisdom of a former monastic headmaster who at a meeting of the Headteachers' Conference claimed: ''But we prepare our boys for death''?' In more practical terms, Cardinal Hume told his audience that the 1988 Education Reform Act was patently failing in its stated aim of promoting the spiritual as well as the material. It is a point he has made many times when discussing the government's reforms. 'I would hope that none of us would subscribe to the view that the purpose of education is primarily to sustain economic prosperity, to promote industry and commerce, to produce competent technicians and managers, men and women of enterprise and initiative. All that is very important and, of course, has its place on our scale of priorities. But training for a job or a profession and education are not co-extensive. Education will often include training for a job, but education is broader and greater and does not always have to serve a utilitarian purpose.'

On this occasion he restricted himself to laying out the Catholic ideal, the Catholic ethos, alongside the Tory business plan. The Cardinal, characteristically casting his net across Europe, quoted from a document addressed to Catholic teachers in France to illustrate his point that education must have the spiritual dimension he found lacking in fact, if not in intention, in the Tory reforms. 'God speaks very gently to children, often without words. The natural creation provides the vocabulary – leaves, clouds, flowing water, a shaft of light. It is a secret language not to be found in books. One sees a child pause suddenly in the midst of some activity, brought to a silent contemplation of some natural object or living creation or picture. . . . Here is the quality of looking and listening which brings him close to God, invoking in one act both the concreteness and the mystery of the world of things. The task of the religious teacher is to go beyond the admiration of the poet and the question of the philosopher as to the ''how'' of things and

133

allow the child to find the bond linking him with the "who" – God the creator.'

The point is, he told the teachers in the audience, that government reforms were in danger of banishing such dreams from the classroom. And it was not just a question of there being no place for God. Even in schools with no denominational or religious base, there would be no place for anything more than mechanistic processes and exercises. 'The heart and the human spirit have needs as well as the mind and body. Pressure in schools created by the demands of examinations, the new national curriculum and the regular testing of pupils encourages the tendency to place increasing emphasis on certain kinds of learning and the acquisition of specific skills. It can deaden creativity, neglect human and affective growth and lead to a somewhat lopsided educational effort. That kind of destruction does not show up in examination results; its effects are felt later in emotional and spiritual deprivation and sometimes in anti-social behaviour.'

What we do in our schools today has profound implications for tomorrow's society, the Cardinal said. And what he saw did not make him optimistic when he looked to the future. Using a tone of condemnation unusual in his vocabulary Cardinal Hume concluded this major address with a damning indictment of government policy in schools. 'I would be more sanguine about the future of education and the whole educational process in our country if it were not for the damaging impact of some current attitudes and approaches. I suspect that the pace and extent of recent changes owe as much to political and social considerations as to purely educational ones. I believe too that the fostering of competition among schools and the introduction of commercial concepts is an undesirable and dangerous development.'

Market forces, the by-word of 1980s Conservatism, the remedy for every malaise in hospitals, factories and broadcasting, had no function in schools, he said. The language of customer and provider of services has no place in the dictionary of education. 'Some of the most important functions in society, some of the supremely human qualities of mind and heart, carry no price-tag, cannot be quantified, are above the rough and ready requirements of supply and demand.' By attempting to introduce market forces into schools, the Conservatives must be aware 'that competitive markets always create losers'. In a dark warning, he concluded that to allow a 'spiritual and religious vacuum at the heart of our own society and of the next generation' was to denigrate democracy and to open the door to tyranny of the sort seen in the 1930s.

In the second of a trio of major and newsworthy attacks on the underlying philosophy of government schools policy, the Cardinal returned to this theme of education leaving young people with no residual values in an address to the Catholic secondary heads of his own Westminster diocese in September 1991. 'We tend in the West and perhaps particularly in Britain to the belief that a value-free education is possible and even desirable. Many in our society today consider education to be primarily a matter of equipping young people to earn a living in a world which is highly complex and constantly changing.' Such a narrow view is at odds with the whole Judeo-Christian tradition that has played such a major part in shaping Britain's school system, the Cardinal said. 'Education must help to develop to the full our spiritual and physical powers and prepare us not only for our earthly tasks but also for our eternal destiny.'

One of the objectives of schools – and again in this speech Cardinal Hume was referring not just to his own constituency but to all institutions, Catholic and not – 'is to teach pupils the importance of moral norms, to underline the objectivity of these norms and to make the all-important distinction between a rightly formed conscience and private judgement'. In a society where 'morality is often regarded as entirely a matter of choice and opinion', a bedrock of values had to be one of the goals of education, he stressed.

In March 1992, speaking to the annual conference of the Secondary Heads Association, Cardinal Hume once more returned to the opening words of the 1988 Education Reform Act and the gap, in his opinion, between the ideal expressed there – 'a vision of what education really is' – and the reality as seen in schools. The theme of value-free education led him into a more profound critique of a society dominated by 'a widespread individualism which emphasises the virtues of independence, self-reliance and personal freedom'.

The Cardinal recalled a conversation with some young people. 'When I explained the traditional Christian moral teaching the response was: "But that's just your opinion". The assumption was that we should simply agree to differ in our views. I was struck by their evident belief that there was no authority to which any of us could appeal, nor, of course, any objective moral norms.' This encounter presented the Cardinal with a disturbing prognosis for the future well-being of our nation. 'If in society there are no "givens", no objective norms which constrain our choices, no duties which place limits on our desires, then morality seems to lose its hold, and to be no more than an outmoded form of coercion. It is almost as if to make any moral judgement is to be judgemental, to make an unwarranted imposition on another person's way of life.'

To halt such a tide, to set out a code of standards, the Cardinal said, was not a task only for church schools. 'Every school can and should by teaching, by its life as a community, and through the collective act of worship, encourage an interest in that search for meaning, purpose and value which is a universal need.' He mentioned in this context a remark he is fond of quoting from a former Archbishop of Canterbury – 'there is a space within each one of us which only God can fill'.

All schools must have an ethos that encourages morality. 'The foundation of such an ethos must be a recognition of the unique dignity of each individual associated with the school. Every person should be treated with respect, and if that is the pervading ideal, the school can have an impact on the self-esteem, kindness and goodness of its pupils. We all need affirmation, and each young person has something they are good at, some gifts to commend and encourage. If a school has a broad enough vision and appropriate facilities to respond then no young person should leave that school feeling a complete failure.' In emphasizing what is often called the whole-person approach, the Cardinal was setting up a model in stark contrast to the government view of the classroom as a place where the learning of particular skills is valued. Schools, whatever their denominational bias or none, are communities, not conveyor belts.

In each of these speeches, the Cardinal made it plain that it was his own opinion that the Christian tradition should be the keystone of the moral standards taught in schools. But he never pressed this view to the exclusion of his more general point that there had to be more than market forces. It is one of Cardinal Hume's unwavering principles that when invited by a secular group – such as the secondary heads or the North of England

Conference – he will talk about 'my thing', as he puts it. He never sidesteps the fact that he is first and foremost the leader of Catholic England, but builds on it, as in these three addressess, to make wider points concerning the environment in which the Catholic Church exists.

The battleground

Successive Secretaries of State for Education have failed to respond to Cardinal Hume's probing of the philosophy behind their reforms. Their attitude to criticism from the Church is akin to the indifference with which they have greeted representations from professional bodies like the teaching unions. Where the state has battled with the leader of English Catholicism has been over the practicalities of the reforms. The most public row, which climaxed in the Cardinal threatening to go to prison rather than agree to reforms that he felt to be ill-advised, was over the Cardinal Vaughan School in west London, part of the Westminster diocese.

Patronized by the offspring of the quieter sort of aristocrat and the arts establishment who congregate in Holland Park, though taking pupils from all across London, the school was heavily over-subscribed on account of its enviable examination result record. Its relationship with Cardinal Hume, the trustee since it was a diocesan school, was in general cordial, although there had been differences of opinion in the past. In May 1988, for example, the Cardinal gave his backing to a London-wide parents' ballot to try to save the Inner London Education Authority, which was facing abolition by the Conservatives. 'The abolition of ILEA was not in the Conservative Party manifesto, and it is inappropriate to treat education in this way', he said. In response the combative Antony Pellegrini, headteacher at the Vaughan School, was enthusiastic about the demise of ILEA: 'It is unquestionably a good idea. The authority is too large to function effectively.'

That difference of opinion about what we would now call subsidiarity – the most appropriate place for control to be exercised – exploded when the Westminster diocese planned a reorganization of its secondary schools in west London. The problem was two-fold. Falling rolls meant that there were empty desks in the classrooms of the other Catholic secondary schools in the area – though not at the Vaughan. And sixth-form provision was proving very difficult, with small numbers in each school offered a very limited range of subjects, and many Catholic 16-year-olds choosing to go to secular further education colleges. (The needs of this particular age group have always been a particular preoccupation with the Cardinal and have found practical expression in such ventures as the annual young adults' pilgrimage to Lourdes, which he leads.)

To tackle the situation in west London, the Cardinal and his advisors at the Westminster Diocesan Education Service came up with a plan in 1985 to close the two secondary schools in the area with the most empty places, and to create a sixth-form college by centralizing the sixth forms of the remaining schools. To the Cardinal Vaughan staff and parents the loss of its own sixth form would ruin the school. They fought the scheme tooth and nail but met the Cardinal in a resolute – they would say dictatorial – mood. When the governors voted down the plan, despite the fact that a majority on the ruling body was appointed by Cardinal Hume, he moved swiftly and decisively to dismiss those of his appointees who had flaunted his wishes. In reply to the howls of anguish from the Vaughan parents, he said that he had to take an overview of what was best for Catholic education in the area and couldn't give in to the well-organized pressure campaign of one school when to do so would be to sell other parents down the river.

When the Conservative Government introduced its opting out proposals, it seemed a God-send to the beleaguered Vaughan School and its supporters. Rather than be crowbarred, as they saw it, into the Cardinal's plan, they would simply opt out of local authority control in favour of direct funding from Whitehall. This would give them control over the destiny of their school, in effect allowing them also to opt out of diocesan control and, more importantly, diocesan reorganization plans. The parents and staff voted for the switch, despite the Cardinal's pleas, and applied to the Department of Education and Science (as it then was). However, before the minister could make a decision, the Cardinal had, as trustee of the school, to name the governors on the application form for directly-funded grant-maintained status. This he refused to do. Furthermore, he said he would rather risk going to prison than put his name to a scheme that he believed would damage Catholic secondary education in west London.

This was an eye-catching and uncharacteristically public gesture, showing just how important Cardinal Hume believed the issue to be. Equally, it showed his critics within the diocese, who occasionally are to be heard comparing the Cardinal's attempt to reach a consensus unfavourably with the more autocratic reign of John Carmel Heenan, that when the going gets tough Basil Hume is prepared to act. However, having taken a forward stance, he was soon forced, on the advice of the diocesan solicitors, to back down and let the application go ahead. The Cardinal Vaughan School opted out – as did the London Oratory, another of the schools covered by the west London reorganization (though the Cardinal was not its trustee) – and the diocesan sixth-form college has had to start its life without the 16–19-year-olds from two of the area's most academically successful schools.

In practical terms Cardinal Hume was defeated by the Vaughan parents and the DES. The clash left a nasty taste in the mouth and served to intensify the disagreement between the Church and the government over the related issues of opting out and parent power.

As early as 1987, the bishops had expressed their concerns about opting out – namely that it would allow parents to go over their heads as trustees to the Secretary of State if they didn't like what was happening to their local schools. The hierarchy asked for Catholic schools to be allowed to opt out of opting out. They gathered the support of some Catholic MPs and peers, and even the influential backing of the former Tory education minister Rhodes Boyson, but the government refused to back down, saying that to accede to the bishops would be to deny Catholic parents the same rights that others enjoyed.

With the passage of the 1988 Education Reform Act there was talk in Catholic education circles of an informal 'gentlemen's agreement' with the DES that the bishops would be listened to carefully when it came to schools opting out where they were trustees. As the Vaughan case was soon to demonstrate, that promise, if it ever existed, wasn't worth the paper it wasn't written on. And even when the local bishop backed a Catholic school's application to opt out – as when Bishop James McGuinness of Nottingham gave his backing to the parents of Blessed Hugh More School in Grantham – it cut little ice with the minister, despite Grantham's being the town that produced Mrs Thatcher.

With every ounce as much gusto as he put into tackling the general thrust of the Conservative education reforms, Cardinal Hume moved swiftly to defend the Catholic system from the threat he saw in the opting-out scheme. Addressing the National Conference of Priests in Birmingham in September 1989, he stressed the bishops' 'special right and responsibility to watch over, support and regulate the Catholic schools in their dioceses so that these may increasingly serve the interests of the community'. The opting-out procedure 'strikes at the heart' of the bishops' role.

By allowing individual schools to choose direct funding from Whitehall and the considerable independence that goes with it, the government 'has created the potential for havoc in the voluntary sector', he said. In a clear reference to the Vaughan battle that was raging at that time, the Cardinal went on: 'what has happened is that, as the bishops feared, it is possible for groups of parents to use the opting-out provisions for another purpose altogether – namely to escape from a school reorganisation plan devised in the interests of the wider community'. However, the Cardinal's core objection to opting out was that the government appeared to be overlooking the Church's special place in the education system – the dual system – and lumping Catholic schools in with all others. 'The essence of the opting-out problem lies in the fact that the 1988 Act fails to distinguish adequately between local education authorities and diocesan authorities. There is more at stake here for a diocesan authority. When an LEA school obtains grant-maintained status, the LEA has no further involvement with the school thereafter. But when a diocesan school gains grant-maintained status, the diocese remains the trustee of the school with the potentially far-reaching responsibilities which that involves, despite the fact that the trustee may have opposed the move because it was not in the interests of the Catholic community.'

The whole notion of community, of a collective responsibility, so alien to the Conservative ideologues of the 1980s and so much a theme of Cardinal Hume's contribution to the education debate, and by association to the national debate, stood in direct opposition to opting out. As in the Vaughan case, the Cardinal tried to make it clear that he was concerned not just for one school, but for all the schools in the area, not just for one set of parents, but for all the parents in the area. The freedom of choice for one group that the opting-out scheme offered was a deprivation of choice for others in the same community, he said.

As an increasing tide of schools applied to opt out, Catholic spokesmen, including the Cardinal, were quick to note that a two-tier system was being created in terms of funding. Grant-maintained schools got a much larger slice of the cake of educational funding, meaning that those choosing to remain in traditional local control got less than their due. This was another violation of the idea of community – a central Christian notion.

For all his fine words, his oratory and the headlines they have commanded, the Cardinal has in practical terms made little progress in winning an opt-out clause for the Catholic system from opting out. In one of the biggest political campaigns he has mounted as Archbishop of Westminster, the tangible benefits are hard to discern. But his criticisms have obviously stung the government, and perhaps even forced it to hold back on more radical schemes. Lady Hooper, a Catholic and an education minister in the House of Lords, was fielded on numerous occasions at Catholic teachers' gatherings to put the other point of view. In April 1988 she told the Secondary Schools Conference that there was no threat in the reforms to the status of the Church system. 'I know that many of you today feel that these proposals represent in some way a threat to the Catholic character of your school', she said, 'but I want to take this opportunity to say firmly that this is not the case.'

In 1991 the Secretary of State for Education himself, Kenneth Clarke, made clear that there was little hope of compromise from the Conservative government. 'I hesitate to lecture the bishops on their theology', he told the *Catholic Herald*, 'but I really don't think there are any theological arguments either in favour or against moving from local authority management of schools to grant-maintained status. I do not see why Catholic parents should be uniquely barred from having the opportunity of voting for grant-maintained status. Nor do I see anything unChristian in giving the headteacher and governors control over all the resources of a school.'

The practical difficulties the Cardinal had laboured to set out were thus brushed to one side. The appointment of a Catholic as Education Secretary after the 1992 election did raise hopes that there might be a little more listening and that the opting-out dispute might be resolved. Within days of John Patten arriving in office, the bishops' conference was writing to him with its concerns. A helpful reply was received, they indicated. However, in the summer of 1992 Mr Patten produced his White Paper on schools, which he claimed would set the tone for the next 25 years. It produced much to make the Cardinal smile in its insistence on moral values being taught in schools. The difference between right and wrong is to be a central feature of the curriculum according to Mr Patten, a traditionalist Catholic whose *Spectator* article in May of the same year on how society divides into the good and the evil caused a few raised eyebrows in the less judgemental corridors of Archbishop's House.

Where Mr Patten showed no inclination to accommodate his Church leader in his White Paper was over the issue of opting out. Indeed, in the two paragraphs in the weighty document dedicated to the Church schools, the only concrete proposal was for more of them to seek grant-maintained status, which would 'build upon the existing freedoms available'. There was a financial incentive. When a Catholic school opts out, it will no longer have to raise its 15 per cent share of capital costs. The glib reassurance that the 'established character and ethos of the school is protected' by Church-appointed governors on the ruling body of opted-out schools did little to answer the detailed criticisms made by Cardinal Hume of the system.

Mr Patten's offer contained a touch of the carrot and the stick. Speaking at the first National Catholic Education Conference in Bradford in July, Cardinal Hume had appealed to the government to give more financial backing to the Church in running its own support services – diocesan education offices and the like. The escalating cost of education was in danger of pricing the Church out of the schools market, the Cardinal warned. In his White Paper, Mr Patten was offering precisely that extra money – if the Church could drop its opposition to opting out. So far the number of individual Catholic schools applying to the Secretary of State for direct funding has been small. They have no doubt been influenced in their reticence by the clear signals coming from the Cardinal and the bishops' conference that such action will not be well regarded, save in exceptional cases. However, there are the beginnings of a breaking of the ranks in the hierarchy. Archbishop Couve de Murville of Birmingham made himself even less popular than he already is with his colleagues by expressing his own support for opting out weeks after the hierarchy had made plain its collective reservations.

So far no blanket condemnation of the practice has come from Cardinal Hume. He has stopped short of saying opting out is wrong, saying merely that it doesn't suit the Catholic system. Such a careful strategy – dealing with the symptoms rather than focusing on the root causes – has left him room to manoeuvre with the DFE. At the same time it is obvious to anyone reading his comments that many of the drawbacks he highlights in regard of Church schools – most notably the damage to the community – apply equally to non-denominational schools. He has pinned his colours to the fence on this issue in the national context while waving a red rag from the top of the mast when it comes to the Catholic sector.

Outspokenness has its price. Cardinal Hume is one of a very select few in this country to enjoy a universally good press. By taking a forward stance on education he has risked the wrath of pundits like the darling of the *Daily Telegraph*, Charles Moore. His address to the Catholic secondary heads in September 1991, quoted above, provoked Mr Moore to confront the Cardinal in print, in the politest terms, over the issue of parental choice. Was the basis of state funding of the Catholic system not to permit parental choice, he asked. And therefore could the Cardinal really justify his attacks on opting out, which in effect simply allows another form of parental choice?

Mr Moore went further and taunted Cardinal Hume, the defender of the traditional values of the state education system, with his previous incarnation as a housemaster at the Benedictine private school, Ampleforth. 'Almost every pupil under his charge was there because of parental choice. . . . I find it hard to believe that the kindly young Basil lost much sleep over the thought that, as a result of this choice, life was hard for potty little St Cake's down the road.'

'Why', Mr Moore asked, 'does the Cardinal think that what works so well for the rich pupils of Ampleforth would be quite unsuitable for the 90 per cent of children who do not have private education? The answer can only be that he lacks faith in the capacity of the majority to order their lives sensibly. He believes that people such as himself, who know better, should order their lives for them. Another way of putting it would be to say that he believes in choice for the few and socialism for the rest.'

Mr Moore is doing Cardinal Hume a disservice by more than the last cheap political jibe. The Cardinal has, it is true, never questioned the value of private education. Although he was not head-teacher at Ampleforth, it is inconceivable that he would have made a success of the role of abbot if his fellow monks had detected even the faintest hint of a doubt in his words and actions regarding the school. It is strange then that he is accused of socialism. But more to the point, or more to the Moore point, the Cardinal has on many occasions confronted head-on the whole thorny area of parental choice.

In the very speech that so angered Mr Moore, Cardinal Hume emphasized a parent's right to choose the best education for his or her child. 'I believe in parental choice, and it would in any case be inconsistent for me not to do so while supporting the right of Catholic parents to choose Catholic schools. My point is that the choice which should exist should never have to be between a school providing a decent education and one providing a poor one.'

In the Cardinal's view, what the government is offering is not choice to parents but something altogether more dangerous to the notion of equality of access to education and hence to society. 'There is a real risk, it seems to me, that the choice will lie not with parents to choose schools, but with popular schools who will be able to choose between children, and the impetus of the system will drive a wedge between successful and unsuccessful schools.' Popular schools will be amply resourced and will have good parental back-up. Unpopular schools will get the scrapings from the barrel of finance and will find themselves caught in the vicious circle of money following parents and parents following money.

If Whitehall has been slow to pay attention to the Cardinal's criticisms, his campaign has at least attracted the attention – and the support – of the Vatican and Pope John Paul II. During their five-yearly *ad limina* visit to the pontiff in the late 1980s, the Westminster bishops were told: 'I know that concern for education has always marked the life of the Church in your ecclesiastical province and country. . . . I commend you for the leadership you are endeavouring to give, and for your vigilance in ensuring that Catholic schools not only survive but flourish.'

Cardinal Hume is emphatic that survival is not under threat. While others have grown alarmed by the national implications of a variety of local disputes – the withdrawal of free travel to Catholic schools in Hertfordshire, a threat to close a South Wales Catholic comprehensive against the wish of the local bishop and force its pupils to travel over 60 miles each day to the next nearest Church school – Cardinal Hume remains convinced that the dual system is in reasonable shape. His principal fear, as made clear in a prolonged and public campaign, has been for the state of the nation's schools, what goes on in their classrooms and the effect that will have on tomorrow's adults and tomorrow's society.

8

Arms or alms?

The world community can continue to pursue the arms race
and build ever larger and more deadly weapons, or it can shift
and move deliberately and urgently towards the provision of
basic needs for our global family.

(Basil Hume, 'Fight World Poverty' lobby, 1985)

One of Basil's more visible 'political' triumphs was to convince
Foreign Secretary David Owen and Prime Minister James Callaghan
in February 1978 that they should halt arms sales to El Salvador. The
US-backed military rulers of that unhappy Central American country were using British-made weapons with great brutality to keep the
lid on a popular rebellion. When local Church people spoke out
against the killings and the 'disappearances' they faced arrest, tor-
ture, abuse, even death. Two years after Cardinal Hume was moved
to act, the leader of the Catholic Church in El Salvador, Archbishop
Oscar Romero, was murdered at his altar by soldiers while he said
Mass.

The Cardinal's El Salvador intervention came as the culmination
of a campaign by various Church organizations like Pax Christi and
the Catholic Institute for International Relations. His willingness
to endorse these protests and give the government a push in the
right direction demonstrates Basil Hume's repeated attempts on a
national and international stage to link the escalation of the arms
race with world poverty. Rather than selling weapons to continue
the civil war in El Salvador, the government should be giving aid
and assistance to the hundreds of thousands displaced from their
homes by the conflict and living in crowded refugee camps.

David Owen was finally won over by the characteristic Hume
strategy of deputations not denunciations. But on other questions
of overseas policy the Cardinal has shown a radical edge, a fire in his

146

public oratory, a willingness to be controversial that has not been anywhere near so obvious in his domestic concerns.

He did not mince words during or after his headline-grabbing visit to famine-stricken Ethiopia in 1984. The situation there was a 'scandal', and the response of European governments simply did not 'compare with what is needed'. This tough talking was followed by a high-profile campaign of visits to 10 Downing Street, TV appearances, and open letters to the EC and to his fellow members of the Council of the European Bishops' Conferences, all geared towards increasing both short-term and long-term aid programmes.

Of course, as any aspiring politician will say, it's easier to make bold gestures on foreign policy. Voters place their crosses on their ballot papers on issues like the economy, education or industrial relations. Overseas aid comes a long way down the list. In recent Conservative governments it hasn't even merited a seat at the Cabinet table. So to an extent Basil Hume is taking a soft option. Yet the Third World has historically been a concern of the Church. Countless thousands of missionaries left these islands to bring God to the 'heathen' in the past centuries. The expansion of the British Empire placed a special duty not just on the Established Anglican Church of the Victorians but also on English and Irish Catholicism to staff the missions. However, Basil Hume's emphasis in this traditional area of activity has been a new one. No longer is it a question of collecting money for 'black babies' or encouraging young men and women to dedicate their lives to the needy in foreign lands. The flood of English and Irish missionaries has dwindled to a trickle. Trainee priests and nuns in the missionary colleges, in common with their colleagues in the domestic seminaries, rattle round in buildings designed for three or four times the numbers they now house.

Policy has had to change to meet this new situation. Because of its long-standing role as a bridge between the Third World and the developed nations, the Catholic Church, and Pope John Paul II in particular, have become a voice on the international stage for the voiceless – the hungry, the refugees, the needy. Old notions of charity have been replaced with an outspoken demand for justice. Basil Hume has played a significant part in spearheading that changing attitude, both in Britain and on a European and world stage, in particular after his visit to Ethiopia.

Overseas aid may be a long way down the politicians' order of priorities, but by his very presence in the food centres of Wollo and

Makele he was challenging the assumptions that had left Ethiopia to suffer out of sight and out of mind for so long. And because his trip was so much a humanitarian one, the work of a man concerned first with people, he made the issue of feeding the hungry in the world a human one that TV viewers at home could understand. On arrival back at Heathrow from Ethiopia the Cardinal said he wanted to be 'an ambassador for the hungry'.

If his work for those in need around the globe shows Basil Hume at his best – combative, determined, outspoken – then on the arms race, the other side of the coin as defined in the quotation that opens this chapter, he has kept his head down and tried, for long periods, to avoid saying anything. We have seen – in the case of the Guildford Four, for example – his willingness to fight in the public forum when he has witnessed an injustice, when he is in possession of all the facts, and is sure of his views. Ethiopia fits into this pattern. On nuclear deterrence, however, the Cardinal has never felt on firm ground, and hence his reaction has been to resort to silence and, when pushed, to ill-defined generalizations.

While he has backed – in words at least – disarmament, an end to the arms trade and the banning of chemical weapons, his stance on nuclear weapons, particularly during the troubled days of 1983 when American Cruise and Pershing missiles arrived in Britain, has hovered uneasily between a horror of their capacity to kill and maim and a defence of the concept of deterrence. Where more radical voices in his own Church – principally Bruce Kent but also heads of religious orders and several of his fellow bishops – have argued that Britain must scrap its nuclear capacity, the Cardinal has struggled to find a consensus line.

This has meant that his fine words about the injustice of the arms trade, for example, have not been matched by his actions. When he raised the issue in a 1985 speech, he was challenged by the Campaign against the Arms Trade to join their fight and give financial support. He has never taken up their invitation to visit their headquarters, while a small cheque arrived with a covering note stressing how financially stretched the Church was.

The Cardinal's 1983 statement on the subject of nuclear deterrence – published in *The Times* – was decidedly mealy-mouthed. The bishops couldn't agree and the Cardinal set the Church's objections to nuclear weapons being targeted on civilian targets against the 'success' of deterrence in keeping the world peace. He avoided any specific reference to such fundamental issues as the inability of weapons like Britain's Polaris deterrent to be accurately targeted within a twenty-mile range, and the implications of this for the Church's unequivocal opposition in the documents of the Second Vatican Council to any risk to civilians in warfare. Equally overlooked was NATO's public commitment with weapons like Cruise and Pershing to a first-use policy. The Cardinal stuck to platitudes.

His unease with the whole issue grew steadily more apparent in the following years as he tried to avoid mentioning it at all costs. Consensus was to be achieved through silence.

War and peace

At the age of 18 Basil Hume had to take a hard decision. He wanted to join the Benedictine community that had taught him. But it was 1941. The war was going very badly for Britain. He was torn between the black habit and the khaki uniform, priesthood and patriotism.

Novice monks were exempt from military service. But what if he found out later that his vocation wasn't to the priesthood, as have many others after taking the first faltering steps down the road to vows and ordination? Would people point the finger? And the Forces ran in his blood. It was a family tradition. His mother's father was a French general.

As we have seen already, Basil Hume is not a man to take snap decisions. And even when set on one course, he can often see the benefits of the spurned alternative. He decided in 1941 to be a monk. But four decades later he was still telling John Mortimer in an interview: 'It was a terrible choice. If it happened again, I think I'd have gone in the army.'

That reluctance to be emphatic, the desire to want to have things both ways, is reflected in Basil Hume's contributions as the leader of English Catholicism to the debate on war and peace. He has been unable to solve the dichotomy of an opposition to nuclear weapons in all but purely military situations and his personal belief that deterrence works. The result has been that he has given little specific guidance to his flock. They have been left, on this crucial moral issue, to make up their own minds, attempting to reconcile the widely divergent guidance offered by some Church leaders and given only generalizations by their Cardinal.

While Basil Hume's reluctance to be firm can be an attractive policy on questions like contraception, where English Catholics have grown used to making their own decisions and would resent clear and unambiguous guidance from the Cardinal, the 1980s saw a great deal of soul-searching about defence policy and the morality of modern weapons. Many were confused by the conflicting claims of the different sides in the nuclear debate. Millions turned out on CND marches and listened attentively to the organization's charismatic leader, the Catholic priest Bruce Kent. The Labour Party stood in the 1983 election on a policy of unilateral nuclear disarmament. British society was split. The Churches had a golden opportunity to give moral leadership on the matter of the moment, nuclear deterrence.

Basil Hume essentially passed the buck. By temperament and feeling he is close to those who rally under the CND banner. 'If I could walk along the Embankment with my banner, I would be a free man – marvellous', he once said. 'But I have to take my responsibilities as a bishop seriously.' His profound desire to see the world free from the threat of a nuclear holocaust is apparent to anyone who listens to the Cardinal's speeches. But as a Church leader in one of the world's handful of nuclear powers, he too often seems, naively, to place his trust in the government to decide what is best for Britain's defence needs. In both the Falklands and the Gulf conflicts, he appealed for peace before the fighting broke out. But once hostilities had started he gave the government his blessing in the battle ahead. In November 1990, for example, he gave Mr Major *carte blanche* in the Gulf. Writing in *The Times*, he said that in deciding on what course to take the government was 'alone in a position to make the decisive assessment' of whether to fight or not. In the early 1980s he was due to visit the Soviet Union, but grew nervous about the trip after Communist forces invaded Afghanistan. He turned for advice to the Foreign Office and when Lord Carrington, then Foreign Secretary, told him not to go he followed the government line.

In April 1980, Basil Hume addressed the launch of the World Disarmament Campaign. He began by firmly establishing his credentials to hold forth on the subject in question. This was not the occasion for drawing lines between priests and politics, nor for fixing his gaze on the life after death. 'Christian idealism demands that we labour to build an earthly city fit for the sons of God in which to live and grow. The struggle will be hard, and sometimes bitter, and the effort must be ceaseless.'

Denying that he was a pacifist, the former abbot upheld the right to self-defence. 'I believe an individual retains this right personally and I believe the state has it on behalf of the citizens.' However, he went on, the advent of nuclear weapons had given a new twist to traditional Church teaching, first set out by Thomas Aquinas in the thirteenth century, about what constituted a just war. The nuclear deterrent had, he judged, preserved 'an unpeaceful peace in an uneasy and unjust world'. For that reason, albeit reluctantly, the Cardinal sided with those who felt it was better to have nuclear weapons than not.

Again he was guilty of generalization. His statement about deterrence keeping the peace is a hard one to justify. British troops have been on active conflict duty in all but a handful of years since the Second World War. And looking round at the trouble-spots of the world, one has to ask what the Cardinal means by peace.

Having sided with those who back the nuclear deterrent, he then attached stringent criteria. Quoting *Gaudium et Spes*, one of the most important Vatican II documents, he argued that using nuclear weapons – or indeed any sort of weapons – to destroy civilian targets 'is immoral and can never be justified'. (During the blanket bombing of Iraqi cities in the Gulf War by the Allies a decade later, the Cardinal was not so quick to reiterate this point.) He could not, he told his audience, 'condemn outright the possession of nuclear arms which are directed to military targets'. Anti-nuclear campaigners would suggest that he was thereby damning Britain's Polaris, with its less than pinpoint accuracy. For the Cardinal, though, as long as a distinction was made between military installations and civilian centres, and provided possession of such strategic weapons did not lead to an escalation in the arms race, then 'deterrent weapons . . . can be morally justified'. The Cardinal was prepared to give nuclear weapons his sanction, hedged with conditions. Some would say that his conditions were impossible for any nuclear power to meet and that he was effectively saying no.

Others within his Church were not convinced and chose to give a much less ambiguous message than their leader. An example is Pax Christi, the international Catholic peace movement, which has branches in Britain and has Basil Hume's auxiliary, Bishop Victor Guazzelli, as its president. Another is the Scottish Catholic Church, which in advance of the 1987 general election argued in an ecumenical statement that it is 'equally immoral' to *threaten* to use nuclear weapons as to use them. And the greatest example is Bruce Kent, today no longer a priest, but still a vociferous campaigner for nuclear disarmament.

Mgr Kent was once Cardinal Heenan's secretary and was one of the diocesan clergy who came under Cardinal Hume's jurisdiction when he arrived in Westminster. Although he continued to do some parish work, Mgr Kent became increasingly involved in CND during the early years of Basil Hume's cardinalate, with the approval of his superior. In 1979 he became secretary of CND, which then had a membership of 3,000. Three years later that figure had leapt to 100,000.

Although Bruce Kent was much in demand in the media and on public platforms, his views were not sought in Archbishop's House. In shaping his own response to the great nuclear debate that gripped Britain throughout 1983, the Cardinal did not take advantage of the fact that Britain's best-known and most articulate exponent of the unilateral nuclear disarmament argument was one of his priests. His presence was overlooked. If the two men met the subject was avoided. If the Cardinal was attempting to reach a consensus position, a base line on which a majority of Catholics could agree, he should at least have been listening to the Christian anti-nuclear lobby.

Although it is known whom the Cardinal did not listen to, who did advise him is harder to discern. For homelessness, the Third World or schools his sources are obvious – the Catholic agencies working in those fields. On defence, the Christian groups were overlooked and the obvious points of reference – like the national Justice and Peace Commission – were silent (some would say silenced).

Believed to be influential was Michael (now Sir Michael) Quinlan, one of the Catholics whose progress to the top of the civil service shows the integration of the 'Romans' into the Establishment. Quinlan rose to be Permanent Under-Secretary of State for Defence and is a believer in the continued relevance and morality of deterrence as 'the keystone of an arch of freedom from war', as he put it in a 1990 address to the Soviet General Staff in Moscow. The retention of an independent British deterrent is 'a military insurance to help prevent war', Quinlan said in a speech that follows much the same line as the Cardinal's own.

As the day in December 1983 when Cruise and Pershing missiles would arrive at Greenham Common and Molesworth air bases drew nearer, tempers on both sides of the debate wore thin. Margaret Thatcher believed wholeheartedly in deterrence and worked closely with the American President, Ronald Reagan, to offer an uncompromising front to the Soviets. She was therefore determined that nuclear missiles should be installed at US bases in Britain. And she never wavered, despite protest marches, petitions, pressure from the opposition and, to the delight of the progovernment tabloid press, the women's peace camp at Greenham Common.

Bruce Kent, at the head of CND, repeatedly questioned the government's policy. His dog collar and his oratory made it harder to dismiss him than the peace campers. His military service history meant that he couldn't be showered with white feathers. Discreet pressure was applied behind the scenes on Cardinal Hume to silence his subordinate. One could almost hear the Defence Minister of the time, Michael Heseltine, demanding 'who will rid me of this turbulent priest?' To his credit, the Cardinal refused to strike the blow. He commented in a letter of April 1983, widely reported in the press, that he had 'serious misgivings' about the increasing politicization of Mgr Kent's role but would not be taking any action.

As the June 1983 election approached, Basil Hume was placed in a very difficult position by some undiplomatic utterances from the Papal Pro-Nuncio in Britain, Archbishop Bruno Heim. Writing to a Catholic Conservative candidate in the election, Edward Leigh, the Archbishop described CND supporters as either 'useful idiots' or 'consciously sharing the Soviet aggression and ideology'. The target of his attack was plain. The Cardinal refused to enter into a public debate. But he had a tussle with the nuncio in private, insisting on his right as the local bishop to deal with disciplinary matters concerning his priests. And he was standing by Bruce Kent.

His resolve was tested again in November 1983 when the CND priest addressed the British Communist Party conference. Another Catholic Tory MP, the late Sir John Biggs-Davison, demanded that the Cardinal take action. Mgr Kent was called to Archbishop's House, and left to continue his work with Basil Hume's blessing. (The Cardinal's defence of the right of his fellow priests, even though technically under his authority, to hold different views from his own has been notable. During the Falklands conflict, Bishop Victor Guazzelli, one of his auxiliaries in Westminster, condemned

British involvement in the war, going against the Cardinal's line. But when Conservative MP Patrick Wall challenged Basil Hume to discipline or disown Bishop Guazzelli, the Cardinal refused.)

In the eye of the storm he refused to yield to outside pressure even though it made life very uncomfortable. In the end it was Mgr Kent who decided that his priesthood and his passionate belief in disarmament were irreconcilable in the prevailing climate. With the 1987 election approaching, and invitations flooding in to outline a CND case that was pretty much akin to the Labour Party's position, Bruce Kent retired from the priesthood so as to be free to speak out without fear of compromising the Church or the Cardinal.

The year of living dangerously

Bruce Kent's activities were just the most visible of a number of conflicting pressures that Basil Hume had to make sense of in 1983. The year began with John Paul II, in his message for Peace Sunday, condemning the futility of war and urging dialogue among the then implacable superpower rivals. The Pope's line was a multilateral one: 'The powers which confront each other ought to be able to proceed together on the various stages of disarmament and to occupy themselves at each point in equal measure'.

That was essentially what Basil Hume had said in his 1980 speech and thereafter. However, any comfort he might have derived from such support from above quickly evaporated when Archbishop Derek Worlock, the Cardinal's second-in-command in the English Church, took a very different line in his own Peace Sunday sermon. The Archbishop referred to Pope John Paul's speech to a United Nations special session on deterrence in June 1982, where he had again given his backing to multilateral disarmament, but had done so on condition that 'mutual, progressive and verifiable' moves be taken towards that goal. 'My personal view', said Archbishop Worlock, (as we have seen earlier, never a man to shy away from taking a stance), 'is that someone has to take the initiative, to give genuine grounds for the confidence necessary for the phased scaling down of the weapons and stockpiles on both sides. I personally believe that we in Britain are probably in the best position to make that first gesture.'

The absence of a single Christian line on the issue was emphasized in the spring when a Church of England working party produced its report, *The Church and the Bomb*, which deemed the possession of nuclear weapons to be as immoral as their use. One of the authors of this report, which effectively pulled the rug from under the deterrence argument, was Catholic moral theologian Fr Brendan Soane, a lecturer at Allen Hall, Basil Hume's diocesan seminary.

On a practical level Catholic priests and nuns were in the front line of peace protests at various US bases in Britain. Fr Timothy Radcliffe, later to become the first Englishman in 777 years to head the 120,000-strong world-wide Dominican order, was among the prominent clerics who took part. He was cautioned for scaling the perimeter fence of the Upper Heyford base. (When a policeman expressed surprise that a Catholic priest should break the law, Fr Timothy replied that it would be more surprising if an English Catholic never broke the law, given the centuries of persecution when they had no choice but to do so.)

On the international Catholic stage all eyes were turned towards America, where the US bishops were working on a pastoral letter on war and peace. Each of its drafts was published. Each took a critical view of the deterrence argument, and such was the interest their discussions aroused that motions were tabled in the House of Representatives condemning them. In May 1983, *The Challenge of Peace* finally appeared. 'The whole world', it said, 'must summon up the moral courage and technical means to say no to weapons of mass destruction.' In October of the same year, the worldwide Synod of Bishops gathered in Rome to debate peace. Agreement was reached on opposition to the stockpiling of weapons and the arms trade, but in the debating hall there was no one prescribed formula on the morality of deterrence. Pope John Paul II was left to write to the Soviet and American leaders to express his fears about the tense international situation.

There was clearly no single Catholic position. Even within the English bishops' conference, different opinions were expressed and a consensus was impossible. On the one side were figures like Bishop Francis Walmsley, Bishop-to-the-Forces, and on the other Bishops Victor Guazzelli and Thomas McMahon, both of whom have close links with the peace movement.

The Cardinal, in an attempt to bring some coherence to English Catholicism on an issue where it was divided and seen to be divided as rarely before, submitted a draft text to the hierarchy meeting in November 1983, at just about the time when the row about Bruce

Kent and the Communist Party speech was at its height. A number of amendments were made and it was published with the bishops' support, but significantly under the Cardinal's name, in *The Times* on 17 November. To this day no authoritative statement akin to *The Challenge of Peace* has emerged from the Catholic bishops of England and Wales.

With the imminent arrival of Cruise and Pershing weighing heavily on the national consciousness, it was no easy task, the Cardinal wrote, 'to see clearly the way forward and to come to terms with these complex and threatening issues'. He balanced this by praising those involved in the peace movements, which of course included many of his own colleagues. 'They bring before us the terrible questions we might otherwise ignore but which must be answered. They rightly alert us to the dangers of nuclear escalation and proliferation. They compel us to question whether new weapons are intended to deter or whether they serve an aggressive purpose.'

He set out in stark terms the moral dilemma. 'On the one hand we have a grave obligation to prevent nuclear war from ever occurring. On the other hand, the State has the right and duty of legitimate self-defence, thus ensuring for its citizens key values of justice, freedom and independence. . . . There is a tension then between the moral imperative not to use such inhuman weapons and a policy of nuclear deterrence with all its declared willingness to use them if attacked.'

Basil Hume, like Derek Worlock earlier, referred to John Paul II's speech to the UN and took it as his yardstick. 'Because of the world situation, deterrence may be accepted as the lesser of two evils, without in any way regarding it as good in itself. Furthermore, this view can be held even by those who reject the morality of nuclear deterrence. It constitutes an acknowledgement that even a morally flawed defence policy cannot simply be dismantled immediately and without reference to the response of potential enemies. To retain moral credibility, however, there must be a firm and effective intention to extricate ourselves from the present fearful situation as quickly as possible.' This was a pragmatic view, the Cardinal acknowledged, 'untidy, risky and provisional'. His unease with what he was saying was apparent. 'If any government in the East or in the West does not take steps to reduce its nuclear weapons and limit their deployment, it must expect its citizens in increasing numbers to be doubtful of its sincerity and alienated from its defence policy.' Yet he never set a time limit for any conditional acceptance of deterrence.

It is worth reflecting, ten years on, that Britain has made no steps whatsoever to reduce its nuclear arsenal despite the changing world conditions and the cuts agreed by Mikhail Gorbachev, Boris Yeltsin, Ronald Reagan and George Bush. Indeed the Trident programme will substantially increase Britain's nuclear capability. By the terms of his 1983 article the Cardinal should now be speaking out, doubting the government's sincerity and moving towards the unilateralist camp. But he shows no sign of doing so. 'Christians must themselves recognise that there is room for differences of opinion in the present situation', the Cardinal went on. 'All of us must retain the right to our conscientious beliefs.' His final remark – 'Those with political power must have the will to discover a better way to achieve peace than through the amassing of nuclear weapons' – handed the baton to governments and left the Churches as by-standers. The Cardinal has political power by dint of his moral authority on a national stage. Yet he was unable or unwilling to exercise it there. Critics were quick to raise these objections and to point out the significant omissions in the text. There was only cursory discussion, for example, of the central question of whether holding nuclear weapons and threatening to use them is as immoral as actually firing them.

As an attempt to throw light on a confused area the statement failed. But it did succeed in putting the defence issue on the back-burner as far as the bishops' conference was concerned until the developing Reagan–Gorbachev *détente* began to defuse the tensions between the superpowers and take the sting out of the arguments.

The Christian peace movement continues to operate, though in much truncated form. Christian CND struggles to fund a full-time worker. Peace protests outside the Ministry of Defence in Whitehall have suffered from the law of diminishing returns. Where once the arrest of nuns made the front pages of national newspapers, today it struggles to get a mention on an inside page of the *Catholic Herald*. Outstanding issues like the status of military chaplains have effectively been buried. In 1988 at its annual gathering the National Conference of Priests, a forum with representatives of all the dioceses of England and Wales, questioned whether it was right that Catholic priests and one bishop should draw a salary from the defence budget. But the debate never really took off. Moves to get the Cardinal to back a nuclear test ban have been met with much wringing of hands but little action. The commitments of the National Pastoral Congress, on behalf of the English Catholic Church, to peace education, a more vigorous Justice and Peace Commission, and an investigation of non-violent alternatives to war have all been forgotten despite the fact that they were voted on and approved.

Only in Scotland have such issues prompted heated and passionate discussion. There the government's decision to order a fourth Trident submarine for the Faslane base on the river Clyde continues to be the focus of protests, church services and even challenges in the courts, with several of the Scottish hierarchy prominent in the campaign.

Perhaps there is something in the English psyche that prefers to play down such matters and Basil Hume, that most English of cardinals, is conscious of that in his reticence on the subject. In March 1992 he broke cover to mark the debut of the first Trident submarine with an article in the *Universe* (now owned by the bishops), backing not only the maintenance of a nuclear deterrence despite the dramatic changes in world conditions following the break-up of the Soviet empire, but also a substantially upgraded and more potent deterrence in the form of the new missile. HMS *Vanguard* was launched on Ash Wednesday and was a reminder, the Cardinal said, of man's capacity to reduce himself into ashes.

He fired a shot across the bows of those who claim that it was the disarmament process, initiated by Reagan and Gorbachev, that brought the Iron Curtain down. 'It is important to note that disarmament has been and is a consequence of peace, not the cause of it.' Historians will be in a position to judge if he was right.

His caution, his willingness to trust in government, came to the surface again during the long run-up to the Gulf War. We have already discussed Pope John Paul II's radical anti-war line on the conflict and how that made it more difficult for Basil Hume to justify his own support of military action against Saddam Hussein. But within English Catholicism too, the Cardinal found himself out of step with many influential voices. In November 1991 several of his fellow bishops and heads of religious orders like the Jesuit and Dominican provincials delivered a peace appeal to 10 Downing Street, urging the Allied forces determined to liberate Kuwait to rely on UN sanctions and negotiations, not force. And in February 1992, in the first days of the fighting, a Christian Coalition for Peace issued an anti-war declaration, based on Pope John Paul II's speeches. Two of the English hierarchy joined theologians, academics and figures from other Christian Churches in rejecting the military option. 'If the Pope was presented with this document', said one of its sponsors at the time, 'then I can see it giving him great satisfaction to sign it.'

It is a measure of the different forces Basil Hume has to balance in leading English Catholicism that on issues like sexual morality radical voices will attack him for not being sufficiently questioning of the Vatican line, while during the Gulf War many of the same voices were attacking him for not doing what the Pope said.

The long build-up to the conflict was undoubtedly an agonizing time for the Cardinal, who was torn between different emotions and political pressures. What caused him most pain was the human tragedy of the war. In February 1992, he spoke to Clifford Longley about his reactions to the start of the fighting. On the night the first Allied shots were fired, he was woken at 1 a.m. by a telephone call. 'I remember I felt all that dread which I had felt in 1939. I relived the whole era of that, which was the end of an era; I remember as a boy of 16 listening to the war about to be declared. And I felt that deep, deep depression. I went through all that again at one in the morning. It was quite uncanny.' In his chapel that night he felt desolation. 'One just felt that situation of Our Lord on the cross – that this is awful.'

Although the cost of the war in terms of human lives appalled the Cardinal, his view that to fight was justified morally did not waver. Speaking on BBC Radio 4's *Thought for the Day* on the day after hostilities broke out – his appearance in this prime slot alongside the Archbishop of Canterbury being a sign of the mantle of national moral leadership the two shared – the Cardinal concluded: 'Saddam Hussein has ignored the resolutions of the United Nations, attempted to wipe a sovereign state off the map and trampled on the rights of so many in his own country and Kuwait. It's for the sake of these thousands of people and it's to uphold the authority of the United Nations that war is now upon us. Only when truth and justice are respected can there be true peace.'

Victims of the arms race

The Cardinal's caution during the Gulf War was a product of his instincts. Although he studied Amnesty International reports on Iraqi outrages, considered texts on the just war, read the Pope's sermons and prayed continuously over the issue, his final response was shaped by what he felt deep down to be right, by the sort of influences we have already seen shaping his behaviour – a concern for people, a natural conservatism, a reluctance to be radical, to take a high profile on an issue where he felt ill at ease. Yet it is those same instincts that have made him such a campaigner for the eradication of world poverty. Although he takes a long time to be convinced of the need to take a bold step, once he gets the bit between his teeth – especially on an issue where he can see human suffering – he can be unstoppable.

The link between the arms race and warfare on the one hand and hunger and starvation on the other is a constant theme in Basil Hume's contributions to any debate on defence issues. In 1980, in his New Year message, he wrote: 'It is a strange logic which justifies vast expenditure on weapons of destruction while tolerating, according to one estimate, that 800 million people should live in a state of absolute poverty'. While praising international efforts to improve health care and education in the world's poorest countries, he felt much more could be done 'if wealthy nations were each to contribute 10 per cent of their defence budgets to development and embarked upon imaginative and large-scale plans for investment in the developing countries. Politicians who understand what needs to be done feel powerless in the face of public indifference and apathy.'

One of the abiding crusades of Basil Hume's cardinalate has been to shake people out of that apathy. He has not been afraid to pitch his message at a populist market. In 1980 he wrote an Easter message for the mass-circulation *News of the World* – a paper that had a long tradition of printing Cardinal Heenan's thoughts, but that had been overlooked by his successor in favour of *The Times*: 'The world spends 450 billion dollars a year on military purposes while we can scrape together only 20 billion on all official development aid'.

As in other areas, words have been matched with action. Cardinal Hume has been an enthusiastic backer of CAFOD, the Catholic Fund for Overseas Development, which during his cardinalate has grown into a major organization, distributing millions through the Church network in many countries around the world. From humble origins in the early 1960s as an offshot of one of the Catholic women's organizations on the margins of the Church, running tombolas to service the needs of missionaries, CAFOD has developed a national and international profile. Run by a lay staff, it has evolved into a role informing and educating both the Catholic and the secular audience about development issues, while at the same time working with other non-denominational agencies to identify priorities for long-term aid, organize appeals for emergency relief and lobby governments. Its expertise is widely acknowledged, a fact confirmed by the fact that some 10–15 per cent of its annual budget of £20 million comes from the British government, while substantial sums arrive via the European Community.

During CAFOD's silver jubilee year of 1987, Cardinal Hume highly praised the organization, an agency of the bishops' conference. CAFOD is, he said, 'a great conspiracy of love that has succeeded in overcoming our insularity and complacency and opening our hearts to the needs of the poor, the disadvantaged and the oppressed'. Indeed the success of CAFOD in making a professional contribution to national life on the issue of the Third World has led to suggestions that what the Church now needs is a 'domestic CAFOD', a single Church agency, perhaps even an ecumenical one, to bring together in one powerful body the various groups working on racism, homelessness and other pastoral needs. The current fragmentation of such efforts, and the accompanying lack of finance, has meant that the 'Catholic lobby' – and indeed the 'Christian lobby' – has not been organized in any coherent shape or form. Various proposals have crossed the Cardinal's desk, but as yet little has resulted.

One notable cross-fertilization between the Cardinal's concern for the Third World and his domestic concerns has been the establishment of a refugees' co-ordinator at the bishops' conference. John Joseet deals not only with the plight of refugees arriving in Britain and with the details of immigration law, keeping the hierarchy informed of any important issues in the field, but also with the refugee situation around the globe.

Out of Africa

When Basil Hume watched Michael Buerk's television news reports of the famine that was devastating Ethiopia in 1984 his instinctive response was to do something, to go and see what was happening so as to be able to lobby on behalf of the millions who were without food.

It was to be one of the most gruelling times – emotionally and physically – in his cardinalate. News of his departure was kept secret until the last moment. CAFOD had laid the plans, and the Cardinal was accompanied by the organization's director, Julian Filochowski, and its Africa Projects Officer, Cathy Corcoran. It was stressed that the six-day visit was very much a personal initiative. Basil Hume was going as a pastor to tend to people in need, not as a politician, a polemicist or, in the wake of Bob Geldof, a pop star. As ever anxious that people should not misinterpret his motives, the Cardinal was determined that his trip should not become a media circus, with the famine victims lined up for photo opportunities.

On his arrival the news crews were kept at arms' length. They accompanied the Cardinal on only one of his visits to a refugee centre, and he refused to answer questions on the politics of the Ethiopian situation. Civil war and the international isolation of the Marxist regime in Addis Ababa were widely held to be as important in bringing on the famine as the absence of rain. But Basil Hume would not be drawn on such matters. He would talk only of the people he had met. One had only to look at his face as he cradled a hungry child to see the effect such enormous human tragedy was having on him.

He travelled round for the most part with local Church figures, the people who were working on the ground to ensure that what aid was coming through got to the people in need. His mission was to find out, as he put it in a brief statement issued on the eve of his departure, 'why there seem to be such delays and confusion in getting help to those who are suffering so much'.

The people of the Ethiopian camps, and on a wider scale the needy around the world, would never be far from Basil Hume's thoughts after that trip. 'This first-hand experience of the effects of prolonged hunger and starvation left me with memories and images which are unforgettable', he wrote the following year. 'To have been face-to-face with a starving child is an experience which gives a totally new dimension and urgency to problems which may other-wise seem distant and academic.' One of his tasks when he returned to Britain was to turn those distant and academic needs into a reality for a domestic audience. Interviews and talks were followed by a special report, aimed specifically at shaking people out of their apathy concerning the Third World. *Africa's Crisis and the Church in Britain*, published by CAFOD and the Catholic Truth Society in 1987, tried to encourage parishes, individuals and those in power to reflect on the extent of poverty and hunger in the world, to ask themselves what they had done as members of a wealthy and afflu-ent society to contribute to that, and how they could work for change.

It was a brave effort, but despite the presence of Chris Patten, a Catholic, as Minister for Overseas Development when the report appeared, it largely fell on deaf ears. The British government's aid budget shrank rather than expanded under Mr Patten, despite his willingness to listen. And among the population at large apathy was hard to dispel. Attention wandered once the worst excesses of starvation were off the television screens. Some memories are only as long as the last disaster. In the heady days before and after Cardinal Hume's dramatic mission to Ethiopia, money flooded in to cathedrals, parishes and CAFOD. But the effort was not sustained at that level, though CAFOD's income over the subsequent years showed a notable boost thanks to the Cardinal's consciousness-raising trip.

It would be fair to add that there is now a noticeably higher degree of involvement in Third World issues at parish level among the Catholic community than in the population at large. CAFOD Friday groups, diocesan Justice and Peace networks and a variety of local organizations have an impressive record in fund-raising and turning out to listen to the overseas speakers to whom CAFOD plays host.

In the immediate aftermath of his trip to Ethiopia, however, Basil Hume's priority was to get food to the people who were starving. He at once secured an invitation to 10 Downing Street to brief Mrs Thatcher on his trip and on the conditions of the seven million at risk. In advance of his departure for Ethiopia he had joined with Robert Runcie and the head of the Free Churches to twist the Prime Minister's arm to send two RAF Hercules transport planes to help with food distribution in the region. British aid – standing at £5 million – was simply not enough, he told her. And plans to reduce the overall aid budget in a government always keen to keep public spending to a minimum were 'a scandal given the present situation'. As much as £1 billion was rumoured to be at risk, but plans were quietly shelved.

Cardinal Hume did not confine his attention to the British government. His Ethiopia trip came during his period as President of the Council of European Bishops' Conferences and he at once fired off letters to his colleagues on the continent, calling for 30,000 tons of grain to be sent each month from EC stocks for the whole of the next year. He asked them to lobby their governments over this proposal. And, he added, long-term development must be upgraded. 'Unless there is investment in agriculture, rural infrastructure and water resources geared to self-sufficiency in food a similar catastrophe will almost certainly recur within a few years.' The EC proved slow in releasing stocks from its grain mountains to send to Ethiopia. But in the end the food aid needed did begin to flow. The Cardinal kept up the pressure. In April 1985 he appealed to the Community's leaders, meeting in Brussels, to make sure that 'the relief operation now underway does not falter for lack of momentum'.

It was not just the EC the Cardinal had to battle with in getting food to the needy. His return from Ethiopia coincided with the publication of a report from the Marxist government in Addis Ababa pledging the regime to 'the immediate launching of a campaign to remove the evils of religion'. It made the front page of *The Times*. The Cardinal was furious. Not only did the publication of the report jeopardize the relief effort, it was inaccurate. Nowhere did *The Times* story mention that the document dated back to 1982. Nor did it add that throughout the Cardinal's own visit Church organizations in Ethiopia spoke of suffering no harassment from the authorities. He was tempted to see the timing of the story as a deliberate attempt to sabotage the relief effort.

It was a rare outburst of anger from Basil Hume. His inbuilt distrust of the media was accentuated – not least because of the role of his favourite newspaper, *The Times*. But he didn't allow such episodes to distract his attention from the task in hand. He dismissed the report and used his moral authority to redirect the nation's attention back to the plight of the starving millions.

His Ethiopia campaign has remained a part of the Cardinal's

interests to this day. He speaks often of his desire to return to Africa. Out of that trip to Ethiopia the Cardinal took on a much higher profile on Third World issues, both nationally and within the Catholic Church. At the 1985 Fight World Poverty lobby at the Houses of Parliament, he tackled 'the stranglehold of international debt', a recurring theme in John Paul II's homilies. Children are dying in the Third World, he told his audience, to meet Western interest charges on debt. As yet, however, the Archdiocese of Westminster has not moved its funds – or its overdraft – to one of the smaller, ethically sound, high street banks.

The Cardinal broached the contraception issue and the need for population control, another favourite theme of the Pope on his world travels. He attacked those 'who would have us ship contraceptive pills rather than grain' to countries where people are starving. 'This response perpetuates the myth that the people of Africa are irrational and irresponsible, while conveniently distracting attention from our underlying responsibility in the northern hemisphere for the grossly inequitable division of the world's goods.'

His stance, like those of CAFOD and of John Paul II, has been a distinctive one. The problems of the Third World are not solved by throwing condoms at them. While he has embraced much of the radical rhetoric and many of the policies of campaigning organizations in this field, Basil Hume has refused to go with the argument that says that any development aid will be redundant if Third World birth rates continue to soar. But population control is not a subject he likes to dwell on.

On the eve of the Rio Earth Summit in the summer of 1992, the Archbishop of Canterbury attacked Rome's refusal to allow artificial birth control and its effects in the Third World. 'We cannot say that population is nothing to do with it. Of course it is. I believe that the issue of population is a challenge facing us all', he said. The Cardinal responded at once. Rome did not ban contraception, he said. It encouraged natural birth control. Significantly he did not challenge the Archbishop of Canterbury's central assertion. Basil Hume has been to developing countries and listened to the people there. He has not taken Western prescriptions for what they must and must not do.

His sensitivity to the real needs of developing countries – as opposed to what the West decides are their needs – has had repercussions for Basil Hume's standing in the eyes of his fellow churchmen in the Third World. His reputation is as one who listens to their point of view, who understands the human tragedies they have to confront daily, who has sympathy for their more liberal theological approaches.

It is not that the Cardinal has stood up and given liberation theology, with its option for the poor, his public endorsement. Because of English Catholicism's lack of academic rigour, the absence of any great theological colleges here, liberation theology has never been an issue of debate. But at synods of bishops in Rome, at meetings in the Vatican's corridors of power, the Cardinal has, his admirers report, defended the liberation theologians' way of acting and their processes with an insight they judge rare for a European. He has been a radical out of sight, but when it matters. 'When we go to Rome we feel we have to keep quiet, that our point of view isn't valued', one Brazilian Cardinal once told me. 'But then Basil Hume speaks up and he says what we want to say but don't dare to. He isn't afraid.'

9

The flesh is weak

The Benedictine tradition is well on the side of the incarna-
tional, that spirituality which takes as its starting point the
Word made Flesh. Christ came not to eradicate human nature
or to obliterate the fields of human activity, but to purify and
exalt them.

(John F. X. Harriott)

When he first arrived at Westminster, Cardinal Hume recalls, he
was told not to be afraid 'to engage in controlled vulgar self-
revelation' – in other words not to be frightened of saying 'I'. Years
of training as a monk to do exactly the opposite have taken their toll,
however, and he remains reluctant to speak of his own life and the
choices he has made. The fact that on several occasions he has gone
on the record as hankering after the benefits of marriage is therefore
significant. In 1981, in an interview with a women's magazine, he
remarked 'it must be marvellous to have a wife'. And ten years later
he said in another newspaper interview that any successful celibate
has to regret he has not married. Debrett took the Cardinal at his
word in May 1988 in its *Distinguished People of Today* and listed
him as having married one Lady Bridget Mullens. He took the
printing error in good spirit. 'Marriages can take place by proxy but
this is going a bit far.'

The significance is not that Basil Hume regrets choosing to be a
monk, but rather in his revelation of a sure and instinctive touch in
handling tricky questions about sexual morality. He puts a human
front on what can become alarmingly technical debates. He shows
that he has an inkling of what goes on in 'ordinary' people's lives,
even if the vow of celibacy he has taken makes him extraordinary.

Basil Hume is not one for pontificating at every given moment on
a subject on which he feels that as a celibate monk he is no great

expert. The Cardinal, it will be recalled from the earlier chapter on his relationship with Rome, decided soon after arriving in London not to talk about sexual ethics. 'I'm not an expert on the subject', he told me, 'and my comments will be interpreted because of that.' You will search in vain for homilies by the Cardinal in the manner of John Paul II, decrying contraception and the 'contraceptive mentality'. The former abbot is equally convinced that too much time and energy are expended by others in the Catholic Church talking about sexual morality. It has all been said and resaid far too many times, and such repetition risks distracting from other matters of concern.

A good example of Basil Hume's feeling that there is very little that is new to say in this area came in a 1980 interview with John Mortimer in the *Sunday Times*. The two had been talking about the nature of evil – in the wake of the deaths in an earthquake in Italy of worshippers at a Catholic church – and faith in adversity. The agnostic interviewer abruptly changed tack. 'And about birth control. . . .' The Cardinal displayed, Mr Mortimer reported, 'a sort of weariness'.

'Journalists always have to ask about that. I don't think that our role is to be the custodians of sex.' Showing what his questioner described as 'a rare modesty in Catholic prelates', Basil Hume went on: 'I think sex looms too large in people's thoughts about Catholicism, after all we have far more interesting things to talk about'. Their conversation then veered away to death, the after-life and the nature of the priesthood, all subjects on which Cardinal Hume felt he had more to offer.

Because of the very nature of Catholicism and the importance it places on the creation and nurture of human life, Cardinal Hume has not always been able to side-step the issue so charmingly. For one thing, the Vatican does not feel any of his diffidence and has over the past couple of decades produced a whole series of statements, documents and encyclicals on sexual morality that have excited dissent and controversy. As the leader of English Catholicism, the Cardinal is inevitably asked to give his opinion. And during his time at Westminster a series of important medical and moral issues have hit the headlines. The Cardinal has not shirked the responsibility intrinsic in his job to make a contribution to the debate. But significantly, on such questions as abortion law reform, the government's response to the AIDS pandemic or legislation on embryo experimentation, he has addressed his comments not just to a Catholic audience but to the whole nation.

Two central themes have linked such contributions: the distinction between the Church's law and the State's law, that what is legal is not necessarily right; and that in each case there are symptoms of a national moral decline that has to be arrested for the public good. In his concentration on morality, the moral high ground, as opposed to specifically Catholic moral teaching, Basil Hume has been listened to by a wide audience, many of whom have grown used, particularly during the debates on embryo legislation, to looking to him as the keeper of the nation's conscience.

There are activists within his own ranks who feel that it is a betrayal of Catholicism for their leader not only to ration his comments on a world that they see as awash with sexual licentiousness and permissiveness, but also to address those he does make to a national audience. They want to hear him banging out the Catholic message on a tribal drum and summoning his community to mass action in the fashion of the old-style fortress Church. This he has steadfastly refused to do, to the evident despair of campaigners like Victoria Gillick, the mother of ten who fought in the courts for a parent's right to be informed if his or her under-age daughter was being prescribed the pill. She pressed the Cardinal to endorse her crusade (of which more later), to make it the *cause célèbre* of every Catholic parish up and down the land. His refusal to do so angered Mrs Gillick so much that she publicly accused him of being lily-livered, while she and her family took to calling him 'Basil Brush', the indecisive and somewhat dim television puppet.

From the Cardinal's point of view, while the point Mrs Gillick was making about parents' rights was an important one, he did not believe the courts were the right place to win the moral argument. Although there have been high-profile legal and parliamentary campaigns in which he has been involved – most notably in this area the campaigns to reduce the upper time limit on abortions and to ban embryo experimentation – his own more usual path has been persuasion not coercion, the human angle not the impersonal directive.

Whatever his own reservations about talking about sexual morality, the Cardinal is not naive. He is not one to bury his head in the sand about prevailing attitudes and come out with a series of idealistic statements that have very little to do with the reality of people's lives. He knows as well as anyone else that the Church's line on contraception and sex before marriage is out of step with prevailing attitudes and is widely ignored by Catholics. A 1992 survey, published in the *British Journal of Family Planning*, found that only 3 per cent of young people believed you had to wait for sex until you were married. Nearly half of those questioned said they had lost their virginity before the age of 16.

He knows young people after many years as a housemaster. Reading them the riot act will not persuade them to change. He once said that his role in the classroom was 'to teach boys to teach themselves', that you don't get anywhere if you work on the basis of rules and regulations. Instead the Cardinal has set individual issues within the broader context of the moral standards of our society. Each of us, by our actions and by our choices, contributes to those standards. If we want things to improve, we have to first remove the splinter from our own eye.

How far this attractive approach has worked is a matter of dispute. Parish churches display a yawning generation gap each Sunday, with few to fill the pews between the very young and their parents and grandparents. But the Cardinal would argue that by not condemning the young who turn their back on Mass attendance and the rules of their Church, he is leaving the door open for an eventual return, usually when they become parents themselves. The fruits of his strategy will not, therefore, be seen for several years.

With older generations Basil Hume's approach has been to listen, to try to understand and to help as far as he can while at the same time making clear the teaching of the Church. It can be a difficult line to walk. He has, for example, given his support and his time to the fledgling Association of Separated and Divorced Catholics (ASDC), a self-help group for those whose marriages have broken down. Divorce is not a sin in the Catholic credo – it is simply not recognized – and therefore the Cardinal's involvement with the group is in a technical sense uncontroversial. However, the prevailing attitude to divorcees in many Catholic parishes continues to be one of suspicion. Too many people whose marriages break down are made to *feel* they have committed a sin. By getting involved with the ASDC, the Cardinal was dispelling such prejudices.

Many who participate in ASDC meetings are angry with their treatment by the Church and refuse to contemplate its complex annulment process as a way of putting themselves on the right side of its laws. Yet that has not stopped the Cardinal saying Mass in

Westminster Cathedral to celebrate the first ten years of the association. He has not made a rigid and uncritical adherence to the letter of the Church's law the condition of his support for organizations, particularly in the domain of issues to do with sex.

While his predecessor Cardinal Heenan approached the pain of marital failure by encouraging a speeding up of the annulment procedure, showing compassion but only within the rules of the Church, Cardinal Hume has extended a helping hand to anyone, whatever their situation. At the same time he has reiterated the Church's line that marriage is for life.

Condemning the sin but loving the sinner is one of the oldest practices in the Church, but with Basil Hume there has often been no need for people to identify themselves as sinners before they get his attention. For sin and sinners, he has substituted principles and people. He is prepared to be uncompromising in his defence of a principle – such as the sanctity of human life – but he will listen to and lend support to people whatever they have done to contravene such principles. It is a policy that shows the Cardinal at his best, his most human. Yet it can also spread confusion, not least among Catholics, as to quite what the Church does allow and what it doesn't.

Implicit in the Cardinal's human touch with regard to sexual morality is his understanding that after *Humanae Vitae* the Church can no longer command unquestioning obedience from its people. It can guide, encourage and provide models for behaviour, but at the end of the day it has no sanction to enforce them. The old resort of denying the sacraments is not an option that Cardinal Hume, with his decidedly liberal pastoral practice, would encourage or contemplate himself.

Even when he does set out the Church's line, he tends to moderation. On homosexuality, for example, the stand taken by the Cardinal and the English bishops, especially in their 1979 statement, was one of the most tolerant and compassionate in the Catholic world. Homosexuality, traditionally the target of fierce condemnation from a Church in which sex remains first and foremost for procreation, was according to the English hierarchy more or less a neutral condition, neither good nor bad in itself. Such a stance was in marked contrast to the 1986 Vatican outburst that to be homosexual is 'a strong tendency towards an intrinsic moral evil'.

Basil Hume will argue that Rome's teaching is not as illiberal as it looks at first sight. When pressed on such points, where one can detect daylight between what he is saying and what the Pope says, he has a habit of remarking 'Please make it clear that I am a loyal son of the Church. I accept the teaching of the Church.' But he never quite makes it plain what, to him, this teaching is, whether it is to be found in Vatican declarations and papal encyclicals, or also perhaps more diffusely in the experiences and day-to-day realities of the Church at large, in the lives of lay men and women. This approach has its roots in his Benedictine upbringing, as the late John Harriott made clear in the passage that opens this chapter. Human nature is not something to be crushed into submission, but rather something to be treasured and nurtured. If our human nature leads us into sins of the flesh, the right course is not to condemn but to show understanding in leading the way back to the light.

In his 'I have a dream' address to the 1980 Synod on the Family in Rome, when he had been asked by the National Pastoral Congress to raise the issue of the ban on artificial contraception, Cardinal Hume outlined his own vision of how bishops and people of any belief should work together: 'We must never fail to listen to other pilgrims. And they need encouraging. We must speak gently, compassionately, co-agonise with them, lead them gradually and speak a language which enables them to say: "yes, that is right; it is now clear, we accept the teaching".'

The touchstone of orthodoxy

In Cardinal Heenan's era, the Catholic Church's stance on sexual morality was associated above all with its teaching on contraception. The Cardinal himself had been a member of a commission that reported in the mid-1960s to Pope Paul VI, recommending that use of the contraceptive pill was not always immoral. In his Trinity Sunday pastoral letter of 1966 the Cardinal seemed to be preparing the way for a change in the Church's teaching: 'Physical science has revealed new facts about nature. Medicine and psychology have made discoveries about human life itself. Although truth remains the same, our knowledge of it is always increasing. Some of our notions of right and wrong have also undergone change.'

In 1968 Pope Paul VI, in his encyclical *Humanae Vitae*, dashed any hopes of change. Each and every act of sexual intercourse must remain open to the transmission of life, he ruled. Pills and condoms were out of the question because they broke the link between what the Pope termed the procreative and the unitive aspects of sex – i.e. sex was still primarily for making babies.

The furore that followed left Cardinal Heenan in a difficult situation. He had to justify a teaching many suspected he did not support. English Catholics, anticipating a relaxation in the rules from Rome, had already started using contraception and saw no reason to stop. This was the crucial point in the break-down of the old authoritarian structures that had dominated Catholic life since the restoration of the hierarchy. Many Catholics turned their backs on the Church as a result of *Humanae Vitae*. Those who stayed learned to make up their own minds. In a survey of Catholic opinion in England published in 1989, the sociologist Michael Hornsby-Smith reported that he could not find a single voice 'raised unambiguously in defence of *Humanae Vitae*'.

This was the Church that Cardinal Hume was called to lead in 1976. When pressed he will emphasize the life values that *Humanae Vitae* sought to defend. He will extol the virtues of natural family planning as taught in several Church-run centres. But in general he has remained silent on the document's best-known teaching. He has made no attempt to turn back the clock.

If contraception has rarely featured on the Cardinal's agenda, then one particular moral issue has come to dominate the public policy of the English Catholic Church during Cardinal Hume's era: abortion, which was legalized in 1967 up to 28 weeks of pregnancy. Where the great contraception debate was essentially fought out within the Church, abortion has become a matter of national controversy, with the Cardinal addressing his comments on the subject to a national audience in the hope of changing prevailing attitudes but with an eye on the continuing legislative struggle.

Catholic teaching is that human life begins at the moment of conception and that to terminate a pregnancy is to kill an unborn child. Since 1967 the Catholic Church has headed a broad coalition of groups trying to translate that Church teaching into the law of the land. It has been a campaign that has generated much heat and not a great deal of light and that, ultimately, has resulted in even more permissive legislation.

In 1990 the Parliamentary crusade headed by Catholic MP David Alton, with the support and encouragement of Cardinal Hume and the bishops, resulted in the upper time limit for abortions being

173

reduced to 24 weeks. However, abortion up to birth was allowed where the mother's life was in danger or the fetus was handicapped. The overall reduction in the number of weeks will save only a handful of children each year, while the new open-ended clause will potentially claim the lives of many more.

The Cardinal's position has always been that his primary aim is not to impose Catholic teachings on others through the law, but to defend human life. The struggle on the floor of the House of Commons was therefore an important focus for him, but not the only one. When he spoke of abortion and what the free availability of it meant about Britain's moral standards, he wasn't addressing his comments only to Catholics or even to MPs, but to a national constituency. He took a new approach, not dealing with abortion in isolation but placing the Church's stance on that issue alongside its work on social justice. Many of those who feel that Catholicism's opposition to abortion is too rigid would at the same time praise its commitment to a more equal world. According to the Cardinal the Church's concern for the unborn child's right to life is indivisible from its demand that the homeless be given a roof over their heads. In 1980 he set out this position in a statement on abortion with his fellow archbishops of Great Britain – a rare joint venture between the English and Welsh Church and their Scottish cousins.

'Our stand against abortion is one aspect of our stand against all practices that degrade human rights and dignity. . . . The bishops have tried to defend the insulted, the despised, the disadvantaged. With other Christians we have resisted racism. . . . The whole of Christian social teaching can be seen as an appeal to the conscience of the relatively well-off and powerful to give practical recognition to the humanity and rights of the poor and weak. And the social teaching proclaims as well the rights of minorities against majorities who treat them with unfair indifference or hostility. . . . These developing human lives may be unborn or silent but they are already our neighbours living in our midst and are part of our human family. They need to be defended. . . . Unborn children in Great Britain today are a legally disadvantaged class; they are weak; they are a minority. . . . Law ought to uphold and embody the principles that are basic to our civilisation and our existing law in every other field; innocent life is to be protected by the criminal law and public policy; no law should countenance discrimination by the strong against the weak.'

174

This attempt to broaden the argument, to link the Church's contentious stance on abortion with its more universally admired work for social justice, has been a recurring feature of Cardinal Hume's policy. In the guidelines he and Archbishop Worlock issued to Catholic voters before the 1992 general election, for example, the right to life was interpreted in its widest sense, 'including the unborn child and also the defence of decent living and working conditions for the individual and for families. One should not go without the other.' Attempts to make Catholic voters place their crosses on the ballot paper on a single issue did not win the Cardinal's blessing.

His attempt to place the abortion question in a fuller social context has not been universally popular among some Catholics, especially those who make up the bulk of Britain's active pro-life lobby. Phyllis Bowman, the general secretary of the Society for the Protection of Unborn Children (SPUC), found the pre-election statement 'so watered down as to be futile'. She held that it was 'utterly empty to talk of living conditions until the right to life is guaranteed'. For Mrs Bowman, and indeed for many of the parish priests who support SPUC's campaigns from the pulpit, opposition to abortion is the touchstone of orthodoxy for a Catholic, and if that means telescoping an entire code of belief into a single-issue pressure group, so be it.

Cardinal Hume, as ever attentive to the views of all his flock, not just a vocal section, can see the folly of such a policy, not to mention its impracticality. The 1989 Hornsby-Smith survey revealed that 40 per cent of the Mass-going Catholics questioned believed that in certain circumstances a women could be justified in choosing abortion.

There is, moreover, a growing lobby even among the activists that feels that the Parliamentary campaign to change the law has absorbed too much energy. If the Church wants to reduce the number of abortions, it is suggested, there are more effective ways forward. Giving pregnant women a real choice is one option that has been pursued by another of the anti-abortion organizations, Life. Its network of safe houses offers pregnant women a place where they can live until after the birth of their child, away from the pressures and judgements of family, friends and society.

Another venture that has enjoyed strong support from Cardinal Hume in his diocese has been the St Joseph's Centre for handicapped children at Hendon. If you are going to tell women expecting a handicapped child that disability is not a good reason to opt for abortion, you have to offer practical support when that baby is born. Sadly this centre is an isolated facility in the broader Catholic world. A glance down the columns of the *Catholic Directory* shows a dearth of specifically Catholic support for parents with children with physical disabilities or learning difficulties.

Cardinal Hume has steadfastly refused to stake all on a change in the law in his policy on abortion. His personal abhorrence of the practice is not in doubt. He commented once that he was coming more and more to realize 'the horror of abortion'. The Cardinal has, however, been realistic. The different camps on abortion, pro and anti, are so polarized that hopes of effective legal reform have been slim throughout his cardinalate. With various governments insisting that it is a matter for the individual consciences of MPs, hopes of Parliamentary progress have always seemed elusive. In 1987 and 1988 David Alton secured a majority for his Private Member's Bill to reduce the time limit on abortions to 18 weeks, but was frustrated by what he called 'procedural mugging' by his opponents.

How far the appeal to society to change its attitudes has succeeded is harder to judge. Will Britain in years to come take to heart the 'horror' of having one of the highest abortion rates in Europe? The Cardinal's bold aim of transforming social trends appears at the moment to have failed. Yet one lesson of history, even in the twentieth century, is that one generation has seen treatment of individuals as second-class citizens which later generations regard as unthinkable. Women, black people and Jews have all been the target of discrimination in this century, but today, in most countries, it is expected that they should enjoy something approaching equality.

Who is to say the Archbishops' comment at the end of their 1980 statement – 'Success has so often appeared to social reformers to be beyond their reach, almost up to the moment when they attained it' – will in the long run prove optimistic? By refusing to launch a single-issue crusade on abortion, avoiding extremes of polarization, the Cardinal may just have hastened the day.

Fighting for the family

If Cardinal Hume and the English bishops have shown a longer-term perspective than the parliamentary campaign to change the abortion law, there is no mistaking their distaste for the vocal crusade of Victoria Gillick and her use of litigation to impose her views on others.

In 1984 and 1985 Mrs Gillick took the Department of Health and Social Security to court over its guidance to doctors on the provision of contraceptive advice and treatment to girls under 16. The Department in a circular advised that in exceptional circumstances it would not be unlawful to prescribe the pill without the girl's parents' consent. The rarity of such occasions was emphasized. But Mrs Gillick felt there should be no such occasions at all and asked the courts to support her. Lining up for the cameras with her own formidable brood, she asked why, if a parent's consent was needed for a 15-year-old to have any other sort of medical treatment, should the prescription of contraceptives be made an exception? This question struck a chord in many homes and parishes throughout the country and various petitions and prayers were organized to wish her well. They were all to no avail. The High Court found against her. She won in the Court of Appeal and lost on a split verdict in the House of Lords, three to two.

As one who made no bones about the connection between her court battle and her Catholicism, Victoria Gillick looked to the Church for support and found it wanting. For a short period in the mid-1980s she became – alongside Cardinal Hume, Mgr Bruce Kent and the Pope – the personification of the Catholic Church in the public mind.

Despite the explicit Catholic connection, Cardinal Hume and the bishops refused to be drawn into Mrs Gillick's court campaign. Their stance was to endorse the role of the family as the primary social unit, to express their concern at teenage sex and pregnancies, but to dispute whether recourse to the law was the best way to make things better. In November 1984, for example, the bishops supported a 2,000-strong petition of doctors. The GPs were asking to be allowed, when they judged it appropriate, to break the confidentiality oath in the case of under age patients and tell their parents that they had asked for the pill. It was not enough for Mrs Gillick. She was not prepared to trust doctors' discretion to the extent that the bishops were. In her autobiography, *A Mother's Tale*, she described the hierarchy as 'wimpish'. She wanted actions not words.

Days after she lost her case in the highest court in the land, she evaluated the reasons for her defeat and pointed an accusing finger at the hierarchy for its 'lack of courage and forthright leadership on Catholic principles' which had 'given comfort to enemies of the family and to those who condone sexual permissiveness in society'. Cardinal Hume would reply – and did when challenged on his coolness to the Gillick crusade – that he had never failed to give leadership on the need to protect the family. It has been a constant theme in his speeches, sermons and writings. In an Advent pastoral letter of December 1991, to pick one example at random, he wrote to his diocese: 'In a world where human love and faithfulness are so often abused, we must restore the home and the family to its proper place in society and in our lives. In our families we learn to be fully human, here we learn to love and relate. If the Church is seen as the most vigorous promoter of family life and of faithfulness in marriage, that will be a beacon of real hope in society.'

Mrs Gillick and her supporters would claim that the beacon would glow all the brighter if the Cardinal had matched words with actions and lent his support. It is a recurring problem for the Cardinal on this and many other issues. What do you do if you tell people the Christian way, the moral way of behaving, and they ignore you? Go to Parliament and ask for a change in the law? Go to the courts and pursue litigation?

His reasons in the Gillick case for not following the latter course were partly to do with factors outlined already: a dislike of appearing to coerce through force of the civil law. He also clearly felt uneasy at Mrs Gillick's brutal attempts to browbeat him into supporting her. Moreover, although in her spoken desire to defend the family unit Victoria Gillick was at one with the Cardinal, in the eyes of the Church there is no strict definition of the point of balance between parental responsibilities and the rights of growing young people. And once again the Cardinal was trying to be realistic. Expert legal advisers said that the Gillick case stood little hope of success. Why get involved in a battle where you are going to lose? More significantly, perhaps, the Cardinal had learnt a lesson from the 1967 Abortion Act and the ensuing battles, namely that if you argue as if the law of the land is the central issue, then when the law is against you, you appear to have lost the moral issue as well. It is much better, goes such a line of thought, to emphasize the difference between the State's laws and the Church's laws, between law and morals, and thereby to allow the Church to maintain its call to moral rectitude. That has been a touchstone of Basil Hume's public policy. If he is going to fight for changes in the law, he will do so only on the occasions when he can see no other option – most notably over embryo experimentation. The bishops' line in the Gillick case showed them adopting this more sophisticated approach on moral issues where Church and State were not at one.

Another factor in Mrs Gillick's apparent abandonment by the hierarchy was her link with a network that might loosely be termed the 'moral majority'. The Reagan era in America saw the rapid growth of a well-organized and well-funded Christian lobby that tried to use its voting power to force politicians, the courts and even the President to do their bidding. Defence of the family was the war-cry, and the battles were fought out over issues like abortion, homosexuality and AIDS. The moral majority campaigners included among their ranks many of the television evangelists who were so popular in the United States in the 1980s – before financial and sexual scandals destroyed the reputations of men like Jim Bakker and Jimmy Swaggert.

The basic message was a simple one. Do what the Bible says and fight all the manifestations of the permissive society with every weapon to hand. It was an aggressive approach that the mainline Churches and particularly the American Catholic bishops tried to steer well clear of. Like Cardinal Hume, as a conference they believed that coercion and the courts were not always the best ways to get the message across.

Attempts to launch a parallel movement in Britain have so far not got off the ground. Broadcasting regulations preclude any attempts to feature tele-evangelists on mainstream British networks – though satellite channels are freer in this respect – and therefore both a high profile and access to funds through screen appeals were out of the question.

Victoria Gillick was the nearest thing the fledgling moral majority ever got to a figurehead. Cardinal Hume realized the danger and gave her a wide berth. His cautious attitude to her crusade has been mirrored by his approach to organizations like the Responsible Society, renamed Family and Youth Concern in an attempt to sound a little more 1980s-friendly, and the Order of Christian Unity. All these organizations dedicate themselves to rallying the socially conservative lobby under the flag of defence of the family. All see the Catholic community, part of a Church unique because of the rigour of its teachings on sexual morality, as a natural ally. All misjudge both the disparity of views within English Catholicism and the amenability of the bishops, who have a much more accurate picture of what Catholics think and a more realistic approach to changing the world.

A *via media*

When it came to formulating a response to the AIDS pandemic, the balancing trick demanded of Cardinal Hume was very obvious. On one wing of English Catholicism there were the conservative voices of the would-be moral majority targeting homosexuals as flag-bearers of the permissive age. On the other were the advocates of the liberal agenda, who feel that sexual morality is a question for individual conscience and that the Church should relax its opposition to condoms in the interest of arresting the spread of the virus.

The identification of AIDS and then of the HIV virus in the early 1980s gave new impetus to the moral majority on both sides of the Atlantic. The fact that AIDS was initially recognized as affecting gay men and drug users in Western countries confirmed all their direst predictions that the world was a sink of licentiousness and was now being punished by God. Those infected by contaminated blood were presented as 'innocent' victims – the implication being that all other high-risk groups were guilty.

The Catholic Church worldwide was slow to respond to AIDS. It was not until the late 1980s that the Vatican organized a seminar on the subject, and even then activists staged a protest at the cautious tone of proceedings. The Church's delay and hesitancy were interpreted in some quarters as the cardinals and bishops saying 'We told you so all along'. Since sexual contact is one of the ways in which the virus is spread, with promiscuity thereby increasing the risks, obedience to the Catholic message of no sex before marriage and heterosexual monogamy thereafter is the perfect protection. However, in Britain the government's decision to launch a national advertising campaign about the dangers of AIDS in 1986, with a leaflet delivered to every household, forced the bishops out of their silence and pushed them once again to consider the tricky relationship between the Church's sexual teaching and public policy.

It was left – as usual in these complex moral issues of Church and nation – to Cardinal Hume to outline the position of the Church in *The Times*. Writing in January 1987, the Cardinal began by dismissing out of hand the suggestions favoured by the moral majority that AIDS was God's punishment of a sinful world. 'It is better seen as proof of a general law that actions have consequences and that disorder inevitably damages and then destroys.' The Cardinal then went on to state emphatically that 'no purpose can be served by recriminations against any section of the population. Something much more radical and constructive is called for than the scourging of other people's vices.'

AIDS, said the Cardinal, was the latest and most deadly symptom of promiscuous sexual behaviour. While the Church had always held that promiscuity was sinful, AIDS was making it suicidal. He criticized the government's safer sex campaign, which urged restraint and the use of condoms, for failing to address the root causes of AIDS and overlooking the best way to eliminate that disease. 'Even in the short term a moral reawakening is society's best hope. That must be part of any national programme of information and education. Condoms and free needles for drug addicts will reduce but not remove the dangers; those most at risk might be led to conclude that a potentially lethal lifestyle can, with precautions, be made safe.'

'The fact to be faced', he said, 'is that all of us in society have to learn to live according to a renewed set of values. That will not be easy. How can any appeal for faithfulness and sexual restraint be heeded when there is on all sides explicit encouragement to promiscuous behaviour and frequent ridicule of moral values? Society is in moral disarray, for which we must all take our share of blame. Sexual permissiveness reflects a general decline of values.' The Cardinal was thus reiterating a constant theme in his thinking about all questions of sexual morality, namely that we live in an age where standards are on the slide, and that if we do not like the results of our actions, we should change our behaviour.

Having given the counsel of perfection, the Cardinal then turned in his article to practicalities. The Catholic Church's teaching rules out the use of condoms because they prevent conception. But if they are preventing the spread of a killer virus, it had been argued, could they not be used? No, said the Cardinal. 'We do not accept that for the unmarried the choice lies solely between condoms and infection. There is a third course of action: refusal to engage in extra-marital sexual activity. Such self-discipline is not emotionally destructive, but can be a positive affirmation of a radical ideal, demanding but not impossible.' Evidence so far from surveys of young people's attitudes has suggested that such radicalism is failing to win converts. Yet on AIDS the Cardinal has maintained, in his public policy contributions, a tough line. He does not seem to be making as many allowances for human nature as he has over, say, contraception. Perhaps it is because he feels that AIDS is precisely the rude awakening society needs from permissive attitudes.

However tough it is, the Cardinal's position has not satisfied the moral majority wing of his Church. Groups like Family and Youth Concern have launched leaflet and poster campaigns against the principal AIDS charity, the Terrence Higgins Trust (THT), with scare stories about supposedly obscene materials being handed out in Catholic schools. Little evidence has been provided for such tales, and attempts to enlist the Cardinal's support in attacking THT have met with silence from Archbishop's House. While some of the educational materials produced by THT put forward the sort of safer sex, 'use a condom' message that the Cardinal was objecting to in his *Times* article, his reluctance to get involved in the attacks shows the clear demarcation in his work between attempting to change attitudes and condemning individual organisations who don't agree with him.

At a practical level, the Cardinal has had to deal with individual patients with AIDS, some of them his own priests. Although Basil Hume has been more reticent than some religious workers in the AIDS field would have liked in focusing on the human dilemma caused by the virus as opposed to the need for a moral reawakening, he has made several gestures. At the Mildmay Mission Hospital, an AIDS hospice run by lay staff but with a board of governors with strong evangelical links, the Cardinal channelled donations made to Westminster diocesan funds towards the setting up of a visitor unit. He also joined the list of patrons of the hospice. A Westminster diocesan AIDS co-ordinator has been appointed (a semi-retired former prison chaplain) and a series of informal gatherings was organized at Archbishop's House for the Cardinal to meet those working with people who are HIV positive. They were occasions for

182

listening to day-to-day needs, not for pursuing the Church's line, times when the Cardinal could show the Church's human face.

There is a danger that such initiatives do not get beyond tea and sympathy. When confronted by one of his auxiliary bishops with the practical dilemma of a priest in his archdiocese who was HIV positive, the Cardinal suggested that the man in question be sent away 'to be taken care of'. Perhaps if the Cardinal really wants to make an impact on the national imagination, to show that the Church does not share the same baseless prejudices that many in society continue to display when confronted by a person living with HIV/AIDS, how much better it might have been if he had stood by the priest not only in private, but also in public, as this particular priest had wanted. The Cardinal is prepared to admit his own humanity, but apparently not always that of priests in his charge.

In the classroom

While disagreements between the bishops on matters like nuclear deterrence are discussed fairly widely in the Catholic community, their differences of opinion on sexual morality tend to remain behind closed doors. It would be hard to pinpoint the disagreements between individual bishops, since the hierarchy as a whole adopts the policy of presenting a united front to the world, and keeps quiet about matters over which they cannot achieve a consensus. Only a couple of more maverick auxiliaries have openly taken an independent line.

Bishop Victor Guazzelli, for example, one of the Cardinal's team in Westminster, has gone on the record on several occasions, most recently in a Channel 4 programme in the winter of 1992, as upholding conscience as the supreme arbiter in sexual morality, and therefore as giving his backing to the use of condoms or pills if the individual Catholic believes in good conscience that is the right thing to do.

On the question of sex education, the hierarchy's inability to agree on a single policy has been more apparent. A 1987 statement from the bishops' conference – *Laying the Foundations for Education in Personal Relationships* – outlined broad parameters, advocating a constructive, positive tone to sex education, but urging that such lessons be slotted into a moral context in the curriculum. On specifics, however, individual dioceses have pursued their own programmes, while many schools have felt free, in the absence of clear-cut central guidance, to shape their own courses in the classroom. Issues such as when to start discussing sex, how much weight to give to the Church's teaching and how much to the reality of youngsters' lives, and which outside organizations if any to involve, have been tackled in different ways in individual dioceses.

In the meantime the government produced a series of directives, pledging itself to present sex education 'within a moral framework'. In a 1986 circular the then Education Secretary, Kenneth Baker, ruled that parents should be consulted by the schools and that pupils should 'be helped to recognize the physical and emotional risks of sexual promiscuity'. The Secretary of State was adamant that all children should receive a basic sex education. No longer could Catholic schools get away with the 'ignorance is bliss' approach of simply not mentioning the subject that characterized the classroom experiences of an earlier generation of Catholics.

In this determination to modernize, Church and State were at one, though the technicalities of how to achieve that goal caused much agonizing in Catholic circles. Again there were conflicting pressures from liberal and conservative wings, with Family and Youth Concern and its allies favouring the shock tactic approach, and those working with the liberal agenda wanting to present the Church's teaching alongside other views. The government's commitment to giving parents and governors more say in what goes on in schools left the door open to both camps to attempt to interfere in what is taught in the classroom.

The Cardinal, with a practical background in nurturing boys at Ampleforth, has occasionally stepped in to separate the warring factions. Two examples suffice to show the different pressures on him. In 1985, the Order of Christian Unity produced a pamphlet, *Children and Contraception: Failure of a Policy*, by Dr Margaret White and Josephine Robinson, a vociferous supporter of many of the conservative groups on the moral majority wing of the Catholic Church. Adopting the language of a moral reawakening favoured by Cardinal Hume, the pamphlet, launched at a press conference by Victoria Gillick, went on to criticize teachers and much of the sex education in schools in anecdotal terms: 'we now have, in some cases, teachers endorsing the natural optimism of youth and telling their pupils that the only thing to fear is pregnancy'. Parents were advised – erroneously it turned out – that they had a statutory right to withdraw their children from sex education lessons if they objected to the content.

Set against that style of approach, which was criticized at the time by Church spokesmen as 'laudable but confused', was the sort of liberal Catholic thinking that produced *A Time to Embrace*, a video made for schools and endorsed by the bishops' conference. It tried to put a human face to the Church's teaching about sexuality in the context of the AIDS crisis but was criticized by teachers for not being specific enough and leaving the children confused. As a result it did not get onto the curriculum in many Catholic schools and reinforced the idea in the staffroom that the bishops were out of touch with youngsters.

It is hard to level such a charge at Cardinal Hume. He has spent most of his working life surrounded by young people and on the rare occasions when he has intervened on sex education, it has been to offer practical, realistic guidance, steering away from the two extremes. In June of 1992, for example, he gave his unequivocal support for HIV and AIDS education in Catholic schools in a letter to the Education Secretary, John Patten. He warned against the 'misplaced anxiety' of parents and governors who might feel that sex education is 'inappropriate or damaging to children'. The classroom should be a place, the Cardinal wrote, where myths are dispelled and the prejudices held against people living with AIDS debunked.

The Cardinal's intervention came in the middle of a controversy over talking about AIDS in schools, with a group of Conservative peers in the House of Lords, backed by traditionalist Church organizations, trying – unsuccessfully it turned out – to insert an amendment to the Education Reform Act allowing parents to remove their children from the classroom if the virus was mentioned. Family and Youth Concern was predictably opposed to AIDS education in schools. The Cardinal was naive to trust teachers, said director Valerie Riches. 'They often get the AIDS unit to come to the classroom and push their line. AIDS is not a heterosexual problem, so I don't see why they have to teach it to children of a tender age.' No substantiation for either of these claims was provided.

Another area where the demands of the Catholic constituency and those of the rest of society have had to be balanced is in shaping what goes into examination syllabuses. There is, of course, a difference between what the Church wants and what is appropriate for the rest of society that does not share Catholic beliefs. A practical compromise has to be achieved in such sensitive subject areas as biology. That was the case in May 1986 when the Cardinal's local London–East Anglia examining board was persuaded by representations from Catholic organizations to delete direct references to birth control from schoolroom biology lessons.

The board, which sets examination papers for schools in the region, Catholic and not, decided to cut out the section that referred to 'contraception, advantages and disadvantages of the pill, condom/sheath, IUD, cap and rhythm methods'. Details of family planning continued to be covered in other parts of the curriculum, but the board at the time admitted that it was pressure from the Catholic lobby, anxious that its beliefs should be given equal space with other points of view, that precipitated the change.

Non-sex

Although Cardinal Hume's appeals for a moral rebirth in Britain have been echoed on many occasions by Church of England bishops, the two Churches have not always agreed in their contributions to public debate on moral issues. They have never disagreed more than over test-tube infertility treatment and experimentation on embryos.

The publication in 1984 of the Warnock Report focused attention on the whole area. Both Churches made representations to the committee, then commented on its report, and finally scrutinized the legislation that the government introduced in 1990. The Anglican bishops viewed with some satisfaction the decision of Lady Warnock's committee to go with their line that experimentation on embryos should be allowed up to 14 days after conception. The Anglican case, put principally by the scientifically trained Archbishop Habgood of York, was a pragmatic one. However, the committee's final recommendations showed considerable dissent, with those who objected to the 14-day limit as too high doing so on moral grounds. The minority view was more in line with the recommendation of the Catholic bishops to the committee against allowing any experimentation because the embryo was a human life.

In the early 1980s, the English Catholic bishops had reserved judgement as to the morality or not of the so-called 'simple case' of *in vitro* fertilization (IVF), where the husband's sperm is used to fertilize one of his wife's eggs, which is then placed back in the womb. Doctors pointed out that such a scenario was unlikely since IVF usually involves the fertilization of several eggs, and potentially the discarding of several more, in order to ensure a good chance of successful implantation. Any discarding of surplus eggs would be, according to Catholic teaching, killing an unborn child.

In 1987, the whole question of the simple case became irrelevant because the Vatican produced its long-awaited encyclical *Donum Vitae*, which ruled out all forms of IVF and artificial insemination and reiterated the ban on abortion and contraception. 'What is technically feasible is not for that very reason morally admissible', the document stressed. By the same logic outlined in *Humanae Vitae*, which said a married couple couldn't have sex without there being a chance of making a baby, *Donum Vitae* argued that they could not make a baby without having sex.

The document did leave the door open to IVF techniques where 'the technical means is not a substitute for the conjugal act', but didn't specifically approve any existing method. As with all Vatican papers, *Donum Vitae* was written in language inaccessible to ordinary Catholics. It was therefore left to Cardinal Hume to stake the Catholic claim to the moral high ground in the test-tube baby debate that followed Warnock.

The long gap between the Warnock committee's report in 1984 and legislation in 1990 made many profoundly uneasy that embryo experiments were going on in the meantime without any legal regulation. In 1985 therefore, veteran MP Enoch Powell launched his Unborn Children (Protection) Bill, aiming at a total ban on embryo experiments. Writing in *The Times* in June 1985, Cardinal Hume reflected on the perception of the Bill's supporters – which included himself and the Catholic bishops – as 'a reactionary group' trying 'to impose its idiosyncratic moral principles on the rest of society by the force of the criminal law'. It was a view he rejected out of hand. Returning to a theme that has dominated his contributions to public discussion on morality, he placed Mr Powell's Bill and indeed the whole embryo discussion in the context of 'a debate about present-day society: how it shall take control of its own future and how this will affect its present character'.

Although in other interventions – most notably the joint 1980 Archbishops' statement on abortion – the Cardinal had hinted at a difference between law and morality, with regard to the Powell Bill he saw an explicit link. 'There is a relationship between law and morality. It is not one of identity. People cannot be forced to be good (though they can be encouraged, helped and taught by law as well as by other means). Nor is it always desirable or feasible to restrain them from doing wrong by force of law. Yet the law is not separable from morality. Legislation cannot remain totally at the level of expediency and practicality without any reference to what is right, just or good. Without these reference points it soon loses the character of law as well as the respect of the citizens.'

In a pluralistic society, the law has to take into account differences of opinion, the Cardinal went on. But there must be a bottom line. 'If the law is merely trying to juggle with conflicting interests in pragmatic terms, is the outcome much more than the prevalence of stronger groups over weaker? Law which is merely enforced but cannot appeal to some fundamental moral principle is in danger of ceasing to be properly law.' If law is to be shaped merely by what is expedient, the Cardinal was in no doubt how the embryo legislation should go. 'The interests of research carried out in the hope of assisting infertile individuals, and of avoiding genetically trans-mitted defects would appear to crush the interests of "collections of human cells visible only under a microscope" as they have been called, incapable of feeling pain or distress, easily reproducible for research purposes, or available from infertility treatment. But surely that is not the whole story. . . . A moral principle is invoked by the expressions "unborn child", "human being with potential", or even "potential human being": that these subjects too are worthy of the protection owing to human beings.'

As a society, we need some absolute principles, the Cardinal stressed. And the sanctity of human life, albeit at that stage just a blob of cells, was one. Whatever the potential benefits of research, certain principles cannot be compromised in the name of benefits. 'The abandonment of objective moral principles and the dogmat-ism of permissiveness have combined in our day to undermine society. This is our crisis.'

These are strong words, stronger than his contributions on other subjects, where he seemed to be suggesting, implicitly perhaps, a distinction between the law and morality. One reason for the Cardi-nal's vehemence was that he felt that the argument over the Warnock proposals was one that could be won. He was speaking, as opinion polls at the time demonstrated, not just for the Catholic community, but for a much broader constituency that crossed traditional conservative/liberal and Christian/secular lines to unite in seeing embryo experimentation as the thin end of the wedge in debasing human life itself.

In 1987, in the wake of *Donum Vitae*, the English and Welsh and Scottish bishops joined forces to make a response to the Warnock recommendations, setting out in simple terms the Church's opposition to experimentation. However, it was left to Cardinal Hume to develop the argument in the public forum. As the government shaped legislation, following the Warnock line, he returned to the columns of *The Times* in March 1990 to reiterate his earlier dire warning that allowing embryo experimentation would lead to the self-destruction of society. 'The vital decisions we reach on human fertilization and embryology will later affect how we regard the status of each individual, his or her human rights, the treatment of people who are handicapped, the fate of the senile and the terminally ill.'

He urged MPs, about to vote on the Embryo Bill, not to be swayed 'by the compassionate objectives of those who demand the freedom to experiment'. Although he had shown that he was a man who could let his judgements be influenced by compassion for individuals on other issues, Cardinal Hume was adamant that what was at stake here left no room for such considerations. 'Once the decision is taken in Parliament, the momentum of science and technology will take over. It will be immensely difficult to introduce later the necessary checks or to reverse what will eventually be seen, I am convinced, as legislation that is fundamentally flawed.'

Changing his attack from moral to practical considerations, the Cardinal attempted to rebut three of the main arguments used in favour of experimentation. The benefits of IVF to infertile couples, he said, were not as great as had been claimed. Its low success rate, he said, could be outstripped by newer methods that aided the body's natural fertilization processes, if more money and research were dedicated to them. He questioned too whether embryo experimentation would really, as claimed, provide a cure for genetically inherited diseases. 'Embryo research, as far as genetic diseases are concerned, is directed, it now seems clear, not at cure but at prevention. By prevention is meant the systematic elimination of live human embryos found to have defects.' In 1986 the Cardinal had withdrawn his patronage of Mencap because of that charity's argument that embryo experimentation would help towards a 'cure' for mental handicap.

The third myth the Cardinal sought to explode was that 'the medical and scientific establishment is not violating the sanctity of human life but taking welcome advantage of the new-found possibility of researching into fertilised cells before they attain human status'. Human life, the Cardinal stated emphatically, begins when egg and sperm meet. 'All subsequent events, including the development of the primitive streak by 14 days [Warnock's benchmark for the start of human life], are but stages of varying importance in human development. . . . It obscures the issues to debate whether this human life can from day one be regarded as a person and whether it is already endowed with an immortal soul. These are philosophical and theological questions which science and legislation are in no position to determine.'

Having in his earlier text made the link between law and morals, the Cardinal seemed here to be saying that the law was overstepping its authority in trying to legislate in the area of the beginning of human life. Individual morality was the higher authority and law could not interfere with that. His conclusion, however, remained the same. The government's Embryo Bill had to be thrown out. Embryo experimentation must be banned. 'This is an issue of life and death, of fundamental human dignity and of the basic and unconditional respect we are bound to have for one another. Until recently our society has consistently recognised these values. Without them it will in future suffer incalculable damage.'

Despite his apocalyptic rhetoric, so uncharacteristic of the Cardinal's usual style in the public forum, the cause was lost. Parliament ignored his warnings and voted for experimentation up to 14 days. Basil Hume was appalled. Never before had he staked so much on a parliamentary vote. What had emerged from the Commons debate of April 1990, the Cardinal said, 'is the lack of a moral foundation for the formation of public policy in this most crucial area, that of human life and death'. By dispensing with the traditional Christian view of the sanctity of human life in their vote, MPs had abandoned Britain's claim to be a Christian society, the Cardinal said. He might have lost the argument, but his remarks made headlines, the front page lead in the *Daily Telegraph*, and were much discussed. Some, including senior Anglican bishops, said that Cardinal Hume represented only one of several Christian views and that his comments were exaggerated. But the Tory MP and government minister, Ann Widdecombe, predicted that 'what the Cardinal has said will be the view of future generations who will look back in disbelief at what we have done'.

In his high-profile campaign against embryo experimentation, Cardinal Hume failed to achieve an aim he always thought was possible – to persuade Parliament to throw out the offending legislation. However, by making the distinction between what was moral and what was legal, he succeeded in rallying behind him a constituency much broader than either Catholics or Christians.

10

Searching for God

I believe we should be on a pilgrimage in search of truth. Full understanding is never possible. The faith is in seeking understanding. That's the pilgrimage. We must keep moving on.

(Cardinal Hume, interview with John Mortimer, 1980)

Cardinal Heenan was a practised and poised broadcaster and preacher, adept at defending the Catholic wicket against all-comers. His radio talks during the Second World War were the first step on a trail that was to see him regularly writing in national newspapers and appearing on the first wave of television shows. He could be funny; he was at ease in the rough and tumble of a group debate; he gave his interviewers as good as he got. What was constant was his combativeness in defence of the Catholic Church and its principles – even when they were not necessarily under attack.

Such a style had made him the perfect man to lead the Catholic Missionary Society in the late 1940s, moving from parish to parish setting out the Catholic credo to the faithful, deepening their belief and strengthening their resolve to stick to it in the face of the already rising tide of secularism. But this approach was less successful when he came to Westminster. His thoughts and words, though often addressed to a national audience, were designed mainly for Catholic listeners, viewers and readers. Cardinal Heenan rarely sought the sort of national moral leadership role that his successor has taken on.

John Carmel Heenan was happier with the spoken word than with books but he did produce several collections of his thoughts and two volumes of autobiography. These tales of his growing up just east of London have a chatty, anecdotal feel to them, but spiritual insights are few and far between. Even when the Cardinal addressed the nature of belief, he tended to do so in a practical, look-and-learn style.

One of his best-known outings in print was *Priest and Penitent*, published before he joined the ranks of the hierarchy. It took as its subject the sacrament of penance and while superficially geared towards an audience of clerics and laity, it focused almost exclusively on the confessor. It began in typically robust Heenan style, slamming what he saw as the faint-hearted soul of Britain. He had harsh words for his erstwhile employer, the BBC.

'Radio religion is the ideal of the twentieth century. It supplies in the nicest and most inoffensive way whatever slight need may still be felt for spiritual uplift. A preacher who is thoroughly orthodox BBC would scarcely offend a militant atheist. But the chief charm of the new religion is that it can be turned off whenever it threatens to become a nuisance or a bore.

'The outlook of the average agnostic may be summed up in these words: the world has grown tired of external religious observance. Church-going is out of date. God can be found on a Sunday morning not only in a stuffy church, but also in the open fields. Denominations are dead. Not in the sense that anyone wished to harm them. Agnostics would be the first to vote against disestablishment. Religions obviously should not be allowed to die out completely. They should be preserved as part of our social service. The bereaved, the poor and the otherwise depressed are quite often consoled by religion. It helps to prevent people with a grievance from becoming communists. In any case on solemn and sentimental occasions there is nothing so satisfying as religious pageantry. Religion is comforting if only as a link with the past. The Church is at least a tradition. It is good that it should be produced on occasion . . . like Black Rod or ancient uniforms. . . . Yet Catholics still go to confession.'

Religion was alive and kicking in the Catholic Church, the young Fr Heenan told his readers. And, with all that talk of traditions and ceremonial occasions, he might just have been hinting that it was not in too healthy a state in the Established Church. It is an interesting passage because Heenan, in his caricature of the agnostic, was predicting many of the attitudes to religion that were to become widespread in the 1960s and 1970s. Yet behind those popularist phrases, the tone is aggressive. You can almost hear him thumping the pulpit. And there is certainty.

The principal pillar of strength is the priest himself, Cardinal Heenan wrote. He must know human nature and guide his flock rather as a parent would guide his erring children. 'During the long years of his [the priest's] training, he must view human nature from every angle. He must know the utmost limits to which human weakness may fall. He must plumb the lowest depths of human depravity, however unpleasant he may find the task, in order that at no time in his future ministry can he be faced with a sinner whose particular difficulties he has not learned to solve. He must become, in a sense, hardened. He must be able to pass from hearing the confession of the pious to that of the careless without showing any sign of surprise or disgust, without even showing preference for the confession of the virtuous.'

For Cardinal Heenan a good priest must have the answers. It was a style of clerical leadership well-suited to the fortress Church, but in the aftermath of the Second Vatican Council the role of the priest changed dramatically. He was one among others of the people of God. He had to go out and be part of his parish, his community, sharing their problems.

Basil Hume's thinking and his spiritual writings are much more in tune with this new era in Catholicism. His constant image is of a pilgrimage, a search for God that goes on throughout life. There are no answers. *Searching for God*, published soon after he was named Cardinal, is a collection of talks delivered by Basil Hume to the community at Ampleforth. 'You are joining a community of extremely imperfect human beings', he used to tell the novices. 'It is like being in a hospital where the matron, as well as the patients, is sick.' His talks ranged widely over the role of the religious, but throughout he is clear about the lack of clarity of their endeavour. 'What then is at the centre of our monastic calling? An exploration into the mystery which is God. A search for an experience of this reality. That is why we become monks. The exploration is a life-long enterprise. And when we come to the end of our lives our task will not have been completed. Such experience as God will grant you will be a limited, pale thing compared to that for which we are ultimately destined.' While the addresses in *Searching for God* were given to a community of monks, there is in them much with which lay Catholics and indeed those with no formal belief can identify. The Cardinal does not set himself above his reader. He does not radiate certainty. He at times frankly admits his doubts.

His whole approach to faith and spirituality is bound up with his Benedictine roots. In September 1980, Basil Hume joined his fellow bishops and monks from all over the world to celebrate the 1,500th

anniversary of St Benedict, the founder, at the Abbey of St Scholas-
tica (Benedict's sister) in Subiaco, Italy. The Cardinal preached the
sermon and reflected on the guidance Benedict had laid down in his
Rule for his followers and indeed for all Christians. 'Life is a pilgrimage out of the valley of man's depressed state to the heights of the
hills where, as was the case with Moses, the glory of God can be seen.
Bishops, with their priests, are spiritual leaders on that journey. St
Benedict can advise us on how we should be, for he has much to say
on spiritual leadership.'

Benedict's model of behaviour was, said Basil Hume, to 'gather
ordinary people around him. Men and women came together in
community and followed his Rule in their own monasteries as they
still do today. He gave them a new way of looking at life, precisely
because they were to learn to put God at the very centre of their
lives. That is the key for all of us.'

St Gregory tells us that Benedict lived out what he wrote. He took
being a leader, being an abbot, to mean being a father – the literal
meaning of the word abbot. It should be remembered that Benedict
was not a priest but a layman. Most of his monks were not ordained
and his thoughts, as encapsulated in his Rule, were therefore
directed to laymen. The emphasis is on joining together in the
search for God. Basil Hume is a follower of that Rule, shaped
around the frailties of man. His humanity, his humility and his
understanding spring from that Benedictine source.

Even when, in *Searching for God*, Abbot Hume discusses questions like compulsory celibacy for clergy, he shows an endearing
honesty. The style of the priests of the old school, as exemplified by
Cardinal Heenan, was to deal succinctly with the question. 'He [the
priest] must have a full knowledge of the facts of life in all its forms.
Knowledge from a healthy source never destroys innocence. The
priest must not have the hands of a child. He must have the clean
hands of a man.' The inference, that not to be celibate is somehow
unclean, creates a gulf between priest and laity. For Basil Hume
there is no such divide. He can see what is on the other side of the
fence and realize its merits. 'At the heart of celibacy there is always
pain. It has to be so, because the celibate lacks something vital. But
the pain is not to be grudged; the celibate forgoes the fulfilment of
his sexual desires precisely because he recognises that his sexuality is
a good thing. He renounces it because he knows that his Master did,
and the Church from earliest times has instinctively known that

other values can be gained as a result of that renunciation. God loves a cheerful giver.'

Making such a gift to God must not make the priest an isolated figure, on a pedestal. 'We have to be good human beings, warm and spontaneous in our relationships with other people, but sane and sensible, recognising our frailty, remembering that we are men and retain our virility and the power to attract and be attracted. A strong interior life of prayer and a love of our monastic life will be our main safeguards in face of the dangers, and will provide the contact within which to work out how to consecrate our celibacy to God and to discover its secret and its value.'

Basil Hume is not a believer in setting himself – or indeed the clergy – up as plaster saints. By stressing the search, the element of pilgrimage in religious life, he dismisses any idea that he is in any way superhuman, or specially blessed. When asked what he had found after his years of searching for God, he replied: 'I suppose a simpler faith. Deeper. Of course it isn't all a cloud of unknowing. God has revealed himself by becoming man.' And on prayer: 'Oh, I just keep plugging away. At its best, it's like being in a dark room with someone you love. You can't see them, but you know they're there.'

The Cardinal is not afraid to admit his doubts. Looking for God can be like a game of hide and seek. In his farewell sermon to the community at Ampleforth as he set off for Westminster, Abbot Hume admitted that 'strangely, in these last few days, I have found a new confidence in God'. He has spoken since his appointment of the difficulties he has with the problem of evil in the world, with suffering. 'In this world I can't understand it. But that doesn't affect my belief. I believe we're a fallen race, that human life is always in the hands of fallen people and when I'm faced with the ghastliness of concentration camps and so on, I can't put it to God at my level.'

Basil Hume comes over as a man who has struggled to find God. His noviciate at Ampleforth was a tough time. In those days before Vatican II the life of trainee monks was not for the faint-hearted. They were not allowed to speak to anyone but each other. They went home once in eight years, spending holidays together under the supervision of the novice master. Life consisted of rising at five and praying for three hours before breakfast, followed by tough manual work. When his younger brother John came to the abbey school,

Brother Basil had to pass him in silence. They met by appointment once a term. The Cardinal has admitted that there were moments when he found the noviciate tedious and the long hours of prayer dispiriting. He was tempted to give it up. One of his exact contemporaries, Fr Martin Haigh, recalled Brother Basil getting very depressed.

Elected as abbot at the age of 40 to succeed the revered Herbert Byrne, Basil Hume guided his abbey through the storms that followed Vatican II. It was a difficult task. His latter years at Ampleforth, according to Fr Haigh, were difficult ones for his personal faith. 'He was emotionally, physically and spiritually tired. He went through a dark night of the soul, one of those periods which comes to nearly all religious – it suddenly goes dark and one can only go on knocking. Some of the radiance of Basil now is that of a man who has gone through darkness into light.'

In one of his talks to the community at Ampleforth, on the occasion of one of the monks abandoning his vocation to the religious life, Abbot Hume gave a glimpse of his own doubts. 'After all, we have given our lives to God and yet, so often, He seems elusive. One comes up against the sudden and supreme difficulty of wanting God with all one's soul and not finding Him. This can be frightening. It can make us want to turn back. The fatal thing to do is to turn back.' It was only on the eve of his departure from Ampleforth, his fellow monks report, that the cloud over Dom Basil lifted. He confirmed as much in the passage from his farewell sermon quoted above.

That understanding of what it is to doubt, to go through a long dark night of the soul, has never left Basil Hume and at Westminster he has turned it to positive effect. One of his most unorthodox moves has been to install a private telephone in his study and give the number to every priest in the diocese – almost a thousand of them – to use when they are in trouble. The telephone is out of bounds to the rest of the Cardinal's staff. When he is away it rings unanswered. It is a mark of the respect that Basil Hume has built among the priests of Westminster diocese that the number has never been leaked.

On a national stage, the Cardinal's pilgrimage of faith, his search for God and his doubts have combined to make him both respected and accessible. He may be the head of the Catholic Church but he comes over as a simple monk, with human frailties, able to understand others' weaknesses. His television appearances tend to come at times of national emergency, or when a pressing moral issue is being debated. He does not indulge in politicians' rhetoric, but speaks in a straightforward way for the Christian tradition, never claiming any direct line to heaven.

11

Quite a legacy

I am becoming increasingly surprised at my own selection. If I was asked to recommend a successor now I can't see myself recommending someone outside.

(Times interview, 1986)

A Gallup Poll in the mid-1980s showed that Catholics made up 11 per cent of the population in Great Britain. Their ranks deviated from the norm, the pollsters said, in that Catholics tended to be younger, more likely to vote Labour, less likely to own a house, and better educated than the rest of the population. There is just a hint there of the old stereotypes of English Catholicism: the working-class Church that developed in the wake of the waves of Irish immigration; the fortress Church that put its faith in bricks and mortar and aimed above all else to build schools for its young; and the papal Church where having children carries more of a premium than elsewhere. Yet the differences were, Gallup said, marginal. Compared with similar surveys carried out in the 1950s, the most recent results show a process of assimilation. English Catholics no longer stand out as a group on the national landscape as once they did. It is a trend that has been charted by other commentators, most notably the Surrey University sociologist Michael Hornsby-Smith.

The successful integration of Catholics into the mainstream of English society and the Establishment after the centuries of persecution and hostility is a story of tolerance to inspire an age when religious and ethnic intolerance is at the heart of so many world disputes. Old prejudices can die. And for other more recent arrivals on the English scene – Muslims, Sikhs, Afro-Caribbeans – who today experience a lack of understanding and discrimination, the example of how the nation has grown to embrace Catholicism is a hopeful one.

Cardinal Hume has not caused that change of heart single-handedly. It was well under way years before he arrived at Westminster, the product of a complex mix of social, economic and internal Church factors. Yet the progression from the defensive, introspective, fortress Church of old had not, until Basil Hume's arrival, been reflected in the leadership of English Catholicism. Cardinal Heenan, for all his strength of purpose and robust defence of the Catholic position, was a prelate of the old school, fighting to reconcile the old certainties with the new wave of change and reform that came in the wake of the Second Vatican Council.

Basil Hume has calmed the storms that rocked the Church in the latter half of Heenan's time at Westminster. Division still exists. Differences of opinion over contraception, over war and peace, and over social policy have been among the themes of this book. Yet no longer does the failure to agree add up to a crisis. English Catholicism has retained its homogeneity but developed diversity. As its leader, the Cardinal has sought to achieve a consensus, to steer a middle course between conflicting demands: Roman centralism and local needs; theology and pastoral practice; traditionalism and liberalism; private and public morality.

He has not always been successful. Sometimes his light hand on the tiller has been applauded. At other moments – principally over defence – steering a middle course has left him open to accusations of muddled thinking. The Cardinal has, over schools policy for instance, made a great deal of noise without achieving any appreciable benefits in his dealings with government. On the other hand, he has achieved some notable political victories by the quiet and patient behind-the-scenes diplomacy that has become his forte, as the Guildford Four would testify.

The institutional legacy of Basil Hume may not be great. He has matched words with actions in his concern over homelessness, and his own office and the bishops' conference are noticeably more professional. Yet mechanisms for the laity to express their views are still few and far between three decades after the opening of the Second Vatican Council. The democracy of the Church of England, with its thrice-yearly synods, is still a long way off for English Catholicism. Indeed, the high point of lay involvement in decision-making, the National Pastoral Congress in 1980, has never been vigorously followed through in the Cardinal's time.

Much of what Basil Hume has achieved has been bound up in his own personality and the impact that has made on the nation. Despite the Cardinal's repeated efforts to direct the spotlight away from himself, he has come to personify Catholicism and, to many, Christianity. He is a man who has God in his shadow. When he speaks out in the public forum, he carries that with him. And the moral authority of his message is therefore all the greater. No longer is Catholicism seen as something strange or foreign. In Basil Hume it has a leader who in his restrained but insistent appeals for a return to moral standards embodies an ideal that remains at the core of English society.

Because so much of what he has achieved is wrapped up in what he is rather than what he has done, Basil Hume will be a hard act to follow when he bids Archbishop's House goodbye and returns to his beloved Ampleforth. But he would not admit to having made much impression as the leader of English Catholicism. His humility has always been one of his most attractive traits in an age where self-interest and self-promotion have become goals to be ruthlessly pursued. 'Trying to be as honest as I can,' he said on the occasion of his golden jubilee as a monk in 1992, 'I do not think I am the right man for this job. I think there are certain parts of it I can do. But I have not got what the man in this job really needs which I think is high intelligence and a very long vision.'

His elevation in 1976 still surprises him. 'For a long, long time in my youth, I thought I was unintelligent. Others probably think that now. I lived in a family where standards were pretty high. My parents were marvellous parents. They did expect high standards. So I did not grow up feeling I was a roaring success as a child.'

In his early years as Cardinal, Basil Hume felt that he was a stop-gap. 'I thought this was a strange interlude. After that it was just a question of getting on with it.' But any hopes of waking up and finding himself back at Ampleforth have as yet proved dreams. After a return visit in 1992, the Cardinal came back thrilled to feel his original vocation confirmed. 'I realized that is where I really like to be.'

Exile from Ampleforth has been a heavy burden. Life in Archbishop's House, the expectations of what a cardinal should be doing and saying, have taken their toll on Basil Hume. 'I used to say to the monks in the community, when I was in a position to say these things, that in an Ampleforth monk there should always be a disappointment that you were not able to be a hermit. There must always be in a monk that kind of nostalgia for God. As a Benedictine I think one brings a certain training, a training in the spiritual life. I have learned in the monastery the value of prayer. I have learned how to pray. I have learned in particular the two loves which I think a monk ought to have: a love of solitude and silence, and a love of community.' Neither has been his lot as Archbishop of Westminster. There are always calls on his time – delegations, telephone calls, diocesan worries. Solitude and silence are rare commodities. And despite the Cardinal's efforts to make Archbishop's House a little more cosy, it lacks the community feel of Ampleforth.

So Basil Hume's return, when it happens, will be a happy one. He took the job out of obedience and he will carry on doing it out of obedience, perhaps until 1998, when he reaches 75, the statutory retirement age for bishops. Rome shows no sign of letting him off the hook sooner. And the Cardinal's role on the international stage of the Church could continue into the next millennium, until his eightieth birthday. That is when wearers of the red hat relinquish their right to vote for the next Pope.

Who will succeed him? The history of the Archbishops of Westminster is one of Rome choosing unlikely candidates: Cardinal Hinsley plucked from semi-retirement, Cardinal Griffin promoted from the rank of humble auxiliary bishop, Cardinal Hume from Ampleforth Abbey. Equally, Rome doesn't repeat its surprises. Even though one of Basil Hume's strengths has been the very Englishness of his Benedictine background, Rome is unlikely to opt for Dom Basil's successor as Abbot of Ampleforth, Dom Ambrose Griffiths, named Bishop of Hexham and Newcastle in 1992.

Among the rest of the hierarchy there are a few obviously strong candidates. Archbishop Worlock is older than Cardinal Hume and his moment has now passed – though Rome might consider rewarding him for his unstinting service in the forefront of English Catholicism with a Cardinal's hat. Having two Cardinals in England is not unprecedented, as a glance back to the age of Manning and Newman confirms.

Bishop David Konstant of Leeds has failed to impress in his battle over Catholic schools, while Bishop Christopher Budd of Plymouth has made little impact despite having the portfolio of family matters. Several otherwise eminently suitable characters have blotted their copybook in Rome by taking a radical stance on matters where the Vatican prefers at the very least a public show of loyalty. Bishop

Cormac Murphy-O'Connor of Arundel and Brighton, who rivals Cardinal Hume for sheer niceness and has a way of putting a human face on even the thorniest of Church teachings, is considered by some of his fellows to have let his doubts on *Humanae Vitae* show through. Bishop Thomas McMahon of Brentwood has been a little too vocal on peace issues and the £5 million he spent on giving his 1960s cathedral a neo-classical face-lift went down very badly in some circles. Bishop Patrick Kelly of Salford, the one outstanding theologian among the hierarchy, has been pursuing various experiments with the age at which children should be confirmed. Innovation is seldom smiled on in Rome.

In the auxiliary ranks Bishop Vincent Nichols, one of the Cardinal's lieutenants in Westminster, might look to the example of Cardinal Griffin, plucked from similar humble origins in Birmingham diocese to be the leader of English Catholicism. A talented man, with a decidedly modern air and media-friendliness, Bishop Nichols is more likely to succeed Archbishop Worlock in his native Liverpool. The rest of the auxiliaries reflect very much the prevailing mood in Rome that they should be less sub-bishops than helpers to their own bishop, 'priests in mitres', as one cynic put it. There are few of the calibre of Cardinal Griffin.

Another of Basil Hume's great plusses in finding a national role has been his Establishment ties. If the Vatican wanted another in this vein, it would have to look no further than Bishop Crispian Hollis of Portsmouth. The son of an MP, the nephew of the former head of MI5, with a Stonyhurst–Oxford–Venerable English College, Rome pedigree, he has already cut quite a dash on the national stage with his regular appearances on radio and television. One of the younger members of the hierarchy, he embodies the sort of liberal pastoral practice and theological conservatism that have been Basil Hume's hallmark.

The fear among liberal Catholics, watching the Vatican's tendency in the rest of the world to appoint men whose loyalty to the official line in public and in private is absolute, is that Archbishop Maurice Couve de Murville of Birmingham will succeed Basil Hume. Traditionally-minded, the Archbishop shares French parentage and good connections in the ruling classes with Cardinal Hume, but little else. He is more in the old mould of a prince of the Church, autocratic in his actions in the diocese and semi-detached from the world outside purely Catholic concerns.

If Bishop Hollis and Archbishop Couve de Murville – who didn't get on at all well when the former was an auxiliary bishop in Birmingham in the mid-1980s – are the front-runners within the hierarchy, Rome might just be tempted after the success of the dark horse it chose in 1976 to cast its net wider in the ranks of the religious orders. The Jesuit Provincial, Fr Michael Campbell-Johnston, has made headlines with his address to the Tory Party Conference and his espousal of social concerns. The recently appointed Master-General of the Dominicans, Fr Timothy Radcliffe, is an attractive figure with a reputation for liberal pastoral practice and an impeccable pedigree from one of England's oldest Catholic families.

But Basil Hume feels that the next Cardinal will not come from 'outide' as he did. As Christianity shapes up to the third millennium, he will leave heightened expectations but no blueprint for leadership and no obvious successor. In the end Catholics will have to rely on the Holy Spirit for their safe deliverance. He – or She – is not spoilt for choice, but has a commendable recent record in picking a man who lifts our eyes to the far horizon while at the same time never losing sight of the here and now. Basil Hume has always been unequivocal as to where any credit for his work at Archbishop's House should go. In his final sermon as Abbot of Ampleforth in February 1976 he spoke of his sadness at leaving and his apprehension of what was ahead. 'The generosity of the press, and the expectations of so many people, expressed in over a thousand letters and close on four hundred telegrams, have been to me personally a profound shock. That, my dearly beloved, is why I need your prayers and your friendship. The gap between what is thought and expected of me, and what I know myself to be, is considerable and frightening. There are moments in life when a man feels very small and in all my life this is one such moment. It is good to feel small, for I know that whatever I achieve will be God's achievement, not mine.'

Bibliography

Cardinal Hume is not a prodigious writer and most of his publications have been collections of sermons and talks. The books he has to his name are:

Searching for God (Hodder, 1977);
In Praise of Benedict (Hodder, 1981);
To Be a Pilgrim (St Paul Publications, 1984);
Prayers for Peace, with Archbishop Runcie (SPCK, 1987);
Towards a Civilisation of Love (Hodder, 1988);
Light in the Lord (St Paul Publications, 1991).

Basil Hume – A Portrait, a collection of essays by writers like Mary Craig, Clifford Longley and John F. X. Harriott, edited by Tony Castle, was published in 1986 (Collins).

Events reported in individual chapters have been checked against reports from the time in the religious and national press. Cardinal Hume's contributions from *The Times* are reprinted with their permission. Books included under the various chapter headings are a combination of titles referred to in the text and those which may give further enlightenment on various points raised but not developed because of the constraints of space and the demands of syntax.

Chapter 2 The reluctant Archbishop

Documents of Vatican II, edited by Austin Flannery (Firepost).
Gerard Noel, *The Anatomy of the Catholic Church* (Hodder).
Michael Hornsby-Smith, *Roman Catholics in England* (Cambridge).
Evelyn Waugh, *Brideshead Revisited* (Penguin).
Flora Thompson, *Lark Rise to Candleford* (Penguin).
Graham Greene, *Brighton Rock* (Penguin).

Chapter 3 A break with tradition

Richard Schiefen, *Nicholas Wiseman and the Transformation of English Catholicism* (Patmos Press).

Brian Fothergill, *Nicholas Wiseman* (Faber).
Ian Ker, *John Henry Newman* (Oxford).
Sheridan Gilley, *Newman* (Darton, Longman and Todd).
E. E. Reynolds, *Three Cardinals* (Burns and Oates).
Arthur McCormack, *Cardinal Vaughan* (Burns and Oates).
Ernest Oldmeadow, *Francis Cardinal Bourne* (Burns and Oates).
Thomas Moloney, *Westminster, Whitehall and the Vatican: The Role of Cardinal Hinsley* (Burns and Oates).
Michael de la Bedoyère, *Cardinal Bernard Griffin* (Rockliff).
Cardinal John Carmel Heenan, *Not the Whole Truth* and *A Crown of Thorns* (Hodder).
Michael Walsh, *The Tablet: A Commemorative History* (Tablet Publications).

Chapter 4 What the Pope doesn't see . . .

David Willey, *God's Politician* (Faber).
Michael Walsh, *The Secret Garden: Opus Dei* (Collins).
John Cornwell, *A Thief in the Night* (Penguin).
David Yallop, *In God's Name* (Grafton).

Chapter 5 Unity in diversity

Archbishop Derek Worlock and Bishop David Sheppard, *Better Together* (Hodder).
Adrian Hastings, *Robert Runcie* (Mowbray).

Chapter 6 Her Majesty's Loyal Opposition?

Paul Misner, *Social Catholicism in Europe* (Darton, Longman and Todd).
Patrick O'Donovan, *A Journalist's Odyssey* (Esmonde Publishing).
Sollicitudo Rei Socialis and *Centesimus Annus* (both available through the Catholic Truth Society).
Faith in the City (Church House Publishing).
Simon Lee and Peter Stanford, *Believing Bishops* (Faber).
Gerry Conlon, *Proved Innocent* (Penguin).
Robert Kee, *Trial and Error* (Hamish Hamilton).
Chris Mullin, *An Error in Judgement* (Chatto, reissued Poolbeg Press).

Chapter 7 Faith in bricks and mortar

Anthony Howard, *RAB: The Life of R. A. Butler* (Jonathan Cape).

Bibliography

Chapter 8 Arms or alms?

Africa's Crisis and the Church in Britain (CAFOD / Catholic Truth
  Society).
Michael Budde, *The Two Churches: Catholicism and Capitalism in the
  World System* (Duke University Press).
Voice of the Voiceless: Sermons of Oscar Romero (Orbis).
Paul Vallely, *Bad Samaritans* (Hodder).
Bruce Kent, *Undiscovered Ends* (HarperCollins).

Chapter 9 The flesh is weak

Vicky Cosstick (ed.), *AIDS: Meeting the Community Challenge*
  (St Paul Publications).
John Mahoney, SJ, *Bioethics and Beliefs: Religion and Medicine in
  Dialogue* (Sheed and Ward).
Dr Margaret White and Josephine Robinson, *Children and
  Contraception: Failure of a Policy* (Order of Christian Unity).
The Facts Behind the Terrence Higgins Trust (Family and Youth
  Concern Factsheet no. 1).
Issues in Human Sexuality: A Statement by the House of Bishops
  (Church House Publishing).
Dr Nicholas Ford in *The British Journal of Family Planning* (July 1992).
Victoria Gillick, *A Mother's Tale* (Hodder).
David Lodge, *How Far Can You Go?* (Penguin).
David Lodge, *The British Museum Is Falling Down* (Penguin).
Michael Hornsby-Smith, *Roman Catholic Beliefs in England*
  (Cambridge).
A Time to Embrace (video available through Catholic Truth Society).
Uta Ranke Heinemann, *Eunuchs for Heaven* (Penguin).
Piers Paul Read, *Quo Vadis* (Claridge Press).
Michael D'Antonio, *Fall from Grace* (André Deutsch).
Professor Simon Lee, *Law and Morals* (Oxford).
Mary Kenny, *Abortion: The Whole Story* (Quartet).

Chapter 10 Searching for God

Cardinal John Carmel Heenan, *Priest and Penitent* (Sheed and Ward).
Richard Sipe, *A Secret World: Sexuality and Celibacy* (Brunner and
  Mazel).
David Rice, *Shattered Vows* (Michael Joseph).

Index